WHAT'S NEW
IN
YOUNG ADULT NOVELS?

and
Ideas for Classroom Use

2010

By Sharon Nehls

ISBN 978-0-578-00444-0

What's New in Young Adult Novels?

After reading 400+ young adult novels, I think I can safely say there are a lot of wonderful new young adult novels for use in the classroom, as well as many that are "fun reads" for middle level and high school readers. The first section of this book includes the bibliographic information about these new books, as well as a short synopsis. I did not attempt to label the books as to their quality. I did, however, suggest an age level for potential readers.

The bibliographic entry includes the author's name, the title of the book, the publisher and copyright date, an age level recommendation, the number of pages and the ISBN number. The age level recommendations are as follows:

MS – appropriate for mature elementary and middle level readers

MS/HS- appropriate for mature middle level readers and high school readers. There may be some disturbing issues presented but they are not dealt with graphically.

HS- appropriate for high school students. Controversial issues are graphically explored in the text and may be disturbing to younger readers and/or their parents.

Example: Anderson, Laurie Halse. **Wintergirls**. Viking Juvenile, 2009. MS/HS. 288 pages. ISBN-13: 978-0670011100

I did not attempt to give a quality rating to the books because I think book preferences are so individual. What appeals to me may not appeal to someone else and vice versa. However, the books that I suggest for use in the classroom in the instructional units are books that in my opinion are relatively well-written and have redeeming social value.

The book bundles section includes books that have similar themes. The fantasy bundle activities focus on the fantasy hero's quest and ideas for using the popular new books about vampires, werewolves, fairies, and angels. I also have a list of "Candy Bar" books which refers to books that may be fun reads for students, but are basically light hearted and are about fairly superficial issues such as strict parents, boyfriend/girlfriend problems, or cliques/popularity. The Books for Boys section suggests titles and activities that are designed to entice the male reader. The Mysteries, Damaged Kids, Teens Dealing with Death, Young Athletes, Sexual Identity, Dystopian Societies and Science Connection bundles include guiding questions that can be used for literature circles.

I hope you are able to find some gems in this list and recommend them to students or use them in your classroom. If I can be of any help to you in your book selections or use of them, I would be happy to consult with you.

Sharon Nehls

snehls@comcast.net

TABLE OF CONTENTS

New Young Adult Novels

Abrahams, Peter. **Reality Check**. HarperTeen; 1 edition, 2009. MS/HS. 336 pages. ISBN-13: 978-0061227660

      Cody Laredo's life begins to unravel when an injury sidelines him from his high school football team in Colorado, and his wealthy girlfriend Clea is sent away to Dover Academy in Vermont. When Clea disappears, Cody drops out of school and heads east to find her.

Adlington, L.J. **Cherry Heaven**. HarperTeen , 2008. MS. 464 pages. ISBN-10: 006143180X

      This companion novel to *The Diary of Pelly D* continues the story with two different narratives which eventually merge. Luka is a seventeen-year-old girl who is a slave laborer in a water-bottling facility. Kat and Tanka are two sisters who move into Cherry Heaven, Luka's abandoned family home, in the New Frontier. The genetic profiling, which has thrown people's lives into turmoil after being identified, continues to plague society. Kat senses the peaceful façade of their new home hides a dark secret which she is determined to discover.

Ain, Beth Levine. **The Revolution of Sabine**. Candlewick; 1 edition, 2008. MS. 224 pages. ISBN-13: 978-0763633967

      In pre-revolution Paris, Sabine Durand, an aristocrat who wants more out of life than a suitable match, contemplates the possibility of determining her own fate. Inspired by *Candide* and Michael, her childhood friend and servant who introduces her to Ben Franklin, Sabine finds the courage to defy her parents' wishes for her to marry and seek her own destiny.

Alexie, Sherman. **The Absolutely True Diary of a Part-Time Indian**. Little, Brown Young Readers, MS/HS. 2007. 240 pages. ISBN-10: 0316013684

      With illustrations by cartoonist Ellen Forney, this semi-autobiographical novel tells the story of a bright hydrocephalic Native American boy, who is the target of bullies and loves to draw. Transferring to a white high school, he attempts to rise above life on the reservation where alcoholism is rampant.

Alvarez, Julia. **Return to Sender**. Knopf Books for Young Readers, 2009. MS. 336 pages. ISBN-13: 978-0375858383

      Tyler's family is forced to hire illegal Mexican workers to save their Vermont farm when his father is injured in a tractor accident. Although he has conflicting feelings about their right to be in the United States, he befriends Mari, the oldest of the three daughters who is worried about her missing mother and incarcerated uncle. Her family lives in constant fear of discovery and Tyler struggles to do the right thing.

Amato, Mary. **Invisible Lines**. EgmontUSA, 2009. MS. 336 pages. ISBN-13: 978-1606840108

      Trevor, who lives in a housing project, finds it hard to fit in at his school, which is in a rich neighborhood. He is asked to join a travel soccer team, but can't even afford new cleats, let alone the participation fee. Torn between his responsibility to his hard working mom and younger siblings and his desire to escape, he finds solace in his drawings which chronicle his observations about life.

Anderson, Jody Lynn. **The Secrets of Peaches**. HarperTeen, 2007. MS/HS. 304 pages. ISBN-10: 0060733087

In this sequel to *Peaches*, Birdie, Murphy, and Leeda begin their senior year in high school, each facing a new set of problems. Birdie pines for her boyfriend who has gone back to Mexico, Murphy longs to head off to NYU but is conflicted about leaving her boyfriend behind, and Leeda's conflicted relationship with her mother begins to taint her relationship with everyone, including her friends.

Anderson, Jodi Lynn. **Love and Peaches**. HarperTeen, 2008. MS. 256 pages. ISBN-13: 978-0060733117

The third and final book in the popular Peaches series finds Murphy, Leeda and Birdie back in Bridgewater for the summer. Murphy's conflicted feelings about her former boyfriend, Leeda's unexpected inheritance and Birdie's heartbreak and fear of losing the family orchard make for a summer of change and decisions about the future.

Anderson, Laurie Halse. **Chains**. Simon & Schuster Children's Publishing, 2008. MS. 320 pages. ISBN-13: 978-1416905851

During the Revolutionary War, enslaved Isabel expects to be freed when her master dies, but instead she and her sister are sold to Loyalists who mistreat them. Enlisted by the rebels to smuggle information to them, Isabel suffers disastrous consequences when her loyalties are questioned and she tries to escape.

Anderson, Laurie Halse. **Twisted**. Viking Juvenile, 2007. HS. 256 pages. ISBN-10: 0670061018

Tyler Miller thinks his senior year is going to be an improvement over the social isolation he has felt in previous years. His improved physique attracts the attention of popular Bethany Milbury, but when she invites him to a party, her drunken behavior turns into a nightmare, as Tyler struggles with issues of integrity and personal responsibility. The situation spirals out of control and Tyler finds himself contemplating drastic solutions to his problems at school and at home.

Anderson, Laurie Halse. **Wintergirls**. Viking Juvenile, 2009. MS/HS. 288 pages. ISBN-13: 978-0670011100

Lia has been hospitalized twice for anorexia. Any progress she has made toward normalcy is negated when her ex-friend Cassie dies alone in a hotel room as a result of her bulimia. As Lia struggles to fight her disease, Cassie's ghost continually haunts her, enticing her to join her in the land of the Wintergirls.

Apelqvist, Eva. **Swede Dreams**. Puffin. 2007. MS/HS. 224 pages. ISBN-10: 0142407461

In this book from the S.A.S.S. (Students Across Seven Seas) series Calista Swanson has followed Jonas, her Swedish exchange student boyfriend, back to Sweden for her own semester abroad. Hoping to escape her problems at home and spend time with Jonas, Calista is bewildered when Jonas does not answer her calls.

Appelt, Kathi. **The Underneath**. Atheneum, 2008. MS. 320 pages. ISBN-13: 978-1416950585

In three separate but entwined stories we meet Gar Face, a sadistic hermit who lives in the Texas bayou, his abused and neglected pet bloodhound Ranger who welcomes a calico cat and her kittens to The Underneath, his home under the front porch, and Grandmother Moccasin, a shape-shifting watersnake. When Puck, one of the kittens, breaks the rule about leaving the safety of The Underneath, he launches a series of catastrophic events that will bring all the characters together.

Arnold, Tedd. **Rat Life**. Dial, 2007. MS/HS. 208 pages. ISBN-10: 0803730209

Todd helps his parents run a motel in upstate New York and dreams of becoming a writer. When he meets Rat, a moody young Vietnam veteran, he becomes fascinated by the damaged young man, who is possibly dangerous. As Todd get to know more about Rat, he begins to wonder if his new friend might have something to do with the unidentified body pulled out of the river.

Asher, Jay. **13 Reasons Why**. Razorbill, 2007. HS. 304 pages. ISBN-10: 1595141715

Clay Jenson receives a mysterious package of cassette tapes from Hannah Baker that are to be circulated among 13 schoolmates. The tapes illuminate the circumstances that led to Hannah's suicide. Alternating between Hannah's voice (italicized) and Clay's thoughts as he listens to the tapes, the story details how seemingly small actions can have dire consequences.

Avasthi, Swati. **Split**. Knopf Books for Young Readers, 2010. MS/HS. 288 pages. ISBN-13: 978-0375863400

16-year-old Jace Witherspoon is thrown out of his Chicago home, after confronting his father who physically abuses him and his mother. Jace heads to Albuquerque to reunite with his 22-year-old brother Christian who fled from home five years before. The two of them develop an uneasy relationship which is haunted by worries about their father finding them and their mother's safety.

Avi. **Crispin – The End of Time**. Balzer + Bray; 1 edition, 2010. MS. 240 pages. ISBN-13: 978-0061740800

Crispin and Troth are still mourning the death of Bear, their protector, and are heading north through France in hopes of making their way to Iceland. They arrive at a convent where Troth decides to stay, so Crispin joins a band of traveling musicians who are actually thieves. When he discovers their plot against him, he decides to escape and take their servant boy with him, in hopes of boarding a ship and finally making it to Iceland.

Avi. **Hard Gold**. Hyperion Book CH, 2008. MS. 240 pages. ISBN-13: 978-1423105190

I Witness: Hard Gold: The Colorado Gold Rush of 1859: A Tale of the Old West is the latest installment in Avi's I Witness series. 14-year-old Early Whitcomb's family is about to lose their Iowa farm, so Early's 19-year-old Uncle Jesse heads to Cherry Creek in Colorado where he hopes to find gold. All he seems to find, however, is trouble. Early sets off with the Bunderly family in their Conestoga wagon to search for Jesse and help him find the gold that will save their family.

Avi. **Iron Thunder**. Hyperion, 2007. MS. 224 pages. ISBN-10: 1423104463

The first of a new series entitled *I Witness*, this historical novel chronicles the tale of thirteen-year-old Tom Carroll, who is enlisted to work on the ironclad ship which is to become the *Monitor*. He works closely with Captain Ericsson in building the ship and then travels to join the Union blockade fleet and enter into its fateful battle with the *Merrimac*. Period newspaper headlines, photographs, and engravings are strategically placed throughout the novel to further bring history to life.

Avi. **Murder at Midnight**. Scholastic Press; 1 edition, 2009. MS. 272 pages. ISBN-13: 978-0545080903

The prequel to *Midnight Magic* chronicles the beginning of the relationship between the magician Mangus and his servant Fabrizio. At first the cantankerous old man wants nothing to do with Fabrizio, but the boy slowly wins him over as they become embroiled in a royal power struggle that results in murder. Fabrizio tenaciously hangs onto his belief in magic, as he seeks to untangle the intrigue at the castle and save his master's life.

Avi. **The Seer of Shadows**. HarperCollins, 2008. MS. 208 pages. ISBN-10: 0060000155
Set in 19th century New York City, this ghost story involves Horace Carpetine, a photographer's apprentice, who is reluctantly drawn into his employer's scheme to dupe a wealthy client, by supposedly capturing her departed daughter's soul on film. Unfortunately, they set lose a spirit bent on revenge.

Avi. **The Traitor's Gate**. Atheneum/Richard Jackson Books, 2007. MS. 368 pages. ISBN-10: 0689853351
This action packed adventure finds young John Huffman unraveling a mystery surrounding his father's bankruptcy and suspected treachery in nineteenth century London. This novel about traitors, spies, family and love has twists and turns that keep the reader eagerly turning the pages.

Bachorz, Pam. **Candor**. EgmontUSA, 2009. MS/HS. 256 pages. ISBN-13: 978-1606840122
Candor is a planned community where people's behavior is manipulated through mind control music. Oscar Banks, son of the town's founder, has found a way to defy the subliminal messages and has developed a business helping teens escape. Then he falls in love with rebellious newcomer Nia, and he can't decide whether to help her escape or find a way for her to stay without losing herself.

Bacigalupi, Paolo. **Ship Breaker**. Little, Brown Books for Young Readers; 1 edition, 2010. MS/HS. 336 pages. ISBN-13: 978-0316056212
In this futuristic dystopian thriller, the world has run out of oil and coastal cities have been swallowed by rising seas. Nailer, a ship breaker, is part of a crew who scavenges for metals on abandoned oil tankers. After surviving a class 6 hurricane, Nailer and his friend Pima find a wrecked clipper ship on the shore. Thinking they are about to become rich, they begin pillaging the wreckage and find a lone survivor, Nita, the "swank" daughter of a shipping tycoon. Nailer convinces Pima not to slit the girl's throat and sell her for body parts, a decision which he constantly revisits as he deals with one problem after another.

Balliett, Blue. **The Calder Game**. Scholastic Press; 1st edition, 2008. MS. 400 pages. ISBN-13: 978-0439852074
Calder, Petra and Tommy are once again involved in the world of art and intrigue when Calder travels to England with his father and goes missing along with a sculpture by Alexander Calder. When Tommy and Petra arrive in Woodstock, England, to help

with the search for Calder, they find mazes, mobiles, puzzles and pentaminoes leading them toward their lost friend.

Baker. E.D. **Wings: A Fairy Tale**. Bloomsbury USA Children's Books, 2008. MS. 320 pages. ISBN-13: 978-1599901930

15-year-old Tamisin has never quite fit in with her high school classmates, but when she begins to grow wings, she realizes how different she really is. Then she learns that she is a halfling fairy and Jak, the new student she admires, is a halfling goblin who has been sent to take her back to the fairy world. When Tamisin meets Titania, the Queen of the fairies, she finds that she and Jak must band together to defeat the goblins, who are plotting against the queen.

Bantle, Lee. **David Inside Out**. Henry Holt and Co. (BYR); 1 edition, 2009. MS/HS. 192 pages. ISBN-13: 978-0805081220

Although high school junior David Dahlgren has a girlfriend, he finds himself more attracted to a cross country teammate Sean. When they begin a secret sexual relationship, David struggles with guilt and the desire to come out to his family and friends. Sean, however, is in denial and their hot and cold relationship has David filled with emotional turmoil which he longs to resolve.

Baratz-Logstead, Lauren. **Crazy Beautiful**. Houghton Mifflin Books for Children, 2009. MS/HS. 208 pages. ISBN-13: 978-0547223070

In this *Beauty and the Beast* inspired romance. Aurora Belle befriends Lucius Wolf, who blew his hands off in a chemical accident. Although Lucius is a loner, who has replaced his hand with hooks rather than prosthetic devices so as to punish himself even further, Aurora finds herself drawn to him. Scorned by the other kids, Lucius is bewildered by Aurora's attentions, even though he is drawn to her. In alternating voices the two explore their feelings for each other in this tale of guilt and redemption

Baratz-Logsted, Lauren. **Secrets of My Suburban Life**. Simon Pulse, 2008. MS. 240 pages. ISBN-13: 978-1416925255

After the death of her mother, Ren D'Arc is distraught about her father's decision to move from Manhattan to Danbury, CT. Her attempts to fit in are thwarted by Farrin, the school's queen bee. Then Ren discovers that Farrin is having an online affair with an older man, and to make matters worse Ren suspects that the man is her own father!

Barkley, Brad and Hepler, Heather. **Jars of Glass**. Dutton Juvenile, 2008. MS/HS. 208 pages. ISBN-13: 978-0525479116

After their mother is committed to a mental institution and their father turns to alcohol to drown his pain, fifteen-year-old Shana and fourteen-year-old Chloe struggle to cope with their broken family. To escape the turmoil at home, Shana turns to the high school Goth scene and Chloe heads off to work at the local Starbucks. Chloe can't understand why Shana doesn't want their mother to return home, until a devastating secret is revealed that brings the girls back together.

Barnes, John. **Tales from the Madmen Underground**. Viking Juvenile; 1 edition, 2009. HS. 544 pages. ISBN-13: 978-0670060818

During six days in 1973, Karl Shoemaker, who is starting his senior year in high school, attempts to enact "Operation Be F***ing Normal," without much success. As he works five jobs, struggling to take care of his alcoholic mother, he realizes that his attempt to distance himself from the other kids forced to endure school therapy, known as the Madman Underground, is futile.

Barron, T. A. **Merlin's Dragon**. Philomel, 2008. MS. 336 pages.
ISBN-13: 978-0399247507

The first book in a new series, which is set between Barron's "Lost Years Of Merlin" and "Great Tree of Avalon" series, focuses on Basil, an unusual lizard who is searching for his true identity. In a quest to save all of Avalon from the evil spirit Rhita Gawr, Basil travels Avalon's seven-root-realms trying to find and warn Merlin, as well as hunt for others of his own kind.

Bauer, Joan. **Peeled**. Putnam Juvenile, 2008. MS. 256 pages. ISBN-10: 0399234756

Aspiring journalist, Hildy Biddle, goes undercover to find out the truth about the mysterious incidents at the Ludlow House, which the townspeople think is haunted. She wonders why the editor of the local paper is fanning the developing flames of hysteria after a dead body turns up at the house and why Madame Zobek, a psychic, suddenly moves to town. In the process Hildy learns a lot about reporting and people who profit from public fear.

Beah, Ishmael. **A Long Way Gone** – **Memoirs of a Boy Soldier**. Sarah Crichton Books, 2007. HS. 240 pages. ISBN-10: 0007247087

Ismael Beah, who is now a children's-rights advocate, recalls his experiences as a young boy growing up in Sierra Leone in the 1990s, during the violent civil war that robbed him of his childhood. In a short period of time he changes from a twelve-year-old boy, who loves rap music and hip hop dancing, to an AK-47 wielding child warrior. When he is rescued and rehabilitated by UNICEF workers, he is tapped as a spokesperson for children in the war torn country.

Beam, Matt. **Getting to First Base with Danalda Chase**. Dutton Juvenile, 2007. MS. 192 pages. ISBN-10: 0525475788

Seventh grader Darcy Spillman is obsessed with baseball and getting to first base with popular Danalda Chase. Using baseball analogies, he tracks his progress with Danalda, as well as his tryouts for the school baseball team. Getting advice from his grandpa, who has Alzheimer's, and a witty new girl who is trying to understand American culture, Darcy fumbles his way toward finding out what he really wants.

Beil, Michael. **The Red Blazer Girls: The Ring of Rocamadour**. Knopf Books for Young Readers, 2009, MS, 304 pages. ISBN-13: 978-0375848148

In the first book of a new series, Sophie, Margaret and Rebecca become amateur detectives to unravel an elaborate puzzle. When the girls meet Ms. Harriman, who lives next door to their all-girls school in Manhattan, she asks them to follow the clues her archeologist father created 20 years ago that will lead to the ring of Rocamadour. The clues challenge their knowledge of math, literature, philosophy and more.

Beil, Michael D. **The Vanishing Violin**. Knopf Books for Young Readers; 1 edition, 2010. MS. 336 pages. ISBN-13: 978-0375861031

The second book in the The Red Blazer Girls mystery series finds the four tween sleuths, not only searching for a violin that was stolen in 1959, but also solving clues that will lead them to a valuable violin that has been promised to Margaret, if they find it. In addition, the girls are forming a band, dealing with a difficult classmate and trying to discover who is mysteriously sprucing up St Veronica's School. Readers once again are able to solve the codes and puzzle clues along with the girls.

Bell, Hilari. **The Last Knight**. Eos, 2007. MS/HS. 368 pages. ISBN-10: 0060825030
     Sir Michael has declared himself a "knight errant" and enlisted the help of Fisk, his indebted but unwilling squire, to rescue those in need. Unfortunately, the first damsel in distress that he rescues is actually an accused murderess. He vows to bring her to justice, and in doing so, embarks on many escapades that require him to use his "magica" which allows him to perform superhuman feats.

Benway, Robin. **Audrey, Wait!** Razorbill, 2008. MS/HS. 313 pages.
ISBN-13: 978-1595141910
     When Audrey breaks up with her rocker boyfriend Evan, he writes a rock song about their breakup that becomes a smash hit and catapults her into fame that she doesn't really want. She finds herself stalked by paparazzi, rock stars looking for a muse and star crazed fans. As Audrey struggles to maintain a normal life and her new romance with her ice cream shop co-worker, she realizes she needs to find a way out of her new found notoriety.

Berk, Josh. **The Dark Days of Hamburger Halpin**. Random House Children's Books, 2010. MS/HS. 250 pages. ISBN-13: 9780375856990
     Being overweight and deaf is a huge handicap for Will Halpin who is trying to make a successful transition from a school for the deaf to Carbon High in a small coal mining town in Pennsylvania. He is befriended by Devon Smiley, another social outcast, who happens to be able to sign. When the school's quarterback dies on a school field trip at the Happy Memorial Coal Mine, the two of them get in touch with their inner Hardy Boy to solve the mystery.

Bingham, Kelly. **Shark Girl.**   Candlewick, 2007. MS/HS. 288 pages.
ISBN-10: 0763632074
     This novel told in verse chronicles the year following a shark attack which claims the right arm of Jane Arrowood, a talented 15-year old-artist. Poems, letters, telephone conversations and newspaper clippings are used to recount Jane's nightmare and subsequent recovery.

Blank, Jessica. **Karma for Beginners**. Hyperion Book CH, 2009. MS/HS. 320 pages. ISBN-13: 978-1423117513
     When fourteen-year-old Tessa's hippie mother pulls her out of school to live at an ashram in the Catskills, Tessa finds herself surrounded by religious zealots and ignored by her mother. She finds solace in a friendship with a 20-year-old outsider named Colin, who fixes trucks for the ashram. As her mother becomes more devoted to the guru and Tessa to Colin, they both struggle to find their way back to each other.

Block, Francesca Lia. **The Frenzy**. HarperTeen, 2010. HS. 272 pages.
ISBN-13: 978-0061926662
     When Liz reaches her thirteenth birthday and turns into a werewolf, she realizes why she only feels at home in the woods and has never really fit in. Her black boyfriend and gay best friend try to help her accept her volatile situation, but as she struggles to

comply with her community's values, she realizes that she must find a way to deal with the "frenzy" of her shape shifting nature.

Bloss, Josie. Albatross. Flux; 1 edition, 2010. MS/HS. 240 pages.ISBN-13: 978-0738714769

Tess, who has recently been uprooted by her newly divorced mom from her friends and home in Chicago, finds herself obsessed with Micah, an abusive but talented pianist who accompanies her for a French horn competition. Knowing that he already has a girlfriend, Tess can't deny her feelings for him, even though her inner voice tells her that she shouldn't tolerate his on-again, off-again attentions.

Blume, Judy. BFF. Two novels by Judy Blume--Just As Long As We're Together/Here's to You, Rachel Robinson. Delacorte Books for Young Readers, 2007. MS. 512 pages. ISBN-10: 0385734077

Stephanie, Rachel and Alison are three junior high school friends who grapple with many issues including divorce, weight gain, problem siblings, and perfectionism, as well as others. The girls find that with two good friends, a girl can deal with just about anything. This is a bind-up of two Judy Blume stories that stand the test of time.

Blundell, Judy. What I Saw and How I Lied. Scholastic Press, 2008. MS/HS. 288 pages. ISBN-13: 978-0439903462

In this National Book Award winning novel, fifteen-year-old Evie and her mother Beverly accompany her stepfather Joe, who has recently returned from WWII, to Palm Beach, Florida, where Evie falls for Peter, an army buddy of Joe's that he's been avoiding. After a boating accident and a suspicious death, her parents become murder suspects, and Evie has to examine her loyalties and consider that her perceptions about her mother may have been wrong all along.

Bodeen. S. A. Compound. Feiwel & Friends, 2008. MS. 256 pages. ISBN-10: 0312370156

Eli lives with his family in a massive underground shelter built by his billionaire father, thinking that nuclear war has destroyed the world he knows. Then the food supply seems to be running out, and, putting aside all morals and ethics, his father comes up with a repulsive cannibalistic solution. Eli, who was already suspicious, begins to investigate the situation and finds himself up against a megalomaniacal monster.

Bosch, Pseudonymous. The Name of this Book is Secret. Little, Brown Young Readers, 2007. MS. 384 pages. ISBN-10: 0316113662

"Warning: Do not read beyond this page." The author cautions the reader on the first page that the book contains a secret that is so dangerous that only the bravest should proceed to read the story of Cass and Max-Ernest and their attempt to rescue a fellow classmate from a mysterious society that is bent on finding the secret to immortality.

Bradbury, Jennifer. Shift. Atheneum, 2008. MS. 256 pages. ISBN-13: 978-1416947325

Best friends, Chris and Win, set off on a cross-country bicycling adventure the day after they graduate from high school. As Win's behavior becomes stranger and stranger and Chris finds thousands of dollars in Win's panniers, their relationship begins to shift. Then Win ditches Chris in Montana, and Chris returns home alone. When the FBI starts investigating Win's disappearance, Chris puts aside his anger and begins to examine clues that are beginning to surface as to what really happened and why.

Bracken, Alexandra. **Brightly Woven**. EgmontUSA, 2010. MS. 368 pages. ISBN-13: 978-1606840382

      After Wayland North, a rogue wizard, ends the drought in Sydelle's village and asks for her as payment, she finds herself accompanying him to the capital in a race to prevent a war with neighboring countries. At first she is furious, but gradually she comes to care for him as she realizes they are together by design, not by accident, and he is harboring a dark secret about their shared destiny.

Bradley, Kimberly Brubaker. **The Lacemaker and the Princess**. Margaret K. McElderry, 2007. MS. 208 pages. ISBN-10: 1416919201.

      When Isabelle, an eleven-year-old lacemaker, is selected to be a playmate for Marie Antoinette's daughter, she is thrown into a world of luxury and decadence. Having been given new clothes and a fashionable name, she forges a fragile friendship with the princess. Then rumors of a revolution surface and Isabelle wonders which side she is really on.

Brande, Robin. **Evolution, Me and Other Freaks of Nature**. Knopf Books for Young Readers, 2007. MS/HS. 272 pages. ISBN-10: 0375843493

      Mena is ostracized by her fundamentalist church friends when she stops the group from harassing a supposedly gay schoolmate. When the next school year begins, she finds herself involved in further drama when they protest the unit on evolution in her high-school science class. Then Casey, her brilliant lab partner, introduces her to his unconventional family and ideas, and her life begins to evolve in some very unexpected ways.

Brasheres, Ann. **Forever in Blue**. Delacorte Books for Young Readers, 2007. MS/HS. 400 pages. ISBN-10: 0385729367

      In the final installment of the Traveling Pants series, Tibby struggles in her relationship with Brian, Lena takes painting classes and falls for a fellow art student, Bridget goes to Turkey on an archaeological dig and gets involved with the married leader of her excavation team, and Carmen goes to Vermont to work as a crew member at a theatrical festival and lands a major role instead.

Brasheres, Ann. **Three Willows: The Sisterhood Grows**. Delacorte Books for Young Readers, 2009. MS. 336 pages. ISBN-13: 978-0385736763

      This new sisterhood series introduces Ama, an overachiever who was born in Ghana, Polly, a curvaceous girl who is longing to be a model, and Jo, a teen who wants to move into the popular crowd, leaving her former friends behind. The girls are spending their first summer apart, and as they go their separate ways, their longstanding relationship seems to be faltering. The issues that brought them together when they were young no longer seem relevant to their lives.

Bray, Libba. **Going Bovine**. Delacorte Books for Young Readers; 1 edition, 2009. MS/HS. 496 pages. ISBN-13: 978-0385733977

      Based on Cervantes' Don Quixote, this fantasy introduces Cameron, a 16-year-old slacker, who has suddenly, becomes the center of attention after he is diagnosed with mad cow disease. In the hospital, he meets Dulcie, an alluring angel, who presents him with a heroic quest to rescue the planet from an otherworldly, evil force and in addition find a cure for his fatal disease

Bray, Libba. **The Sweet Far Thing**. Delacorte Books for Young Readers, 2007. MS/HS. 832 pages. ISBN-10: 0385730306

In the final book of Bray's trilogy Gemma Doyle has to decide whether to fight or join the many creatures of the realms who want access to the magic. As she faces her upcoming social debut, Gemma has more on her mind than dresses and tea parties.

Broach, Elise. **Masterpiece**. Henry Holt and Co. (BYR), 2008. MS. 304 pages. ISBN-13: 978-0805082708

Marvin, a beetle who lives with his overprotective family in an apartment on the Upper East Side, befriends James, the human boy who lives there with his family. A cityscape that Marvin drew for James by dipping his two front legs in ink is mistaken for James' work, so his artist father takes him to the Metropolitan Museum to see similar work by Albrecht Durer. James and Marvin soon find themselves involved in creating a Durer forgery and then having to discover a way to communicate in order to catch the thief of a Durer masterpiece.

Brooks, Kevin. **Being.** The Chicken House, 2007. MS/HS. 336 pages. ISBN-10: 0439899737

Accused of a crime he did not commit, Robert Smith, a lonely teen who finds he is not totally human, is on the run. With the help of Eddi, a girl who makes fake ID's, he escapes to a house in Spain. Unfortunately, he is followed by "the men in suits" who threaten to destroy Eddi and Robert's idyllic beachside existence.

Brooks, Kevin. **Black Rabbit Summer**. Push, 2009. HS. 512 pages. ISBN-13: 978-0545060899

After a night of drug-induced revelry at a summer carnival, Pete finds himself searching for clues to the disappearance of his best friend and a teen celebrity. Raymond, a troubled loner who seeks advice from his black rabbit, was last seen with Stella Ross, a self-obsessed, vapid teen starlet. Although Raymond is the prime suspect, Pete doesn't believe that he could have had anything to do with Stella's disappearance. Pete's investigation leads him into a complicated world of betrayal and blackmail.

Brothers, Meagan. **Debbie Harry Sings in French**. Henry Holt and Co. (BYR); 1st edition, 2008. MS/HS. 240 pages. ISBN-13: 978-0805080803

After Johnny's father dies and his mother withdraws from life, he sinks into a bout of alcoholism that results in his going to rehab, where he discovers solace in the music of Blondie, a punk rock band whose lead singer is Debbie Harry. He loves her voice, her fierce look and the power behind her music. When his mother sends him to live with his uncle in South Carolina, he falls in love with Maria, a fellow outcast, who encourages him to find his "inner Debbie Harry" by competing in a drag contest in Atlanta.

Bunce, Elizabeth C. **A Curse Dark as Gold**. Arthur A. Levine Books, 2008. MS. 400 pages. ISBN-10: 0439895766

This Rumpelstiltskin tale finds Charlotte Miller struggling to run Stirwaters, her family's cursed textile mill. With massive debt and a string of bad luck and vandalism, Charlotte makes a deal with a mysterious man who can spin straw into gold. As she fights a conniving uncle and financial ruin, she almost loses her infant son.

Burd, Nick. **The Vast Fields of Ordinary**. Dial, 2009. HS. 320 pages.
ISBN-13: 978-0803733404

During an eventful summer before college, Dade Hamilton watches his parents marriage implode, his relationship with sort of boyfriend Pablo fizzle, and the media's obsessive coverage of an autistic girl's disappearance unfold. He toils away at a boring job at Food World and feels lost and invisible, until he meets Alex Kincaid, an openly gay drug dealer, with whom he falls in love.

Burg, Ann. **All the Broken Pieces**. Scholastic Press, 2009. MS. 224 pages.
ISBN-13: 978-0545080927

In this novel-in-verse Matt Pin, a twelve-year-old Vietnamese boy who has been adopted by an American family, is haunted by his past in which his father abandons him, his little brother is maimed by a land mine and his mother sends him off to America. He is adored by his new little brother and is a star pitcher on the school baseball team, but he struggles with the prejudice of his teammates and his memories of the atrocities of war.

Bushnell, Candace. **The Carrie Diaries**. Balzer + Bray, 2010. MS/HS. 400 pages.
ISBN-13: 978-0061728914

In this prequel to the wildly popular *Sex and the City*, Carrie Bradshaw navigates the drama of senior year in high school. She dates bad boy Sebastian, who can't seem to stick with one woman, mourns the death of her mother, and dreams of becoming a writer. Hoping to attend a summer writing seminar in New York City, Carrie experiments with finding her voice, as she takes on writing for the school newspaper.

Cabot, Meg. **Airhead**. Point, 2008. MS. 352 pages. ISBN-10: 0545040523

Video game playing tomboy, Emerson Watson, suffers a terrible accident and wakes up in the hospital one month later in the body of the hot teen supermodel Nikki Howard. Em, a self proclaimed feminist, has to reexamine her values and her relationship with her best friend and secret crush Christopher, as she adjusts to the idea that maybe Nikki was more than just an airhead.

Cabot, Meg. **Being Nikki**. Point, 2009. MS. 352 pages. ISBN-13: 978-0545040563

The sequel to *Airhead* finds Em, the tomboy in a supermodel's body, now the "Face of Stark Enterprises." Unfortunately, her friend Christopher is determined to destroy Stark to avenge what he believes to be her death. Then Nikki's brother shows up demanding that Em help him find their missing mom. As the novel ends, Em discovers some shocking news that will have fans eager to read the next book in the series.

Cabot, Meg. **Runaway**. Scholastic Inc.; 1 edition, 2010. MS. 320 pages.
ISBN-13: 978-0545040600

The final book in the *Airhead* series takes up where the second, *Being Nikki*, ends with Emerson Watson, whose brain has been transplanted into super model Nikki Howard's body, being held captive by Brandon Stark, the son of the Stark Enterprise owner. She learns that Christopher is right about the nefarious plans of Stark Enterprises, and she enlists his help to engineer her escape and expose them to the world

16

Caletti, Deb. **The Nature of Jade**. Simon & Schusters Children's Publishing, 2007. MS/HS. 304 pages. ISBN-10: 1416910050

Eighteen-year-old Jade, who suffers from panic attacks, finds watching the elephants on Seattle Zoo's webcam a calming influence. She ultimately meets and falls in love with Sebastian, a single father whom she observes watching the elephants; but he has a secret that threatens to destroy both their dreams.

Caletti, Deb. **The Fortunes of Indigo Skye**. Simon & Schuster Children's Publishing, 2008. MS/HS. 304 pages. ISBN-10: 1416910077

Indigo Skye is a high school student who is a part-time waitress at a diner frequented by eccentric customers. When one of them leaves her a $2.5 million tip, her world is turned upside down. Indigo's struggles to deal with her instant wealth test her ability to decide what is truly import in life.

Caletti, Deb. **The Secret Life of Prince Charming**. Simon Pulse, 2009. MS. 336 pages. ISBN-13: 978-1416959403

When seventeen-year-old Quinn Hunt finds out her father has collected trophy items from each of his wives and lovers, she hits the road to return them to their respective owners. As she, her sister, her half-sister, a musician and a Big Boy statue make their way from one delivery to another, she learns lessons about life and love.

Card, Orson Scott. **Ender in Exile**. Tor Books, 2008. MS/HS. 384 pages. ISBN-13: 978-0765304964

Ender in Exile takes place between the author's immensely popular *Ender's Game* and its sequel *Speaker for the Dead*. After wiping out the Buggers' alien civilization, Ender is sent to be the governor of one of the new human colonies. Hailed as a hero by some and reviled as a murderer by others, Ender struggles with the philosophical issues related to his role in the deaths of so many. Accompanied by his sister Valentine, he travels to the end of the universe trying to find meaning in his life now that he has accomplished his destiny.

Carey, Janet Lee. **Stealing Death**. EgmontUSA, 2009. MS. 368 pages. ISBN-13: 978-1606840092

When fire destroys his family farm killing his mother, father and brother, 17-year-old Kipp vows to find a way to protect his young sister and make sure no one he loves ever dies again. He makes a pact with a witch, allowing him to steal the soul sack from the grim reaper. However, possessing it is an overwhelming responsibility, which is more than he can handle.

Carman, Patrick. **Into the Mist**. Scholastic Press, 2007. MS. 304 pages. ISBN-10: 0439899524

In this Land of Elyon chronicle Ronald Warvold tells Alexa Daley the story of his boyhood. He and his brother Thomas were raised in a horrible orphanage, but escape to find their destiny in a strange unknown world of magic.

Carter, Ally. **Heist Society**. Hyperion Book CH, 2010. MS. 304 pages. ISBN-13: 978-1423116394

Katarina Bishop, daughter of one of the world's foremost art thieves, decides to retire from the family business and attend a New England boarding school. However, when her father's life is threatened, Kat returns to her team of teenage burglars in an attempt to stage a heist that will save her father's life.

Carter, Ally. **I'd Tell You I Love You, But Then I'd Have to Kill You.**
Hyperion, 2007. MS. 288 pages. ISBN-10: 1423100042

15-year-old Cammie Morgan is a student at the Gallagher Academy, a top-secret boarding school for girls who are spies-in-training. Her troubles begin when she falls for Josh, a local boy who has no idea about her true identity. Cammie's double life leads to some hilarious encounters as she navigates the mysteries of boy/girl relationships that seem much more difficult for her than studying covert operations and cultural assimilation at spy school.

Carter, Ally. **Cross My Heart and Hope to Spy**. Hyperion, 2007. MS. 240 pages. ISBN-10: 1423100050

In this sequel to *I'd Tell You I Love You, But Then I'd Have to Kill You*, Cammie Morgan still is training to be a spy at the Gallagher Academy for Exceptional Young Women. After having to give up her non-spy boyfriend Josh, who has been brainwashed to forget her, she is shocked to learn that boys from the Blackthorne spy school for boys will soon be joining them. When the boys finally arrive, gorgeous, but obnoxious, Zak is assigned to be her covert-operations partner. Will he replace Josh in her heart?

Carter, Ally. **Don't Judge a Girl by Her Cover**. Hyperion Book CH, 2009. MS. 272 pages. ISBN-13: 978-1423116387

The third book in the Gallagher Girls series finds Cammie, Bex and Liz on the campaign trail with Macey whose father has been nominated for vice president of the United States. After a failed kidnapping plot, they must protect Macey from an unknown assailant and use their spy training to expose the truth.

Carter, Ally. **Only the Good Spy Young**. Hyperion Book CH; 1 edition, 2010. MS. 272 pages. ISBN-13: 978-1423128205

In the fourth book of the Gallagher Girl series, Cammie Morgan finds herself hiding from an ancient terrorist organization that is trying to kidnap her. When one of her favorite teachers is revealed as a rogue double-agent, Cammie doesn't know who to trust. With the help of her friends, she tries to get to the bottom of the mystery and determine the right path for her future as a spy.

Cashore, Kristin. **Graceling**. Juvenile, 2008. MS. 480 pages. ISBN-13: 978-0152063962

In the fantasy world of Cashore's debut novel, the "Graced" are individuals who are gifted in a particular way. Katsa's Grace is that she is a virtually invincible fighter. She serves her tyrannical uncle, who is king of one of the seven kingdoms. Although she is forced to punish people for infractions against him, she has secretly organized the Council, which tries to find justice for victims of his abuse. As the story opens, she is on a mission to rescue the father of the Lienid king, who has been abducted. In the process she meets Prince Po, the captive's grandson, who is also graced. He joins Katsa on this quest, which is filled with danger, as well as romance.

Cashore, Kristin. **Fire.** Dial , 2009. MS/HS. 480 pages. ISBN-13: 978-0803734616

In the prequel to *Graceling*, we meet Fire, an irresistibly beautiful monster, who can control the minds of those around her. King Nash, whose rule is being contested by neighboring lords, enlists her help in keeping his throne. Although her childhood friend longs to marry her, she is attracted to the king's brother, the commander of his armies, who resents her because of the role her father had in the downfall of the previous king.

Cassidy, Kay. **The Cinderella Society**. EgmontUSA , 2010. MS/HS. 336 pages. ISBN-13: 978-1606840177

The first book in a proposed series introduces Jess Parker who, after a year spent in new girl anonymity, is invited to join the Cinderella Society (TCS) at her high school. At first she thinks membership is all about a makeover and attracting the attention of Ryan Steele, the high school quarterback. She then finds out that TCS is dedicated to protect the Reggies (regular kids) from the popular mean kids known as the Wickeds. As she gets more involved with TCS, she realizes that membership includes a lot of responsibility.

Castelluci, Cecil. **Beige**. Candlewick, 2007. MS/HS. 320 pages. ISBN-10: 0763630667

When Katy is sent to L.A. to spend two weeks with her father, an aging punk rocker known as the Rat, she is determined not to make a fuss. Even though Katy doesn't want to be there and is disgusted by Rat's filthy apartment and uncouth friends, she quietly bides her time until she can go home. Then, when plans change and she has to stay there all summer, she decides she will no longer be the nice girl, who everyone refers to a Beige.

Chaltas, Thalia. **Because I Am Furniture**. Viking, 2009. HS. 368 pages. ISBN-13: 978-0670062980

This novel-in-verse explores the struggles of a high school girl whose father abuses her sister and brother, but ignores her. Although Anke knows her mother is in denial and her father's behavior is devastating the family, she longs for his attention. Against his wishes she joins the school volleyball team and finds the courage to stand up to her father and help her family begin a new life.

Charlton-Trujillo, E.E. **Feels Like Home**. Delacorte Books for Young Readers, 2007. MS/HS. 224 pages. ISBN-10: 0385733321

When their father dies, Danny returns to attend the funeral and see his sister, Michelle, whom he hasn't seen in six years. Danny had always been Michelle's hero, until he got involved in a fireworks accident that killed his best friend and left town, consumed with guilt. Having a hard time forgiving him for abandoning her, Michelle remembers a quote from their favorite book *The Outsiders* and realizes that "nothing gold can stay."

Childs, Tera Lynn. **Oh. My. Gods**. Dutton Juvenile, 2008. MS. 224 pages. ISBN-13: 978-0525479420

Just as Phoebe Castro's dream of winning a cross-country scholarship to USC seems about to come true, her mother whisks them off to an island in the Aegean where Phoebe is enrolled at a top-secret school where all the students are ascended from one or more Greek gods. As Phoebe struggles with her evil stepsister sabotaging her attempts to fit in, making the cross-country team, and dealing with her crush on a fellow teammate, she begins to wonder if she will survive this unconventional year abroad.

Childs, Tera Lynn. **Goddess Boot Camp**. Dutton Juvenile, 2009. MS. 224 pages. ISBN-13: 978-0525421344

In the sequel to *Oh. My. Gods.*, Phoebe, a descendant of the goddess Nike, continues to adjust to her new life at a boarding school for the descendants of Greek gods. She has problems controlling her new divine powers, so her stepdad enrolls her in a Goddess Boot Camp. Unfortunately, her mean stepsister is her camp counselor. In addition to this, she is training for the Pythian games and is worried that her boyfriend is cheating on her. What's a goddess to do?

Choldenko, Gennifer. **Al Capone Shines My Shoes**. Dial, 2009. MS. 288 pages. ISBN-13: 978-0803734609

In the sequel to *Al Capone Does My Shirts* Moose Flanagan thinks he is indebted to the mobster and worries his family will be kicked off Alcatraz Island if anyone finds out. With his mentally impaired sister off at the Esther P. Marinoff school, he thought his problems were solved, but he receives a gangster's note in his laundry that may mean they've just begun.

Choldenko, Gennifer. **If a Tree Falls at Lunch Period**. Harcourt Children's Books, 2007. MS 224 pages. ISBN-10: 0152057536

On his first day at the new private white school, Walk, an African American student, meets Kirsten, who is weathering her parents escalating feud and her best friend's defection to the queen bee's clique. Little do they know that they will soon discover a secret that will change their lives.

Choyce, Lesley. **Wave Warrior**. Orca Book Publishers, 2007. MS/HS. 105 pages. ISBN-10: 1551436477

Sixteen-year-old Ben Currie, who lives in Lawrencetown, Nova Scotia, has often wondered why anyone would be crazy enough to surf in the cold waters of the northern Atlantic. Never-the-less he tries it and is not only injured, but humiliated in front of the other surfers. Then he meets Ray Cluny, a kahuna or old surfer from California, who challenges him to become a wave warrior, one who "embraces his fear, knows why it's there and respects both the fear and the wave."

Clare, Cassandra. **City of Bones**. Simon Pulse, 2008. MS/HS. 512 pages. ISBN-10: 1416955070

When Clary Fray witnesses three teenagers murder another teen, she learns that the teens are Shadowhunters, humans who hunt and kill demons. Shortly after this discovery, she finds out that her mother is also a Shadowhunter and the only one who knows the location of The Mortal Cup, a dangerous magical item that turns humans into Shadowhunters. When her mother disappears, Clary and her friend Simon must find the cup before all hell breaks loose.

Clare, Cassandra. **City of Ashes**. Margaret K. McElderry, 2008. MS/HS. 464 pages. ISBN-10: 1416914293

The sequel to *City of Bones* finds Clary's mother in a magically induced coma. Clary's only hope of helping her mother is to hunt down her father, the evil Valentine. To complicate matters, someone in New York City is murdering vampire, werewolf and faerie children. Is Valentine behind the killings -- and if he is, what is he trying to do? When the second of the Mortal Instruments, the Soul-Sword, is stolen, the terrifying Inquisitor suspects Clary's brother Jace. Clary wonders if Jace is willing to betray everything he believes in to help their father?

Clare, Cassandra. **City of Glass**. Margaret K. McElderry, 2009. MS/HS. 560 pages. ISBN-13: 978-1416914303

In the final installment of the Mortal Instrument series, Clary goes to the City of Glass in search of a remedy for her dying mother. There she gets involved in a battle between the Shadow hunters and Valentine's army of demons in a last ditch effort to save the world. Romantic issues are resolved and surprising relationships are revealed in a satisfying ending to the popular series.

Clement-Davies, David, **Fell**. Amulet Books, 2007. MS. 432 pages. ISBN-13: 978-0-8109-1185-7

This sequel to *The Sight* finds Fell, a black wolf, who has the gift of seeing into the minds of others, coming to the aid of a human. The villagers believe that fifteen-year-old Alina is a changeling. When she must flee the village, Fell helps restore her to her family and in doing so, reunites a divided kingdom.

Clement-Moore, Rosemary. **Prom Dates from Hell**. Delacorte Books for Young Readers, 2007. MS/HS. 320 pages. ISBN-10: 0385734123

Maggie Quinn is six weeks from high school graduation, when she realizes something strange is going on. When weird things start happening to the school's ruling clique, Maggie realizes it's up to her to play Nancy Drew and find out who unleashed a demon before all hell breaks loose.

Clements, Andrew. **Extra Credit**. Atheneum, 2009. MS. 192 pages. ISBN-13: 978-1416949299

To avoid being held back a year, Abby, an eleven-year-old girl in central Illinois, takes on an extra-credit assignment that involves writing to a pen-pal in Afghanistan. Her letters are answered by Sadeed, a gifted student who attends a one-room school in Kabul. His sister must dictate and sign the letters, because it would be considered improper for a boy to be corresponding with a girl, but Sadeed can't resist telling Abby about his own hopes and dreams. Through their correspondence the two develop a bond that transcends the literal and figurative distance between their two homes.

Cohn, Rachel. **Cupcake.** Simon & Schuster Children's Publishing, 2007. MS/HS. 256 pages. ISBN-10: 1416912177

The third in the series, *Cupcake* finds Cyd Charise living in New York's Greenwich Village with her half brother Danny, working as a barista, and missing her surfer boyfriend, Shrimp. When Shrimp shows up on her doorstep, CC needs to decide what direction she wants her life to take.

Cohn, Rachel. **You Know Where to Find Me**. Simon & Schuster Children's Publishing, 2008. MS/HS. 208 pages. ISBN-10: 0689878591

In a first-person narrative employing essays and flashbacks, Miles, an eighteen-year-old Goth, chronicles the suicide of her cousin Laura, which leads to a year of grieving and growing drug addiction. Set in Washington DC where racial stratification and political turmoil are rampant, the story discusses teenage angst with graphic realism.

Cohn, Rachel. **Very LeFreak**. Knopf Books for Young Readers; 1 edition, 2010. HS. 320 pages. ISBN-13: 978-0375857584

Veronica, aka Very, is obsessed with technology. Attending class and listening to her Columbia University professors aren't nearly as interesting instant messaging, texting, meme-ing and tweeting. A co-creator of the Grid, an underground student networking site, Very is also busy organizing flash mobs and illegal parties. In danger of flunking out, Very is finally sent to tech-rehab when her friends do an intervention.

Colfer, Eoin. **Airman**. Hyperion Book CH, 2008. MS. 416 pages. ISBN-13: 978-1423107507

Conor Broekhart, who was born aboard a dirigible in 1878, is determined to learn to fly. He grows up in the Saltee Islands off the coast of Ireland, is best friends with Princess Isabella, daughter of King Nicholas, and seems to be destined for greatness. Then he is framed for the death of King Nicholas and ends up in prison. Conor engineers an aerial escape and is determined to get revenge on the scheming Marshall Bonvilain who derailed Conor's life.

Collins, Suzanne. **The Hunger Games**. Scholastic Press, 2008. MS/HS. 384 pages. ISBN-13: 978-0439023481

In the not-too-distant future in Panem, a dystopian state in North America, 24 teens are selected by lottery each year to compete in The Hunger Games. The games are televised as the teens are forced to eliminate their competitors until only one teen is left alive. In District 12, the poorest district in Panem, 16-year-old Katniss takes her 12-year-old sister's place along with Peeta, the town baker's son. Although they are pitted against stronger contestants, their cooperation just may allow them to survive.

Collins, Suzanne. **Catching Fire**. Scholastic Press, 2009. MS. 400 pages. ISBN-13: 978-0439023498

The sequel to *The Hunger Games* finds Katniss and Peeta on a victory tour which reveals the unrest in the districts of Panem. As Katniss struggles to understand her feelings for Gale and Peeta, the 75th Anniversary of the Hunger Games is approaching. Will she obediently marry Peeta and appease President Snow, or will she lead a rebellion against the oppression which is becoming intolerable?

Collins, Suzanne. **Mockingjay**. Scholastic Press, 2010. MS/HS. 400 pages. ISBN-13: 978-0439023511

In the final book of the Hunger Games series, Katniss Everdeen, who has survived the Hunger Games twice, becomes the figurehead for the rebel forces who are plotting to overthrow the Capitol. She is living in District 13 with her mother and sister and has reconnected with Gale, her hunting partner from her childhood. Peeta, her Hunger Games mate, is being held captive by President Snow. It is up to Katniss to help those who are trying to change the leadership of Panem and secure the future of those she loves.

Colasanti, Susane. **Something Like Fate**. Viking Juvenile, 2010. MS/HS. 288 pages. ISBN-13: 978-0670011469

Lani and Erin, best friends since childhood, are obsessed with exploring the concept of fate. When Erin starts dating Jason, Lani is happy for her, until Lani realizes that she and Jason are fated to be together. Although Jason breaks up with Erin to pursue a relationship with Lani, Lani struggles between remaining loyal to her friend and being with the boy whom she believes is her soul mate.

Condie, Ally. **Matched**. Dutton Juvenile, 2010. MS. 369 pages.ISBN-13: 978-0525423645

The first book in a new dystopian trilogy is set in a tranquil, rational futuristic world where choice has been virtually eliminated. Seventeen-year-old Cassia, who is looking forward to her matching ceremony where she will be introduced to her future husband, is also dreading her grandfather's upcoming Final Banquet, where he is scheduled to die. But then, as events go vastly awry, she begins to rebel against the societal dictates she has followed blindly for years.

Cooney, Caroline. **Diamonds in the Shadows**. Delacorte Books for Young Readers, 2007. MS. 240 pages. ISBN-10: 0385732619

When his family takes in a refugee family from war torn Sierra Leone, Jared suspects that something is not right. Although the family's strange behavior could be blamed on the horrors they have experienced, Jared thinks it has something to do with the uncut diamonds he finds in the "ashes" of their ancestors.

Cooney, Caroline. **Enter Three Witches**. Scholastic Press, 2007. MS/HS. 288 pages. ISBN-10: 0439711568

Inspired by Shakespeare's *Macbeth*, *Enter Three Witches* chronicles the events of the play through the eyes of Lady Mary, the 14-year-old ward of Lord and Lady Macbeth. After Mary's father betrays King Duncan and is hung, Mary is demoted to scullery maid, a position from which she then watches with horror the violence that sweeps through the Scottish court as the MacBeths vie for power.

Cooney, Caroline. **If the Witness Lied**. Delacorte Books for Young Readers, 2009. MS. 224 pages. ISBN-13: 978-0385734486

Jack Fountain's family has been overwhelmed by tragedy. His mother fatally foregoes cancer treatment in order to give birth to his baby brother Tris, and then Tris allegedly causes the death of their father and leaves them in the clutches of "Aunt" Cheryl. Their older sister Madison moves in with her godparents and younger sister Smithy heads off to boarding school, leaving Jack to cope. Now Cheryl is selling the family story as a reality TV show, and the kids reunite to uncover the truth and put an end to their nightmare.

Cornwell, Autumn. **Carpe Diem**. Feiwel & Friends, 2007. MS/HS. 368 pages. ISBN-10: 0312367929

Sixteen-year-old overachiever Vassar Spore has every minute of the next ten years planned out. Then somehow she ends up spending the summer with her bohemian grandmother, who has blackmailed Vassar's uptight parents into letting her go backpacking through Malaysia, Cambodia and Laos. Vassar finds herself hiking through jungles with Grandma and an Asian cowboy bodyguard, who rescues her from one disaster after another. As Vassar learns to "live in the moment," she comes closer and closer to uncovering the family secret that will change her world forever.

Crane, E.M. **Skin Deep**. Delacorte Books for Young Readers, 2008. MS. 288 pages.
ISBN-10: 0385734794

Winner of the 2006 Delacorte Press First YA Novel contest, this book details the relationship between a lonely sixteen-year-old girl and an eccentric artist who is battling cancer. When Andrea is hired to dog sit for Honora's St. Bernard Zena, while Honora undergoes chemotherapy, a relationship blossoms, which enables Andrea to embark on a journey of self discovery.

Creech, Sharon. **The Castle Corona**. Joanna Cotler, 2007. MS. 336 pages.
ISBN-10: 0060846216

This comic fairy tale set in feudal Italy begins with Pia and Enzio, orphaned peasant children, finding a stolen pouch. In a parallel story the slightly ridiculous royal family members let their need to appear "royal" interfere with what they really want to do. When the king fears for his life, Pia and Enzio are hired as royal food tasters. Ultimately, the contents of the stolen pouch are revealed and transform all their lives.

Creech, Sharon. **Hate that Cat**. Joanna Cotler , 2008. MS. 160 pages.
ISBN-10: 0061430927

In a companion book to *Love that Dog*, Jack's teacher continues to introduce him to the poetry of the masters. He still misses his dog and resists the suggestion that he adopt a cat, as he studies William Carlos Williams and other poets.

Crowley, Suzanne. **The Very Ordered Existence of Merilee Marvelous**.
Greenwillow, 2007. MS. 384 pages. ISBN-10: 0061231975

Merilee Monroe is autistic and her only way of coping with the world is through following a routine she calls her Very Ordered Existence. (V.O.E.) When two strangers come to town, Biswick, a boy with fetal alcohol syndrome, and Veraleen, a nurse who has been dismissed from the hospital, Merilee's V.O.E. is derailed, and she must learn to deal with the chaos that caring about people entails.

Crutcher, Chris. **Deadline**. HarperTeen, 2007. HS. 320 pages. ISBN-10: 0060850892

18-year-old Ben Wolf is diagnosed with an aggressive form of leukemia and decides to decline treatment and keep his illness secret from his family and friends. Free from long-term consequences, he joins the football team where his brother is the star quarterback, dates a girl he's had a crush on, and annoys his biased U.S. Government teacher. Hoping to have a "normal" senior year at his small Idaho high school, he tries to pack a lifetime of living into a single year.

Curtis, Christopher Paul. **Elijah of Buxton.** Scholastic Press, 2007. MS. 288 pages.
ISBN-10: 0439023440

Eleven-year-old Elijah Freeman was the first free black born in Buxton, an actual Canadian settlement established in 1849 by the abolitionist Reverend William King. Elijah's mother frequently admonishes him that he is too fragile, so he sets out to prove her wrong. His adventures take him many places including across the border where he risks capture by slave catchers and experiences the dangers of the Underground Railroad.

Dasher, James. **The Maze Runner**. Delacorte Books for Young Readers; First Edition edition, 2009. MS. 384 pages. ISBN-13: 978-0385737944

The first book in a proposed trilogy introduces Thomas, who is an amnesiac thrust into an enormous maze named the Glade where other teens are struggling to survive. No one knows why they are there, but each day elected maze runners search the monster ridden labyrinth to find a way out. When the first girl arrives in the Glade, she triggers memories in Thomas about the world outside the Glade, giving him clues as to how to escape.

Davis, Deborah. **Not Like You.** Clarion Books, 2007. MS/HS. 272 pages. ISBN-10: 061872093

Kayla's mother has always referred to their abrupt moves as "starting a new chapter," but 15-year-old Kayla knows they are really running from problems caused by her mom's alcoholism. When they move to New Mexico and Kayla gets involved with a 24-year-old musician, Kayla hopes that this move will be different.

Dean, Claire. **Girlwood**. Houghton Mifflin; 1 edition, 2008. MS. 256 pages. ISBN-13: 978-0618883905

Polly's concern over the plans for cutting down the woods near her Idaho home to put in a subdivision are compounded when her older sister Bree runs away and Polly believes she is hiding in the woods. To complicate matters their parents are separated and their herbalist grandmother, who is trying to help find Bree, is ill. As Polly struggles with these issues, she is also trying to learn all she can about herbal remedies and her ability to see auras, as well as save the magical forest which has always been her refuge.

de Guzman, Michael. **Finding Stinko.** Farrar, Straus and Giroux , 2007. MS. 144 pages. ISBN-10: 0374323054

Newboy, an abandoned child who is an elective mute, escapes from his eleventh foster home into a hostile city where he is robbed and assaulted. Then, he finds a smelly discarded ventriloquist's dummy that he names Stinko and has him do the talking for him. Befriended by a dancer with artificial feet, Newboy learns to take chances and finds friends among other street children he meets.

De La Cruz, Melissa. **Masquerade: A Blue Bloods Novel.** Hyperion, 2007. MS/HS. 320 pages. ISBN-10: 0786838930

In the sequel to *Blue Bloods* Schuyler Van Alen has headed off to Italy to find her grandfather, who will hopefully help her find out why young blue blood vampires are being murdered. Meanwhile, the other blue blood teens are planning the Four Hundred Ball. Schuyler returns and as she gets ready to attend the ball, she struggles with her feelings about her "familiar" Jack and a new guy in town.

De la Cruz, Melissa. **Revelations**. Hyperion Book, 2008. MS. 272 pages. ISBN-13: 978-1423102281

The third book in the Blue Bloods vampire saga finds Schuyler Van Alen struggling with her relationships with friends and foes. Her grandfather has gone off to Rio, her mother is in a coma and Schuyler has been left stranded in the Force household with Mimi her nemesis and Jack her secret lover. As the Silver Bloods breach the Gates of Hell in Rio, Schuyler comes to the aid of the Conclave with the help of her familiar and best friend Oliver.

de la Pena, Matt. **Mexican WhiteBoy**. Delacorte Books for Young Readers, 2008. MS. 256 pages. ISBN-13: 978-0385733106

Biracial baseball player, Danny Lopez, doesn't feel like he fits in with his dad's Mexican culture, nor the white culture at school. The baseball field is the only place he is comfortable. If he could only get control of his blazing fast ball, it might be his ticket to acceptance. When he meets Uno, an African American street thug with issues of his own, they team up on and off the field to navigate their problems.

De la Pena, Matt. **We Were Here**. Delacorte Books for Young Readers, 2009. MS/HS. 368 pages. ISBN-13: 978-038573667

This story is written as a court ordered journal that Miguel Castenada is required to write while in a group home in San Jose. Fed up with the group home environment, Miguel and two other inmates, Mong and Rondell, break out and attempt to flee to Mexico. Miguel continues to chronicle their adventures in the journal, slowly revealing the stories leading to each boy's incarceration and the tragic event that changed Miguel's life forever.

De Lint, Charles. **Dingo**. Puffin, 2008. MS. 224 pages. ISBN-10: 0142408166

Lainey and her twin sister Em, Australian shapeshifters who are being pursued by an ancient dingo spirit, have just moved to the Point where Miguel Schreiber lives. Miguel falls in love with Lainey and the town bully is attracted to Em. Together they try to free the girls from the clutches of Warrigal, the first dingo, who needs their blood to free himself from a fig tree where he is trapped in Australian dreamtime. Australian folklore permeates this story of mythic battles and romance.

De Vita, James. **The Silenced.** Eos, 2007. MS/HS. 512 pages. ISBN-10: 0060784628

This dystopian novel takes place in a futuristic world where the Zero Tolerance Party controls everything. Listening devices are in every home and citizens are forbidden to read or write. Marena, in the spirit of her murdered mother, forces a resistance group called the White Rose to fight the tyranny.

Despain, Brea. **The Dark Divine**. EgmontUSA, 2009. MS/HS. 384 pages. ISBN-13: 978-1606840573

Sixteen-year-old Grace Divine, a pastor's daughter, can't deny her attraction to Daniel, her foster brother who returns after disappearing for three years. Her brother Jude begs her to stay away from Daniel, but Grace keeps thinking she can save him. When she finds out he's a werewolf, she realizes she may be in over her head.

Despain, Bree. **The Lost Saint**. EgmontUSA, 2010. MS/HS. 416 pages. ISBN-13: 978-1606840580

In the sequel to *Dark Divine*, Grace, who sacrificed her soul save Daniel Kalbi in the first novel, finds herself struggling to deal with her mother's death, as well as her own evolution into a werewolf. While her absentee father is out searching for her missing brother Jude, Grace befriends Talbot, a newcomer who promises to help her. Her relationship with Daniel, who is now free of the werewolf curse, is threatened as he refuses to help her harness her newfound powers.

Dessen, Sarah. **Along for the Ride**. Viking Juvenile, 2009. MS. 384 pages.
ISBN-13: 978-0670011940

   After her parents' divorce Auden is spending what she hopes will be a carefree summer with her dad and his new wife. Auden, who is always studying in an attempt to please her demandingly academic mom, has missed out on a normal teenage life. Then she meets Eli, who is struggling to deal with the guilt he feels over the death of a friend. Both insomniacs, they meet on nightly nocturnal sojourns. Together they embark on a quest to find out what the town has to offer at night and end up discovering a lot about themselves and each other.

Dessen, Sarah. **Lock and Key.** Viking Juvenile, 2008. MS/HS. 432 pages
ISBN-10: 067001088X.

   When social services finds out Ruby is living alone after her neglectful, alcoholic mother disappears, they place Ruby with her estranged sister Cora, whose husband is the wealthy founder of a popular social networking site. All of a sudden Ruby is attending a private school and living a life of privilege she's not sure she really wants.

Dionne, Erin. **Models Don't Eat Chocolate Cookies**. Dial, 2009. MS. 256 pages.
ISBN-13: 978-0803732964

   Thirteen-year-old plus-size Celeste is mortified, when her aunt enters her in the Husky Peach modeling contest. She is sure she will be taunted and humiliated if anyone at school finds out. Instead she finds friendship and a new self confidence as she goes through the pageant process.

Doctorow, Cory. **Little Brother**. Tor Teen, 2008. MS/HS. 384 pages.
ISBN-13: 978-0765319852

   Techno-geek Marcus and his gaming buddies are ditching school when terrorists blow up the Bay Bridge in San Francisco. Agents from the Department of Homeland Security find the kids suspicious and detain them for six days of intensive interrogation and torture. After his release, Marcus uses his technological skills to fight back against governmental electronic surveillance and restrictions which threaten to take away people's privacy and personal freedom.

Doctorow, Cory. **For the Win**. Tor Teen; 1 edition, 2010. MS/HS. 480 pages.
ISBN-13: 978-0765322166

   In the near future, gaming has evolved into big business. Young gamers are recruited all over the globe for gold farming, accumulating virtual gold and weaponry to be sold for real money to monied players. The gold farmers, under the control of brutal bosses, endure horrible working conditions and earn slave wages. Leonard in LA, Mala and Yasmin in Dharavi, and Matthew and Lu in Shenzhen, under the guidance of Big Sister Nor in Singapore, decide to unionize the gaming world to demand fair treatment and protection from organized crime for the workers.

Dogar, Sharon. **Waves.** Chicken House Ltd, 2007. MS/HS. 352 pages. ISBN-10: 1905294247.
   While fifteen-year-old Charley lies comatose in a hospital bed, her younger brother Hal begins to channel her memories, connecting her injury to the brother of the girl Hal loves. Will Hal be able to solve the mystery, so his sister can rest in peace?

Donnelly, Jennifer. **Revolution**. Delacorte Books for Young Readers, 2010. MS/HS. 496 pages. ISBN-10: 0385737637

After her brother's murder sends Andi into a suicidal tailspin, her father takes her to Paris where he is doing DNA tests on a heart thought to belong to Louis XVII, the doomed son of Marie Antoinette. While there, Andi finds Alexandre Paradis's diary which chronicles the royal family's last days during the French revolution. Andi feels a cosmic connection with Alex, as well as Virgil, a hip-hop musician she bonds with over their shared love of music.

Dowd, Siobhan. **Bog Child**. David Fickling Books, 2008. MS. 336 pages. ISBN-13: 978-0385751698

While pilfering peat in the Irish hills, eighteen-year-old Fergus McCann discovers the perfectly preserved body of a dwarf, who was apparently murdered 2000 years ago. Archeologists are called in to study the find, and Fergus falls in love with Cora, the lead archeologist's daughter. As he worries about his brother who is a Long Kesh political prisoner on a hunger strike, smuggles packages for the IRA and pursues Cora, Fergus begins dreaming about the life of the bog child whom he names Mel. In stories alternating between the past and present the author explores the theme of sacrifice in the name of peace.

Downham, Jenny. **Before I Die.** Definitions, 2007. HS. 336 pages. ISBN-10: 1862304874

Terminally ill, Tessa decides there are ten things she wants to experience before she dies, including sex, petty crime, drugs, and true love. With the help of her best friend she sets out to accomplish her goal. Tessa's internal monologues allow the reader to experience her highs and lows as she spends her remaining time living not dying. . Downham's lyrical language makes the poignant journey an experience that is heartbreaking, yet inspiring.

Doyle, Marissa. **Bewitching Season**. Henry Holt and Co. (BYR), 2008. MS/HS. 352 pages. ISBN-13: 978-0805082517

Twins Persephone and Penelope are to be presented at court in London during the 1837 social season. Pen can't wait, but Persy would rather be studying magic with their governess, Ally. Then Ally disappears and the girls must employ their magical skills to find her. In doing so, they uncover a plot against the young Queen Victoria that they must thwart, and Persy struggles to untangle her involvement with Lord Seton, whom she has loved since childhood. She has cast a love spell on him and can't determine whether his attentions are true love or the result of her magic potion.

Doyle, Marissa. **Betraying Season**. Henry Holt and Co. (BYR), 2009. MS/HS. 336 pages. ISBN-13: 978-0805082524

The sequel to *Bewitching Season* finds Persy happily married to Lord Seton and Pen in Ireland studying magic with Ally who is now married to Michael Carrighar. When Niall Keating begins to court her, Pen is charmed. Little does she know that he has been ordered by his sorceress mother to seduce her for nefarious purposes. Although Pen's magic skills are becoming increasingly powerful, they may not be enough the combat the sorceress's evil plan.

Doyle, Roddy and others. **Click.** Arthur A. Levine Books, 2007. MS/HS. 256 pages. ISBN-10: 0439411386

Many of the world's well-loved authors each contribute a chapter in the life of the mysterious George "Gee" Keane, photographer, soldier, adventurer and enigma. Through the eyes of people who knew him, a portrait emerges of a man, his family, and many of the subjects he met during his complicated tangle of a life.

Draper, Sharon. **Fire on the Rock**. Juvenile, 2007. MS/HS. 240 pages. ISBN-10: 0525477209

When Sylvia is chosen as one of the first black students to integrate the white high school In Little Rock in 1957, she is not sure she wants to go. If she stays at her old school, she is guaranteed a good education and a social life. If she goes to the white school, she will be prohibited from participating in extracurricular activities and will be in danger, but she will make history.

Draper, Sharon. **November Blues**. Atheneum, 2007. MS/HS. 320 pages. ISBN-10: 1416906983

The sequel to *The Battle of Jericho* involves November Nelson, whose boyfriend Josh died in a hazing incident, and his cousin Jericho, who cannot bear the pain of his loss. When November finds out she is pregnant with Josh's child, she and Jericho struggle to deal with this problem that maybe bigger than both of them.

Duff, Hilary. **Elixir**. Simon & Schuster Children's Publishing, 2010. MS/HS. 336 pages. ISBN-13: 978-1442408531

The first book in a new paranormal series, which Duff co-wrote with Elise Allan, introduces Clea Raymond, a young photojournalist whose famous parents make her a paparazzi target. When her father goes missing, Clea notices that a mysterious stranger is showing up in many of her photographs. When she finally meets him, she finds that she has known him in past lives, and he may be able to help her solve the mystery of her father's disappearance.

DuPrau, Jeanne. **The Diamond of Darkhold**. Random House Books for Young Readers, 2008. MS. 304 pages. ISBN-13: 978-0375855719

The last book in the *City of Ember* series finds Lina and Doon in Sparks, where the shortages brought on by the arrival of the Emberites are becoming a serious problem. Doon comes across a book that hints about an artifact that will provide help after the citizens leave Ember, but most of the pages have been used to start fires. He and Lina journey back to Ember, hoping to retrieve supplies to relieve the scarcity in Sparks and at the same time look for the artifact that was hinted about in the book.

Duprau, Jeanne. **The Prophet of Yonwood.** Yearling, 2007. MS. 304 pages. ISBN-10: 0440421241

After Nickie's grandfather dies, she accompanies her aunt to Yonwood, NC, to sell his house. When they arrive, they learn of a prophet's prediction of fire and disaster which the townspeople hope to avert by giving up sinful diversions. Nickie succumbs to this brainwashing until the Prophet's spokesperson tells everyone they must give up their pets, at which point Nickie confronts the Prophet and finds out the truth. Although this is billed as a prequel to City of Ember, the relationship isn't revealed until the last chapter.

Ehrenberg, Pamela. **Ethan Suspended.** Eerdmans Books for Young Readers, 2007. MS. 336 pages. ISBN-10: 0802853242

Ethan Oppenheimer is sent to live with his old fashioned grandparents in Washington, D.C., after he is suspended from his suburban school in Pennsylvania. The only white student at his new junior high school, he finds it impossible to fit in. As he struggles to adjust to this new world, he also worries about his parents' separation and the mysterious events surrounding his suspension.

Elkeles, Simone. **Perfect Chemistry**. Walker Books for Young Readers, 2008. MS/HS. 368 pages. ISBN-13: 978-0802798220

When Brittany Ellis, the school's golden girl, and Alex Fuentes, a Latino Bloods gang member, are assigned as chemistry lab partners, they clash immediately. However, as they get to know each other, they are surprised to find they have a lot in common and an undeniable attraction begins to smolder. Complications in both their lives find them turning to each other for support and ultimately romance.

Elkeles, Simone. **Rules of Attraction**. Walker Books for Young Readers, 2010. MS/HS. 336 pages. ISBN-13: 978-0802720856

In the sequel to *Perfect Chemistry* Alex and Brittany are attending the University of Colorado. When Alex's younger brother Carlos gets into trouble in Mexico, their mother sends him to live with Alex, who finds Carlos more than he can handle. Then Carlos is framed for narcotics possession, and one of Alex's professors takes him in. He gets involved with the professor's daughter Kiara, who finds herself attracted to Carlos, despite his hard headed combative behavior.

Engle, Margarita. **The Firefly Letters: A Suffragette's Journey to Cuba.** Henry Holt and Co. (BYR), 2010. MS. 160 pages. ISBN-13: 978-0805090826

This novel-in-verse chronicles the three months suffragette Fredrika Bremer spent in Cuba in 1851. The story focuses on three oppressed women: Fredrika, an upper class girl from Sweden, Cecilia, a teenage slave who is her translator, and Elena, a teenager whose family owns Cecilia. Elena, who is kept a virtual prisoner on her family's estate, finds herself envying the other two women's relative freedom.

Engle, Margarita. **Tropical Secrets: Holocaust Refugees in Cuba**. Henry Holt and Co. (BYR); 1 edition, 2009. MS.208 pages. ISBN-13: 978-0805089363

This companion book to *The Poet Slave of Cuba* and *The Surrender Tree*, tells the story of Daniel, a German Jewish refugee whose ship is allowed entry into Cuba, and Paloma, a Cuban girl whose father is getting rich selling visas to the refugees. Defying her father, Paloma helps the refugees and develops a friendship with Daniel who is also aided by David, an elderly man who immigrated to Cuba from Russia.

Ephron, Delia. **Frannie in Pieces.** HarperTeen , 2007. MS/HS. 384 pages. ISBN-10: 0060747161

When Frannie's dad dies, she finds an elaborate puzzle he made and labeled "Frances Anne 1000." Thinking it is her birthday present, Frannie starts to put the puzzle together and begins magically entering the puzzle. Her trips into the puzzle take her into the world of her parents' past, before and after their divorce, enabling her to come to terms with her grief.

Eulberg, Elizabeth. <u>The Lonely Hearts Club</u>. Point; 1 edition, 2009. MS.320 pages. ISBN-13: 978-0545140317

Penny Lane Bloom's passion for the Beatles inspires the name for the Lonely Hearts Club, which she starts after a being devastated by the boy she thought was her sole mate. Many of her friends join, including Diane, her former best friend who just broke up with the boy who came between the girls several years before. The club grows and their social clout cannot be ignored. Unfortunately, their no dating rule becomes a problem when Penny falls for Diane's ex.

Fantaskey, Beth. <u>Jekyl Loves Hyde</u>. Harcourt Children's Books; 1 edition, 2010. MS/HS. 288 pages. ISBN-13: 978-0152063900

This spin off from Robert Louis Stevenson's classic introduces good girl Jill Jekyl who meets bad boy Tristen Hyde at her murdered father's funeral. When their teacher throws them together to enter a chemistry contest, the two decide to try to recreate the original Dr. Jekyll's formula, to combat the monster Tristen thinks is growing within him.

Fantaskey, Beth. <u>Jessica's Guide to Dating on the Dark Side</u>. Harcourt Children's Books; 1 edition, 2009. MS/HS. 368 pages.ISBN-13: 978-0152063849

Mathlete Jessica Packwood, who was adopted as an infant in Romania, lives in rural Pennsylvania with her vegan parents. She is horrified when foreign exchange student Lucius Valdescu arrives and informs her that she is a vampire who has been betrothed to him since infancy. A family pact decrees that she must marry him to unite their vampire clans and avert war. But just when she convinces him that their marriage is out of the question, she begins to have a change of heart.

Farmer, Nancy. <u>The Land of the Silver Apples.</u> Atheneum/Richard Jackson Books, 2007. MS. 496 pages. ISBN-10: 1416907351

The sequel to *The Sea of Trolls* finds Jack searching for his sister Lucy, who has been stolen by the Lady of the Lake. He reunites with Thorgil and together they battle kelpies, yarthkins, and elves in their quest to right the many wrongs that have occurred.

Feinstein, John. <u>Change-Up: Mystery at the World Series</u>. Knopf Books for Young Readers, 2009. MS. 320 pages. ISBN-13: 978-0375856365

Two teen investigative reporters, who are covering the World Series between Boston and Washington, D.C., uncover a suspicious incident in a rookie pitcher's past. Nobert Doyle, a career minor league player, is called up at the last minute to play for the Nationals. Fortuitously, the teens interviewed him before his winning game and are able to parlay the information he divulged into a front page story. However, they face an ethical dilemma in deciding whether to expose him and ruin his fairytale story.

Ferguson, Alane. <u>The Circle of Blood</u>. Viking Juvenile, 2008. MS/HS. 256 pages. ISBN-10: 0670060569

In this forensic mystery Cameryn Mahoney, assists her father, the Silverton county coroner, in investigating crime scenes, as well as attending autopsies. When she and her mother pick up a mysterious young hitchhiker, Cameryn intuits that the girl is a runaway, but before she can investigate, the girl is found dead. Although the authorities want to rule it a suicide, Cameryn suspects it is murder and is determined to find out the truth.

Ferguson, Alane. **The Dying Breath: Forensic Mystery**. Viking Juvenile, 2009. MS/HS. 234 pages. ISBN-13: 978-0670063147

The fourth book in The Forensic Mystery series finds teen assistant coroner, Cameryn Mahoney, stalked by a sociopathic killer with whom she became involved in an earlier book. Kyle O'Neil is leaving creepy love notes for her and no matter what the Deputy Sheriff does to protect her, Kyle seems to find a way around it. Finally, it is up to Cameryn to put an end to Kyle's schemes, before he kills again.

Ferris, Aimee. **Girl Overboard**. Puffin, 2007. MS/HS. 224 pages. ISBN-10: 0142407992
This S.A.S.S. novel is about a six-week marine biology study in the Caribbean. Marina, who wants to be a marine biologist, decides to apply for the trip, not only to pursue her passion for dolphins, but also to take time out from her three-year relationship with her boyfriend Damon. When she falls for her gorgeous Australian boatmate, her life gets even more complicated.

Fisher, Catherine. **Incarceron**. Dial, 2010. MS. 448 pages. ISBN-13: 978-0803733961

In the first book of a new trilogy, we meet Finn, who is imprisoned in Incarceron, a sentient prison which is a failed experiment meant to imprison undesirables in a model utopia. After he finds a crystal key that opens any door, he is determined to use it escape. The crystal key connects him with Claudia, the warden's daughter who is trying to avoid an arranged marriage. She believes Finn is the True Prince of the Realm, to whom she was engaged. Together they attempt to engineer his escape.

Fitzpatrick, Becca. **Hush, Hush**. Simon & Schuster Children's Publishing, 2009. MS/HS. 400 pages. ISBN-13: 978-1416989417

Nora Grey, budding journalist, uses her researching skills to investigate several new transfer students at her school. Elliott, the key suspect in a suspicious death at his former prep school, and his silent best friend intrigue Nora and her best friend. Then there's Patch, Nora's new bad-boy lab partner, whom she discovers is a fallen angel who wants to become human. All three are entangled in a mysterious relationship she is determined to unravel.

Fitzpatrick, Becca. **Crescendo**. Simon & Schuster Children's Publishing, 2010. MS/HS. 432 pages. ISBN-13: 978-1416989431

The sequel to *Hush Hush*, finds Nora Grey in love with Patch, who is now her guardian angel; but the archangels have forbidden their involvement. In a fit of jealousy, Nora breaks up with him, only to discover she has thrown him into the arms of her archenemy Marcie Millar. As Nora struggles with her lingering feelings for Patch, she begins seeing visions of her dead father and wonders if Patch had something to do with his death.

Flanagan, John. **The Icebound Land.** (The Ranger's Apprentice: Book 3).
Philomel, 2007. MS. 260 pages. ISBN-10: 0399244565

    After a battle with Lord Morgarath in *The Burning Bridge*, Will and Evanlyn have been taken captive by the Skandians. Halt has sworn to rescue Will, but must defy the king to do so. Joined by Will's friend Horace, Halt travels toward Skandia, hoping he is in time to save Will from a horrific life of slavery.

Flanagan, John. **The Battle for Skandia.** (The Ranger's Apprentice: Book 4).
Philomel, 2008. MS. 272 pages. ISBN-10: 0399244573

    In the fourth book of this popular series Will and Evanlyn escape slavery in Skandia, only to have Evanlyn be taken captive by a Temujai warrior. Will's attempt to rescue her is futile, until he is aided at the last minute by Hult and Horace. Before they can celebrate their reunion, they discover the entire Temujai army has breached Skandia's borders and their next target is Afaluen. Will the two kingdoms put aside their quarrels and band together to defeat this ruthless enemy?

Fletcher, Christine. **Ten Cents a Dance**. Bloomsbury USA Children's Books; 1st edition, 2008. MS/HS. 368 pages. ISBN-13: 978-1599901640

    In this historical novel set in Chicago in the 1940s, 15-year-old Ruby quits school and secretly takes a job as a dance hall instructor to support her ailing mother and sister. She's drawn to the easy money, the pretty clothes and "bad boy" Paulie, who is a mobster wannabe. Although she seems to be able to avoid the advances of the men at work, she is drawn into the Paulie's gangster lifestyle and wonders how she can avoid being a bad influence on her impressionable younger sister.

Flinn, Alex. **Beastly**. HarperTeen , 2007. MS. 320 pages. ISBN-10: 0060874163

    Kyle Kingsbury, a gorgeous, rich, ladies man at a private high school in New York City may be beautiful on the outside, but he is cruel and arrogant on the inside. When he angers a Goth girl, who is actually a witch, he is turned into a beast who can only be transformed by finding true love. In chat room sessions he seeks advice from other fairy tale characters, who root for him as he tries to woo Lindy, a fellow student whom he lures and then holds captive in his Brooklyn Brownstone.

Flinn, Alex. **Kiss in Time**. HarperTeen, 2009. MS.384 pages. ISBN-13: 978-0060874193

    In this inventive retelling of Sleeping Beauty, Princess Talia of Euphrasia has been sleeping for 300 years when Jack, a Miami teen who is on an educational tour of Europe, awakens her with a kiss. He spirits her off to Florida where she discovers the wonders of the twenty-first century. However, their happy ending is thwarted by the evil fairy, who put the spell on Talia, and they must return to Euphrasia to put an end to her magical interference in their lives.

Forman, Gayle. **If I Stay**. Dutton Juvenile, 2009. MS/HS. 208 pages. ISBN-13: 978-0525421030

    Mia, a talented cellist, and her family are in the family car heading to a bookstore when a truck broadsides them, leaving her parents dead and Mia and her brother in critical condition. Through flashbacks, flash-forwards and out-of-body reports on what is going on around her, Mia contemplates the situation and wonders, Should I stay?

Although life ahead seems bleak, her loving grandparents, alt-rock boyfriend and best friend Kim are begging her to choose life.

Foxlee, Karen. **The Anatomy of Wings**. Knopf Books for Young Readers, 2009. HS. 368 pages. ISBN-13: 978-0375856433

Ten-year-old Jennifer loses her beautiful singing voice when her older sister Beth dies in a tragic accident. Jennifer and her best friend's search for her voice turns into a search for how and why her beautiful sister became a stranger as she turned to a life of drugs, alcohol and casual sex. As they investigate Beth's decline, they find out what it means to leave childhood behind.

Frankel, Valerie. **American Fringe**. NAL Trade, 2008. HS. 272 pages ISBN-10: 045122292X

When Adora Benet is chosen to write a teen advice column, she has no idea the havoc it will create. Her advice to a reader asking if his mom should go back to work launches a presidential campaign and a flirtation that threatens her relationship with boyfriend Nate. And why can't the teen advice queen help her best friends patch up their differences? Solving other people's problems, not to mention her own, is much more difficult than she ever imagined.

Franklin, Emily. **At Face Value**. Flux, 2008. MS. 264 pages. ISBN-13: 978-0738713076

This adaptation of Cyrano deBergerac finds eighteen-year-old Cyrie longing for a nose job. Although she is the high-achievening editor of the school newspaper, she struggles with cruel jokes about her nose and her secret crush on Eddie Roxanninoff, who is smitten with her friend Leyla. As Cyrie begins editing the inarticulate Leyla's emails to Rox, Cyrie longs to let him know how she feels.

Frazer, Megan. **Secrets of Truth and Beauty**. Hyperion Book CH, 2009. MS/HS. 352 pages. ISBN-13: 978-1423117117

Dara, a former Little Miss Maine, is now more than pleasingly plump. When she is assigned a multimedia autobiographical project at school, she decides to focus on society's obsession with thinness. After her parents and teacher overreact to what they think is her mental instability, Dara leaves Maine to visit her estranged older sister who works on a goat farm which harbors homeless lesbian teens. There Dara finds acceptance and friendship which give her a self-confidence she has long been lacking.

Fredericks, Mariah. **In the Cards: Love**. Aladdin, 2007. MS. 288 pages. ISBN-10: 0689876556

This first book in a planned trilogy employs Tarot cards as the catalyst for a makeover for Anna, self proclaimed "blah nobody." She has a crush on Declan and her Tarot card reading indicates they'll get together. Unfortunately, when they do, Anna neglects and alienates her best friends Eve and Syd to spend time with him.

Fredericks, Mariah. **In the Cards: Fame.** Atheneum/Richard Jackson Books, 2008. MS. 288 pages. ISBN-10: 0689876564

In the sequel to *In the Cards: Love* the focus is on Eve who is determined to gain fame on the stage. After asking the tarot cards "Will I make it?" and getting a positive response, she decides to try out for the school play, *Cabaret*. When the daughter of a famous reality show host gets the lead, Eve turns to her best friends to help her cope.

Freitas, Donna. **The Possibilities of Sainthood**. Farrar, Straus and Giroux (BYR); 1st edition, 2008. MS. 280 pages. ISBN-13: 978-03743608

Fifteen-year-old Antonia spends much of her time petitioning the Vatican to appoint her the first living saint. Her petitions include creating positions for patron saints of figs, secret keeping, gelato or more importantly the first kiss. As Antonia longs for her first kiss from her crush Andy Rotellini, she fends off the attentions of Michael McGinnis, a neighborhood flirt, who just may be a better option.

French, S. Terrell. **Operation Redwood**. Amulet Books, 2009. MS. 368 pages. ISBN-13: 978-0810983540

Twelve-year-old Julian Carter-Li, who is living with his corporate executive uncle while Mom is in China, discovers his uncle's firm has acquired an old growth redwood forest that he plans to cut down. With the help of his best friend Danny and Robin, who lives next door to the grove, Julian attempts to save the redwoods. Although he's supposed to be at math camp, he heads off to Robin's family farm where he and his friends take up residence in a tree house in the Redwoods to draw attention to the problem and thwart the logging plans of the corporation.

Friedman, Aimee. **The Year My Sister Got Lucky**. Point, 2008. MS. 384 pages. ISBN-10: 0439922275

Sisters, Katie and Michaela, ballerinas from New York City are transplanted to a rural town in upstate New York. Michaela, the star of the ballet school, surprisingly, adjusts easily, making new friends and finding a hot boyfriend. Katie, however, mourns the loss of her New York world and her sister's attentions.

Friesner, Esther. **Nobody's Princess.** Random House Books for Young Readers, 2007. MS/HS. 320 pages. ISBN-10: 0375875281

Beautiful Helen of Sparta is determined to hunt and fight like her brothers, even though her family expects her to be a proper young princess. She learns to use a sword, hunt and kill game, and ride a horse, which get her into various dangerous situations. The abrupt ending leaves readers anxious to read the sequel *Nobody's Prize*.

Friesner, Esther. **Nobody's Prize**. Random House Books for Young Readers, 2008. MS. 320 pages. ISBN-10: 037587531X

In the sequel to *Nobody's Princess*, Helen accompanies Jason and the Argonauts on their quest for the Golden Fleece, disguised as a weapons carrier. When they find out she's a woman, she pretends to be the famous huntress Atalanta. Helen, of course, gets more than she bargained for on this adventure.

Fukuda, Andrew Kia. **Crossing**. AmazonEncore, 2010. MS/HS. 217 pages. ISBN-13: 978-1935597032

Xing Xu has always felt a little out of step with the kids at school, but he counted on his relationship with Naomi, the only other Chinese student, for support. When he and Naomi begin to drift apart, he finds solace in singing and lands a part in the school musical. However, students are disappearing from his high school and the suspects and victims all seem to be in some way involved with him.

Fukui, Isamu. **Truancy**. Tor Teen, 2008. MS/HS. 432 pages. ISBN-10: 0765317672

In a totalitarian society, where a dictatorial mayor rules a repressive school system designed to make students obedient automatons, a group of dropouts known as the Truancy fight to destroy the system by any means possible. Fifteen-year-old Tack, whose sister gets killed in the crossfire between the Educators and the Truants, seeks vengeance by infiltrating the Truancy. But he soon finds himself torn between his sympathy for the Truants and his desire for revenge.

Funke, Cornelia. **Igraine the Brave.** Chicken House Ltd, 2007. MS. 224 pages. ISBN-10: 0439903793

Princess Igraine , who lives with her magical family in Pimpernel Castle, wants to become a knight. When the nephew of the baroness-next-door shows up, he's got a dastardly plan to capture the Pimpernel Castle and claim the singing spell books that belong to Igraine's magician parents. To make matters worse, at the very moment of the siege, her mom and dad botch a spell, turning themselves into pigs! Aided by a Sorrowful Knight, it's up to Igraine to save the day.

Gaiman, Neil. **The Graveyard Book**. HarperCollins, 2008. 320 pages. ISBN-13: 978-0060530921

This Newbery award winning story begins when an independent toddler escapes the murder of his family by climbing out of his crib and toddling away from the house and into the local graveyard. He is adopted by Mr. and Mrs. Owens, who unfortunately are ghosts. They raise the child they name Nobody Owens or Bod, with the help of the other ghostly inhabitants of the graveyard. The murderer, however, was actually after Bod and has not stopped pursuing him. Although his ghostly parents have given him some of the powers of the dead such as fading and dreamwalking, he may not be able to evade the assassin forever.

Galante, Cecilia. **The Patron Saint of Butterflies**. Bloomsbury USA Children's Books; 1st edition, 2008. MS/HS. 304 pages. ISBN-13: 978-1599902494

Having grown up in the Mount Blessing religious community, Agnes and Honey have been shielded from the outside world. However, Agnes is devoted to their leader Emmanuel, whereas Honey is looking for a way out. When Nana, Agnes' grandmother, finds out about the physical discipline imposed on the children, she is outraged. Then Agnes' brother is injured and Emmanuel tries to heal him with a miracle. Nana sneaks the three children out of the compound to medical help and freedom.

Gallagher, Liz. **The Opposite of Invisible**. Wendy Lamb Books, 2008. MS/HS. 160 pages. ISBN-10: 0375841520

When a popular football player, Simon, courts Alice, who has always hung out with the "artsies," she is filled with conflict. To complicate matters, her best friend Jewel, a talented artist, has just kissed her and is devastated when she decides to go out with Simon. Set in offbeat Seattle, this story puts a clever spin on the clash of the cliques novel.

Gardner, Sally. **The Red Necklace.** Dial, 2008. MS. 384 pages. ISBN-13: 978-0803731004

The French Revolution is the backdrop for this tale of intrigue when Gypsy magician Yann and the young heiress Sido are pitted against the evil Count Kalliovski.

Sido's father, who loathes her, has promised her to the count and Yann is determined to save her. However, a series of murder victims begin to surface with a necklace of garnets around their necks, and Yann and Sido find themselves in danger of becoming the next victims.

Gehrman, Jody. **Confessions of a Triple Shot Betty**. Dial, 2008. HS. 256 pages. ISBN-10: 0803732473

Geena, who works at a Sonoma Valley coffee shop, is looking forward to spending the summer working with her caustic friend Amber and her prim cousin Hero, who is returning from boarding school. Unfortunately, the girls immediately detest each other. However, they put aside their differences to exact revenge on the local golden boy who posts faked nude pictures of Hero on her My Space page.

George, Jessica Day. **Sun and Moon, Ice and Snow**. Bloomsbury USA Children's Books, 2008. MS. 336 pages. ISBN-13: 978-1599901091

This retelling of Beauty and the Beast mixes Norse legend with the popular fairy tale. Pika, who can understand the speech of animals is taken by a great white bear to live in his ice castle for a year and a day. When events conspire to separate them, Pika has to fly on the winds to the land "East o' the Sun and West o' the Moon" to rescue him and find her destiny.

George, Madeline. **Looks**. Viking Juvenile, 2008. MS. 240 pages. ISBN-13: 978-0670061679

Meghan, who is obese, and Aimee who is anorexic, seem to have nothing in common; however they have both been targets for humiliation by Cara, a popular girl at school. After Meghan discovers that Cara has plagiarized one of Aimee's poems, they set out to exact revenge on the girl who has brought them both pain.

Giles, Gail. **Right Behind You**. Little, Brown Young Readers, 2007. MS/HS 308 pages. ISBN-10: 0316166367

After setting his seven-year-old neighbor on fire in a fit of anger, Kip spends four years in a juvenile offenders' facility. When he is released, he and his family move and assume new identities. When Kip self destructs again, by revealing his past, his family then moves to Texas where he has a last chance for happiness and a normal life. But will he take it?

Gill, David Macinnis. **Black Hole Sun**. Greenwillow Books, 2010. MS/HS. 352 pages. ISBN-13: 978-0061673047

Durango is a teenage mercenary, who, along with Vienne, his second in command, and Mimi, the AI planted in his brain, takes on a job on Mars protecting miners from the cannibalistic monsters known as the Draeu. Blood and guts fly as Durango and his team fight their enemies with courage and witty repartee.

Godbersen, Anna. **The Luxe**. HarperCollins, 2007. HS. 448 pages. ISBN-10: 0061345660

The first in a new series that could be titled Nineteenth Century Gossip Girls introduces Elizabeth Holland, a wealthy young New York City socialite who is secretly in love with a servant but engaged to an eligible bachelor of her social standing. Her fiancé Henry Schoonmaker is a playboy who must marry Elizabeth or be disinherited. A scheming ingénue, who wants Henry for herself, and a bitter servant girl, who has been rejected by Elizabeth's lover, add to the intrigue involving the upcoming wedding.

Godbersen, Anna. **Rumors: A Luxe Novel**. HarperCollins, 2008. HS. 432 pages. ISBN-10: 0061345695

After Elizabeth's disappearance rumors continue to circulate about her mysterious death, and her mother focuses on marital possibilities for her mischievous sister Diana, who is in love with Henry Schoonmaker, Elizabeth's supposedly grieving fiancé. Meanwhile, Penelope Hayes and Elizabeth's former maid Lina Broud are scheming to get Henry to marry Penelope.

Godbersen, Anna. **Envy: A Luxe Novel**. HarperCollins, 2009. MS/HS. 416 pages. ISBN-13: 978-0061345722

The third installment of the Luxe series finds Elizabeth grieving over Will's death, Diana lamenting Henry Schoonmaker's marriage to Penelope, Lina, now Carolina Broad, hoping to capture the heart of a Manhattan socialite and Penelope scheming as always to manipulate the lives of those around her. As the girl struggle to maintain appearances, they find themselves unable to deny what is truly in their hearts.

Going, K.L. **King of the Screwups**. Harcourt Children's Books; 1 edition, 2009. MS/HS. 320 pages. ISBN-13: 978-0152062583

Liam Geller, the son of a high-powered CEO and a retired super model, is a party animal who constantly aggravates his father. After a particularly flagrant screw-up, Liam is sent to live with his glam rocker uncle in a "run down trailer park in the middle of nowhere." Hoping to regain his father's approval, Liam decides to change his persona from Mr. Popularity to Mr. Studious Nerd, but the makeover isn't as easy as he had hoped.

Golding, Julia. **The Diamond of Drury Lane**. Roaring Brook Press, 2008. MS. 432 pages. ISBN-10: 1596433515

The first book in the Cat Royal quartet introduces Catherine Royal, an orphan who lives in the Drury Theater in 18th century London, where she was abandoned as a baby. When the theater owner tells her there is a diamond hidden on the premises, she vows to help him protect it. However, gang leader Billy Boil gets wind of the diamond and Cat and her friends have a devil of a time protecting it.

Golding, Julia. **Cat Among the Pigeons**. Roaring Brook Press, 2008. MS. 384 pages. ISBN-13: 978-1596433526

The second installment in the Cat Royal Adventures finds Cat trying to protect Pedro from his former master who is trying to take him back to the West Indies. Cat gets involved with abolitionists and ends up hiding out at Lord Francis's school and pretending to be a boy. When her efforts are thwarted, it is up to Cat to rescue Pedro and save the day.

Golding, Julia. **Den of Thieves: A Cat Royal Adventure**. Roaring Brook Press, 2009. MS. 432 pages. ISBN-13: 978-1596434448

In the third book of the Cat Royal series, the theater on Drury Lane is being torn down and Cat finds herself homeless. Her patron sends her off to Paris to report on the Revolution and there she has to rescue many old friends and get to know some new ones, including Jean Francois, the self-proclaimed king of thieves.

Gonzalez, Julie. **Imaginary Enemy**. Delacorte Books for Young Readers, 2008. MS. 256 pages. ISBN-13: 978-0385735520

Bubba is Jane's imaginary enemy who takes the blame for all the misfortunes in her life. She has been writing him since second grade, when he takes the blame for her spilt milk in the cafeteria. Nothing is ever her fault. Her slacker attitude and mischievous pranks are exasperating to her parents and amusing to her peers, including Sharp, the boy-next-door, who patiently waits to be more than a friend. As Jane navigates the trials of adolescence, she continues to write accusatory missives to Bubba, but then Bubba writes back and wants to meet face-to-face!

Goodman, Allegra. **The Other Side of the Island**. Scribe Publications, 2008. MS. 272 pages. ISBN-13: 978-1921372292

After a catastrophic flood the remaining islands on Earth have been enclosed and are ruled with an iron hand by the Earth Mother Corporation. Honor and her rebellious parents are living on Island 365 when her parents are "taken" and she must brave the other side of the island to rescue them.

Gordon, Roderick and Williams, Brian. **Tunnels**. The Chicken House, 2007. MS. 480 pages. ISBN-10: 0439871778

The first book in a planned series introduces Will Burrows and his archeologist father, who are tunneling underneath an unused train station. Secretly engaging in separate digs, they both find "The Colony," a dangerous society hidden since the 1700s in a network of tunnels underneath the city. Its citizens have their own religion and social hierarchy, and they feel lethally superior to "topsoilers." As Will discovers his roots, experiences betrayal, and struggles to save those he cares for, the stage is set for the sequel.

Gray, Claudia. **Evernight**. HarperTeen, 2008. MS. 336 pages. ISBN-13: 978-0061284397

Bianca's parents have taken teaching positions at Evernight Academy, an elite boarding school where she is to be a student. She is dreading her first day until she meets Lucas, a handsome outsider with whom she shares a special connection. However, they both have deep secrets that may threaten to keep them apart.

Gray, Claudia. **Stargazer**. HarperTeen; 1 edition, 2009. MS/HS. 336 pages. ISBN-13: 978-0061284403

In the sequel to *Evernight*, Bianca, sophomore at the Evernight Academy for vampires, fakes a relationship with Balthazar, a three-hundred-year-old vampire, so that she can sneak out to see Lucas, her lover who is a member of the vampire-hunting Black Cross. To complicate matters, wrathes have appeared at the academy and seem to be targeting Bianca.

Gray, Claudia. **Hourglass**. HarperTeen; 1 edition, 2010. MS/HS. 352 pages. ISBN-13: 978-0061284410

In the third installment of the Evernight series, Bianca, the daughter of two vampires, has taken refuge with her boyfriend Lucas in the Black Cross vampire hunters enclave. However, an email to her parents brings Evernight Academy vampires straight to them and then two Black Cross members witness Bianca drinking a bag of blood, so she and Lucas are on the run again. For some reason Bianca's body temperature is falling and she is feeling weaker and weaker. To complicate matters, Charity, a rogue vampire, and her minions are also after Bianca and Lucas. Will the lovers find refuge from all the beings that are stalking them?

Green, John. **Paper Towns**. Dutton Juvenile, 2008. MS/HS. 320 pages.
ISBN-13: 978-0525478188

Quentin has always idolized Margo Roth Spiegelman, the girl-next-door who was his best friend until she dumped him for the popular crowd in high school. When she enlists him as her driver in a night long escapade of revenge and spontaneity, he enthusiastically participates, thinking their friendship might be renewed. However, she vanishes the next day and he begins discovering clues that he is sure she left for him. He spends the remainder of senior year enlisting his quirky friends to help him follow the bread crumb trail of clues that he hopes will lead him to her.

Greenwald, Lisa. **My Life in Pink and Green**. Amulet Books, 2009. MS. 272 pages.
ISBN-13: 978-0810983526
Twelve-year-old Lucy, who is an aspiring makeup artist, finds a foreclosure notice in the mail for her family owned pharmacy. While her mother and grandmother argue about how to handle the crisis, Lucy begins hatching a plan to turn it into an eco spa. As Lucy runs into one roadblock after another, she longs for the day when "adults take kids seriously."

Grisham, John. **Theodore Boone: Kid Lawyer.** Dutton Children's Books; 1 edition, 2010. MS. 263 pages. ISBN-13: 978-0525423843

Theo Boone, the only child of two lawyers, hangs out in his parents' law office and hands out free legal advice to his middle school classmates. He is understandably excited about an upcoming murder trial, where the prosecution has only circumstantial evidence against the defendant. Then an illegal immigrant, who witnessed the crime, comes to Theo with incriminating evidence, but he wants his identity kept a secret. Should Theo betray him and tell the authorities, or should he let the criminal go free?

Guttman, Dan. **Getting Air**. Simon & Schuster Children's Publishing, 2007. MS. 240 pages.
ISBN-10: 0689876807
Skateboarders, Jimmy, David and Henry are headed to California, when their plane is hijacked by terrorists. They take action and defeat the terrorists, but their plane crashes in the wilderness and all they have are their skateboarding skills to help them survive.

Haddix, Margaret Peterson. **Found**. Simon & Schuster Children's Publishing, 2008. MS. 320 pages. ISBN-10: 1416954171
The first book in a new series begins when a plane filled with 36 unattended babies, lands, bewildering airport personnel. The babies are adopted out, and as the story begins thirteen years later, the adoptees all receive mysterious letters about their origins. Adoptees Chip and Jonah, along with Jonah's sister Katherine, attempt to solve the mystery only to find more questions than answers.

Haddix, Margaret Peterson. **Sent**. Simon & Schuster Children's Publishing, 2009. MS. 320 pages. ISBN-13: 978-1416954224

In the second book of The Missing Series, Jonah and Katherine attempt to save Alex and Chip, the royal princes who were snatched out of time before their deaths in

London in 1483. The four kids travel back in time and try to thwart the murder plans of the boys' evil uncle, Richard III, without altering history more than necessary.

Haddix, Margaret Peterson. **Sabotaged**. Simon & Schuster Children's Publishing, 2010. MS. 384 pages. ISBN-13: 978-1416954248

The third book in the Missing series finds Jonah and Katherine traveling back in time with Andrea who is Virginia Dare, the first child born in the Roanoke Colony. Along the way the lose the Elucidator, which allows them to time travel. Andrea meets her grandfather and the kids find out their trip has actually been sabotaged by an adult known as Second.

Halam, Ann. **Snakehead**. Wendy Lamb Books, 2008. MS. 304 pages. ISBN-13: 978-0375841088

In this retelling of the story of Perseus slaying Medusa, Perseus and Andromeda cooperate to complete the quest and right the wrongs at home. Readers will recognize many of the characters from Greek myth, including Jason and the Argonauts, who populate this story with a modern day twist.

Hale, Shannon. **Book of the Thousand Days.** Bloomsbury USA Children's Books, 2007. MS. 320 pages. ISBN-10: 1599900513
This retelling of a classic Grimm's fairy tale is set in the Central Asian Steppes. Lady Saren and her maid Dashti are shut in a tower for 7 years, because Saren refuses to marry a man she despises. When the two women finally escape, it's into a barren world of warring societies.

Hall, Barbara. **The Noah Confessions.** Delacorte Books for Young Readers, 2007. MS/HS. 224 pages. ISBN-10: 0385733283
Expecting to receive a car for her sixteenth birthday, Lynnie is shocked and disappointed to receive a worn-out bird charm bracelet that belonged to her deceased mother. Her ungrateful, rebellious behavior warrants a second gift, a manuscript detailing her family's secrets, lies and tragedies which begin to make her doubt her own future.

Halpin, Brendan. **How Ya Like Me Now.** Farrar, Straus and Giroux (BYR), 2007. MS/HS. 208 pages. ISBN-10: 0374334951
After his widowed mother checks into rehab, Eddie goes to stay with his aunt and uncle in Boston, where he attends an alternative school with his underachieving cousin Alex. Finding friendship and support he's never had before, Eddie struggles with conflicting emotions about reuniting with his mother and returning to his former pain-filled life.

Han, Jenny. **The Summer I Turned Pretty**. Simon & Schuster Children's Publishing, 2009. MS. 288 pages. ISBN-10: 1416968237
Belly's family shares a beach house every summer with her mother's best friend whose two sons have been Belly's lifelong friends. Now fifteen, she has turned into a beauty and the only one who seems to be immune to her charms is Conrad, the older brother she adores but who treats her like an annoying little sister. As they struggle to provide support for the boys' mother who has terminal cancer, Belly and the boys navigate a summer filled with changing feelings and relationships.

Hanley, Victoria. **Violet Wings**. EgmontUSA, 2009. MS.368 pages. ISBN-13: 978-1606840115

When Zaria, a twelve-year-old fairy in Feyland, receives her wand and a watch which reveals her inborn levels of magic, she is astounded to find out she and her friend Leona are two of the most powerful fairies alive. Zaria, however, is "Earth struck" and can't stop thinking about her family's disappearance there. As she struggles to deal with the loss, she must also battle her evil mentor and plot against her for control of the governing council of Feyland.

Harazin, S. A. **Blood Brothers.** Delacorte Books for Young Readers, 2007. MS/HS. 240 pages. ISBN-10: 0385733649.

Clay's job at the hospital is the only thing in his life that makes him feel worthwhile. He wishes he could be like his best friend Joey, who has a great family, money, a car and is headed to Duke. Then Joey overdoses at a party and clings to life at the hospital where Clay works. Even worse, Clay may be blamed for Joey's condition.

Harper, Suzanne. **The Juliet Club**. HarperTeen, 2008. MS. 416 pages. ISBN-10: 0061366919

After being dumped by her boyfriend, Kate wins a Shakespeare essay contest and heads off to a school in Verona, determined to avoid all romantic entanglements. There she and classmates must answer letters to Juliet asking questions about love. Of course, romantic complications ensue when Kate and lothario Giacomo discover a plot to make them fall in love, while they profess to detest each other.

Harris, Joanne. **Runemarks.** Knopf Books for Young Readers, 2008. MS. ISBN-10: 0375844449

A rigid, witch hunting order has declared Norse myths blasphemous, just as 12-year-old Maddy finds she's the daughter of Thor. Advised by Odin and guided by Loki, Maddy travels to a fantasy world where she is hoping to prevent a prophesied war between the old gods and the new.

Harrison, Mette Ivie. **The Princess and the Hound**. Eos, 2007. MS. 416 pages. ISBN-10: 0061131873

Prince George possesses animal magic which is forbidden in the beleaguered kingdom he will one day rule. Beatrice, unwanted daughter of a king from a rival kingdom, is inseparable from her hound. When their fathers forge an alliance through their engagement, George and Beatrice meet and think they have little in common, but each has a secret that must be hidden at all costs.

Hartinger, Brent. **Split Screen: Attack of the Soul-Sucking Brain Zombies/Bride of the Soul Sucking Brain Zombies**. HarperTeen, 2007. HS. 304 pages. ISBN-10: 0060824085

In this companion to *Geography Club* two books in one tell the stories of best friends Min and Russel who sign up to be extras on the set of a zombie film. In *Attack of the Soul-Sucking Brain Zombies,* Russel must choose between his long-distance boyfriend and a close-to-home ex who wants to get back together. In *Bride of the Soul-Sucking Brain Zombies,* Min struggles to accept her cheerleader girlfriend's decision to stay in the closet.

Harvey, Alyxandra. **<u>Hearts at Stake</u>**. <small>Walker Books for Young Readers; 1 edition, 2010. MS. 256 pages. ISBN-13: 978-0802720740</small>

The first book of the Drake Chronicles introduces two best friends: Solange, who is waiting for her sixteenth birthday when she will change into a vampire and is prophesied to become the vampire queen, and Lucy, the feisty human, who is in love with Nicholas, one of Solange's seven vampire brothers. Lady Natasha, who is currently the queen, is determined that Solange won't live to celebrate her birthday. It is up to Lucy, Solange's family, and Kieran, a vampire hunter who is looking to avenge his father's death, to save Solange, so that she may fulfill her destiny.

Harvey, Alyxandra. **<u>Blood Feud</u>**. <small>Walker Books for Young Readers, 2010. MS. 272 pages. ISBN-13: 978-0802720962</small>

The sequel to *Hearts at Stake* focuses on Solange's brother Logan and his attraction to Isabeau St Croix, a vampire from the Hounds Clan, who arrived at the eleventh hour to help rescue Solange. Isabeau survived the French Revolution, only to be attacked by the vampire Greyhaven and then buried for two hundred years until the Hounds rescued her. Logan is immediately attracted to her, but although she reciprocates his feelings, she is focused on finding Greyhaven and getting revenge.

Hautman, Pete. **<u>All-in.</u>** <small>Simon & Schuster Children's Publishing, 2007. MS/HS. 192 pages. ISBN-10: 1416913254</small>

In this sequel to *No Limit* seventeen-year-old Denn Doyle is in Las Vegas parlaying his ability to read "tells" and calculate odds into a fortune. That is, until he meets Cattie Hart, a dealer who steals his heart and his money. When his old enemy, Artie Kingston, hosts a million-dollar Texas Hold 'Em tournament, Denn has to play for all or nothing.

Hawking, Lucy and Stephen. **<u>George's Secret Key to the Universe</u>**. <small>Simon & Schuster Children's Publishing, 2007. MS. 304 pages. ISBN-10: 1416954627</small>

This is the first volume of a projected trilogy. George Greenby's eco-activist parents have tried to shelter him from the dangers of the modern world. However, when he meets his new neighbor Annie, her scientist father and his super-computer Cosmos, he is not only introduced to new technology, but is also able to travel instantaneously throughout the universe.

Headley, Justina Chen. **<u>Girl Overboard</u>**. <small>Little, Brown Young Readers, 2008. MS/HS. 352 pages. ISBN-13: 978-0316011303</small>

Syrah Cheng, daughter of a billionaire cell phone magnate, finds anonymity and fulfillment in snowboarding. Then she narrowly escapes an avalanche and blows out her knee and her parents ban her from the slopes. With her workacoholic parents ignoring her and her best friend not returning her calls, Syrah turns to manga and helping a new friend who is dealing with her sister's cancer to find self-worth.

Headley, Justina Chen. **<u>North of Beautiful</u>**. <small>Little, Brown Young Readers; 1 edition, 2009. MS. 384 pages. ISBN-13: 978-0316025058</small>

Sixteen-year-old Terra defines herself by her port wine birthmark on her face, even though she is an excellent student and accomplished artist. The she meets Jacob, a gorgeous Asian Goth guy who has a cleft lip scar that doesn't seem to phase him. When she and her mother accompany Jacob and his mother to China to visit her brother and the orphanage where he spent his first three years, Terra begins to see that strength and beauty come from within.

Henkes, Kevin. **Bird Lake Moon**. Greenwillow, 2008. MS. 192 pages. ISBN-13: 978-0061470769

Mitch and Spencer, who live next door to each other at Bird Lake, are each experiencing loss. Mitch's parents are divorcing and Spencer is visiting the lake for the first time since his brother drowned there. Although the boys get off to a rocky start, they forge a new friendship; then events occur that threaten to cut short their summer idyll.

Hennesy, Carolyn. **Pandora Gets Jealous**. Bloomsbury USA Children's Books, 2007. MS. 272 pages. ISBN-10: 159990196X

In the first book of a new series, Mythic Misadventures, Pandora, daughter of Prometheus, sneaks the fabled box of evils out of the house for show and tell and accidentally releases the plagues of humanity. Zeus sentences her to retrieve them and in this first adventure she and her gal pals, Alcie and Iole, set off to retrieve jealousy.

Henry, April. **Torched**. Putnam Juvenile, 2009. MS/HS. 224 pages. ISBN-13: 978-0399246456

In a deal that allows her hippie pot-growing parents to stay out of jail, sixteen-year-old April agrees to go undercover and join a local activist group, Mother Earth Defenders (MEDs). Participating in acts of eco-terrorism to prove herself, April is appalled to find out that the group is planning a deadly protest mission. To complicate matters, she has fallen for Coyote, one of the activist leaders. How far will she go to do what's right when the moral complexities of environmental activism blur the lines between right and wrong?

Hepler, Heather and Brad Barkley. **Dream Factory.** Dutton Juvenile, 2007. MS/HS. 256 pages. ISBN-10: 0525478027

When the character actors at Disney Land go on strike, Ella and Luke are among the teens hired as replacements. Ella portrays Cinderella and Luke is Dale the chipmunk, one of the "fur characters." When they are paired for a team building scavenger hunt, which is designed to uncover the magic kingdom's hidden treasures, they discover more than they ever imagined possible.

Helpler, Heather. **The Cupcake Queen**. Dutton Juvenile, 2009. MS. 240 pages. ISBN-13: 978-0525421573

Penny, whose parents are recently separated, has moved from Manhattan to Hog's Hollow, her mother's tiny hometown, where she is employed at her mother's cupcake bakery. Penny hones her artistic skills through cupcake decorating, as she worries about her parents' relationship, the mean girls at school and the enigmatic Marcus, who is grieving for his deceased mother.

Herlong, M.H. **The Great Wide Sea**. Viking Juvenile, 2008. MS. 288 pages. ISBN-13: 978-0670063307

Two months after the death of their mother, the three Byron boys are uprooted by their father and taken on a year long sailing trip. 15-year-old Ben is not happy to leave behind everything he knows and obey his grieving father's orders. 11-year-old Dylan retreats into his intellectual pursuits and 5-year-old Gerry develops irrational fears. Then Dad disappears and the boys are lost at sea in a violent storm, ultimately ending up on a deserted island where they must struggle to survive.

Hernandez, David. **No More Us for You**. HarperTeen, 2009. MS/HS. 288 pages. ISBN-13: 978-0061173332

Narrating the story in alternating chapters, Carlos and Isabel recount the events that bring them together after they are introduced by a mutual friend at the Long Beach Contemporary Museum where Carlos is a security guard. Their relationship slowly evolves as they struggle to deal with many issues including the results of a tragic car accident.

Hiaasen, Carl. **Scat**. Knopf Books for Young Readers, 2009. MS. 384 pages. ISBN-13: 978-0375834868

This environmental mystery begins with a suspicious wild fire in the Black Vine Swamp and the disappearance of Mrs. Starch, the unpopular science teacher who is leading a school field trip when the fire breaks out. Nick and Marta, two students who were on the field trip, are determined to find out who set the fire and what happened to Mrs. Starch. During their investigations they encounter a motley crew of characters including evil oilmen and an eccentric millionaire eco-avenger, who enlists their help in saving an endangered panther and her cubs.

Higgins, F. E. **The Black Book of Secrets**. Feiwel & Friends, 2007. MS . 288 pages. ISBN-10: 0312368445

After fleeing his parents who are trying to sell his teeth for gin money, Ludlow Fitch finds work with Joe Zabbidou, a "secret pawnbroker." In the village of Pagus Parvus Joe buys people's secrets and Ludlow records them. Most of the people's troubles are created by an evil landlord who is determined to bankrupt the destitute town. As Ludlow records the town's litany of woes, he never guesses what the future has in store for him.

Higson, Charlie. **Double or Die**. Puffin Books, 2007. MS. 391 pages. ISBN-10: 0141322032

In a north London cemetery an Eton professor is kidnapped at gunpoint, and it is up to Young James Bond and his classmates to rescue him. They receive a letter filled with seven cryptic clues. After they decipher them, James has 48 hours to rescue the professor or the future of the world is in jeopardy. This is the third book in Young James Bond Series.

Hijuelos, Oscar. **Dark Dude**. Atheneum, 2008. HS. 448 pages ISBN-13: 978-1416948049

Rico Fuentes is a "dark dude" in 60's Harlem. Although he is Cuban-American, his light skin makes him the target of bullies of all races. He takes refuge in comic books and science fiction; but when harassment at school becomes unbearable, his best buddy turns to drugs, and his parents threaten to send him to military school, he heads off to a hippie commune in Wisconsin where he discovers, "Where you are, doesn't change who you are."

Hillmer, Timothy. **Ravenhill.** University of New Mexico Press, 2007. HS. 239 pages. ISBN-10: 0826339859

One fateful day at Ravenhill High School in 1997, an act of violence leaves five people dead and a community in shock. Told from four points of view, the story explores who is responsible when tragedy occurs.

Hobbs, Will. **Go Big or Go Home**. HarperCollins, 2008. MS. 192 pages. ISBN-10: 0060741414

A meteor breaches Earth's atmosphere and lands in Brady's bed in the Black Hills of South Dakota. After being exposed to the meteor, Brady begins to notice he is quicker and stronger, almost superhuman. When he and his cousin Quinn consult a local scientist, he suggests that exposure to long-dormant microbes in the meteor might be causing the transformation. Then Brady loses the meteor just as the process seems to be reversing itself. Will Quinn and Brady regain the meteor in time to save his life?

Hoffman, Mary. **The Falconer's Knot: A Story of Friars, Flirtation and Foul Play.** Bloomsbury USA Children's Books, 2007. MS/HS. 288 pages. ISBN-10: 1599900564

Set in Renaissance Italy, this is a tale of a young nobleman who seeks sanctuary in a friary after being wrongly accused of murder. Parallel stories include one about a young novice, who has been sent to live at the neighboring monastery and another woman who has been forced to marry a man she does not love. Multiple murders, romance and betrayals combine to create a page turning mystery.

Hooper, Mary. **Newes from the Dead**. Roaring Brook Press, 2008. MS/HS. 272 pages. ISBN-13: 978-1596433557

Hanged for the crime of infanticide in England in 1610, Anne, a teenage housemaid, regains consciousness in her coffin. Meanwhile Robert Matthews, a young medical student, is getting ready to assist surgeons who are going to dissect her. When he notices movement of her eyelids, he alerts the surgeons who attempt to revive her. The nobleman whose grandson took advantage of her demands justice, while people are lining up to view the miraculous messenger from God. Based on a true story.

Hopkins, Ellen. **Fallout**. Margaret K. McElderry, 2010. HS. 672 pages. ISBN-13: 978-1416950097

The final book in the trilogy that includes *Crank* and *Glass*, focuses on meth-addict Kristina's three teenager children. Hunter, lives with his grandparents, Autumn, bounces between foster homes and her father's trailer when he's out of jail, and Summer lives with her aunt, unaware of her siblings.

Hopkins, Ellen. **Identical**. Margaret K. McElderry, 2008). HS. 576 pages. ISBN-10: 1416950052

Kaeleigh and Raeanne are identical twins who are both harboring a secret. Their mother is a politician who is constantly on the campaign trail, and Kaeleigh is the inappropriate focus for her father's love. Raeanne, who is jealous, resorts to drugs, alcohol and sex. What can save the twins from their separate nightmares?

Hopkins, Ellen. **Impulse.** Margaret K. McElderry , 2007. HS. 672 pages.
ISBN-10: 1416903569

    After failed suicide attempts, three teens bond in a psychiatric hospital. In alternating chapters in verse the stories of Vanessa, Tony, and Conner are told, revealing dysfunctional family relationships and damaged psyches. Rather than the professionals, they rely on each other for help in fighting the demons within.

Hopkins, Ellen. **Tricks**. Margaret K. McElderry; 1 edition, 2009. HS. 640 page. ISBN-13: 978-1416950073

    Five teens driven to prostitution through five different journeys all end up in Las Vegas where they struggle to find a way out of the hopelessness that has come to define their lives.

Hornby, Nick. **Slam.** Putnam Juvenile, 2007. HS. 304 pages. ISBN-10: 0399250484

    Sam, a fifteen-year-old skateboarder, finds his life turned upside down when his girlfriend informs him she is pregnant and keeping the baby. He seeks advice from a sort-of-imaginary friend: the world's greatest skater, Tony Hawk, whose poster Sam talks to when he has problems. Does Tony really answer him, or has Sam read Tony's autobiography so many times that he is able to remember quotes from the book that apply to his situation?

Horowitz, Anthony. **Snakehead.** Philomel, 2007. MS. 400 pages. ISBN-10: 0399241612

    Alex Rider has just crash landed on the coast of Australia after he reenters the earth's atmosphere from his last adventure in outer space. The Australian Secret Service recruits him to infiltrate a gang known as snakeheads, who smuggle drugs, weapons and people. Alex accepts the assignment because it is a chance to work with his godfather and learn more about his parents, whom he barely knew before they died.

House, Silas. **Eli the Good**. Candlewick, 2009. MS. 304 pages.
ISBN-13: 978-0763643416

It's the summer of 1976 and ten-year-old Eli Book's usual summer routine is interrupted by the arrival of his Aunt Nell, who has just been diagnosed with breast cancer. An anti-war activist, Nell tangles with Eli's Vietnam vet father, who is struggling with flashbacks, and runs interference between Eli's rebellious sister and their mother. As Eli watches his family combust around him, he wonders how he can help them find peace.

Howell, Simmone. **Notes from the Teenage Underground.** Bloomsbury USA Children's Books, 2007. HS. 335 pages. ISBN-10: 1582348359

    Seventeen-year-old Gem feels like she's beginning to drift away from her best friends, Lo and Mira. In the spirit of Andy Warhol and his Happenings, Gem comes up with the idea to make an underground film to screen at a party. She thinks this project will bring the three girls back together again. As scriptwriting and production begin, however, she realizes that the project is getting out of control.

Hughes, Mark Peter. **Lemonade Mouth**. Delacorte Books for Young Readers, 2007. MS/HS. 352 pages. ISBN-10: 0385733925

    When Stella, Mo, Wen, Charlie, and Olivia meet in detention and begin to sing along with a radio jingle, the band Lemonade Mouth is born. Certified geeks, the band members are empowered by their new friendships to take on their own problems and in the process empower others as well.

Hyde, Catherine Ryan. **The Year of My Miraculous Reappearance.** Knopf Books for Young Readers , 2007. MS/HS. 240 pages. ISBN-10: 0375832572

With an alcoholic mother, thirteen-year-old Cynnie has been the primary caretaker for her 3-year-old brother Bill, who has Down syndrome. When her grandparents take custody of Bill, Cynnie is devastated and turns to alcohol herself. Through Alcoholics Anonymous she struggles to overcome her problems and find a stable adult in her life, so she can be reunited with her brother.

Ingold, Jeanette. **Paper Daughter**. Harcourt Children's Books, 2010. MS. 224 pages. ISBN-13: 978-0152055073

Maggie Chen, an aspiring journalist who is still reeling from her father's death, takes an internship at a Seattle newspaper, where she uncovers a story that links her father's death to political corruption. At the same time she is investigating her father's lies about his family origins, which are related to a story about Fai-yi Li, a Chinese immigrant, whose narrative alternates with Maggie's.

Jablonski, Carla. **Silent Echoes**. Razorbill, 2007. HS. 288 pages. ISBN-10: 1595140824

This historical fantasy alternates between nineteenth century and present day New York City and involves sixteen-year-old Lucy, who in 1882 puts on sham séances for the wealthy, and Lindsay, who in the present day struggles with an alcoholic mother and abusive stepfather. When Lindsay hides in her closet to avoid their fighting, she is surprised and bewildered when Lucy answers her call for help.

Jay, Stacey. **You Are So Undead to Me**. Razorbill, 2009. MS. 272 pages. ISBN-13: 978-1595142252

High school sophomore, Megan Berry, is a Zombie Settler; she helps the dead resolve issues so that they can rest in peace. Then someone starts using black magic to turn the undead into flesh-eating zombies, and it's up to Megan find the mysterious mastermind and stop her before the homecoming dance turns into a blood bath.

Jenkins, A.M. **Repossessed.** HarperTeen, 2007. HS. 224 pages. ISBN-10: 0060835680

One of the devil's minions decides to take over the body of a teenager named Shaun, who is about to be killed by a car. The minion's job is to mirror the self-loathing and regret of the souls who are relegated to hell. Wanting to experience the physical sensations of the living, he descends to earth and inhabits Shaun's body, causing a drastic change in Shaun's personality, which confuses all those involved with him on Earth.

Jinks, Catherine. **Genius Squad**. Harcourt Children's Books, 2008. MS. 448 pages. ISBN-13: 978-0152059859

In the sequel to *Evil Genius* Cadel is living in foster care with nothing to do and a bully who makes his life miserable. It almost seems too good to be true when he and his best friend, the multiply handicapped Sonja, are moved to Clareview Estates, where they join the Genius Squad, a group of geeks secretly working to bring down corrupt genetic corporation GenoME. When Prosper escapes from jail, Cadel is in grave danger, as are those he loves.

Johnson, Maureen. **Suite Scarlett**. Point, 2008. MS. 368 pages. ISBN-10: 0439899273
    Following family tradition, Scarlett Martin inherits her own suite at the family-owned Hopewell Hotel in Manhattan, just as her family falls on hard times. Then Mrs. Amberson, an aging wealthy actress, moves into the suite and it is Scarlett's responsibility to keep her happy. Mrs. A meddles in the lives of Scarlett and her siblings creating one disaster after another, which Scarlett valiantly tries to avert.

Johnson, Maureen. **Scarlett Fever**. Point; 1 edition, 2010. MS. 352 pages.
ISBN-13: 978-043989928

    In the sequel to *Suite Scarlett*, Scarlett continues her job as personal assistant to Mrs. Amberson, who is now a theatrical agent. Recruited to spy on Max, the brother of Mrs. Amberson's newly signed starlet, Scarlett finds herself vacillating between being annoyed and intrigued by him. Meanwhile, her brother has landed a part in a TV show, her sister has married "Number 98" and Maureen has become alarmingly nice. The Martin family financial woes continue in the second book of this madcap trilogy.

Jones, Carrie. **Need**. Bloomsbury USA Children's Books, 2008. MS. 320 pages.
ISBN-13: 978-1599903385

    After the death of her beloved stepfather, Zara is devastated. Her mother sends Zara to live with her grandmother in Maine where she makes several new friends including Nick whose dangerous vibe is very enticing. Then Zara discovers the man who has been stalking her since her stepfather's heart attack is actually the pixie king, who has been kidnapping local boys. At first she is frightened, but then she realizes it is up to her and her new friends to stop him once and for all.

Jones, Traci L. **Finding My Place**. Farrar, Straus and Giroux (BYR), 2010. MS. 192 pages.
ISBN-13: 978-0374335731
    In 1975 Tiphanie, a talented African American girl, finds herself transferring to a predominately white school, when her parents, veterans of the civil rights movement, insist she must "uphold the race." Although she struggles at first, she is befriended by Jackie Sue, a hippie from the trailer park, who hides her problems behind a brash personality and a large vocabulary. Their complicated friendship enables Tiphanie, who is struggling with parental pressure, as well as racism at school, to cope; but ultimately it is she who has to be the strong one, as Jackie Sue's problems spiral out of control.

Joyce, Graham. **TWOC (Taken Without Owner's Consent).** Viking Juvenile, 2007. HS. 224 pages. ISBN-10: 0670060909
    Matt and his older brother Jake take cars without their owner's consent. Then Jake dies and Matt is haunted by his ghost. Why? Matt can't remember if he killed him as a result of some ill-advised stunt driving. It's clear, though, that he has been deeply traumatized by the accident. To help Matt come to terms, his counselor sends him and two other troubled kids off to the country for a weekend of activity-based therapy, which will have dramatic consequences.

Juby, Susan. **Another Kind of Cowboy**. HarperTeen, 2007. MS/HS. 352 pages.
ISBN-13: 978-0060765170
    Alex, who is struggling with his sexuality, has longed to switch from competing in Western riding to dressage. Through fortuitous circumstances he ends up a

competition worthy dressage horse and enrolls in lessons at a local stable. There he meets Chloe, a spoiled rich girl with an attitude and a hard-to-handle horse, and the two forge an unlikely friendship. When Chloe gets involved in too much partying and Alex "comes out," they depend on their friendship to help them navigate their problems.

Kadohata, Cynthia, **A Million Shades of Gray**. Atheneum; 1 edition, 2010. MS. 216 pages. ISBN-13: 978-1416918837

Y'Tin, a 13-year-old Vietnamese elephant handler, dutifully attends school, but all he really cares about is taking care of Lady, his elephant. When the Americans leave South Vietnam in 1975 and the North Vietnamese massacre his village, Y'Tin flees, but then finds himself trying to protect Lady and survive in the jungle, while searching for his family in the midst of war.

Kadohata, Cynthia. **Outside Beauty**. Atheneum, 2008. MS. 272 pages. ISBN-13: 978-0689865756

Twelve-year-old Shelby and her three sisters have different fathers, but they couldn't be closer. When their beautiful Japanese-American mother has a disfiguring accident, she sends them each to live with their respective fathers while she recuperates. When her recovery doesn't go as expected, the girls begin to wonder if they'll ever be together as a family again.

Kagawa, Julie. **The Iron King**. Harlequin; Original edition, 2010. MS. 368 pages. ISBN-13: 978-0373210084

The first book in a proposed trilogy introduces Meghan Chase whose life changes drastically on her sixteenth birthday, when her four-year-old brother is replaced by a changeling and her longtime friend Robbie Goodfell admits that he is actually Puck, the fairy. Together they go to Nevernever where Meghan hopes to rescue her brother. There she meets Ash, the Unseelie Prince, as well as her real father King Oberon and Queen Mab, who are both fighting to keep her in their courts.

Kantor, Melissa. **The Breakup Bible**. Hyperion Book CH; Reprint edition, 2008. MS. 288 pages. ISBN-13: 978-0786809639

When school newspaper reporter Jen Lewis's boyfriend breaks up with her and she is wallowing in self-pity, her grandmother gives her *The Breakup Bible* to help her move on. At first Jen tosses it aside, but when she finds out her ex, who is the school newspaper editor, dumped her for a fellow reporter, she digs the book out of the trash for advice.

Kantor, Melissa. **Girlfriend Material**. Hyperion Book CH; 1 edition, 2009. MS. 256 pages. ISBN-13: 978-1423108498

Kate's hopes for a wonderful summer with her friends in Utah are dashed when her mom takes her to Cape Cod for the summer to avoid dealing with her failing marriage. Although Mom finds the support she needs from old friends, Kate struggles to connect until she meets Adam, who looks like the perfect summer fling. As Kate's feelings for Adam grow, she begins to wonder if she is girlfriend material?

Karr, Kathleen. **Born for Adventure**. Marshall Cavendish Children's Books, 2007. MS. 200 pages. ISBN-10: 0761453482

Young Tom Ormsby yearns for a life of adventure and joins Henry Morton Stanley on his 1887 expedition to Africa. However, Tom quickly becomes disillusioned as he struggles to survive jungle diseases, wild animal attacks and political intrigue in this thrilling historical tale.

Kelly, Jacqueline. **The Evolution of Calpurnia Tate**. Henry Holt and Co. (BYR); 1 edition, 2009. MS. 352 pages. ISBN-13: 978-0805088410

Thwarting societal expectations, 12-year-old Callie pursues her desire to become a scientist in rural Texas in 1899. Although she has six brothers, only one other family member shares her interest, her gruff intimidating grandfather, who happens to own a copy of Charles Darwin's new book, *The Origin of the Species*. Callie and Granddaddy bond over their curiosity about the natural world and discover a new plant species along the way.

Kephart, Beth. **The Heart is Not a Size**. HarperTeen; 1 edition, 2010. MS. 256 pages. ISBN-13: 978-0061470486

Georgia, who suffers from panic attacks, and her friend Riley, who is hiding her anorexia, must face their demons when they join the Good Works team and head to Juarez, Mexico to do a community service project. In the small village of Anapra, where girls routinely disappear, Georgia and Riley are confronted by the sparse beauty of the landscape and the dire poverty of its people. Their friendship is threatened when Georgia finally voice her concerns about Riley's health.

Kephart, Beth. **Undercover.** HarperTeen, 2007. MS/HS. 288 pages. ISBN-10: 0061238937

A loner and a talented writer, Beth operates an undercover business ghostwriting love letters for guys who struggle to express their feelings. When her parents' marriage begins to fall apart, she spends more and more time at a secluded pond, where she finds her inspiration in nature, and, in winter, she teaches herself how to skate. Then she falls for one of her clients and incurs the wrath of the very girl she has been wooing for him.

Kerr. M.E. **Someone Like Summer**. HarperTeen, 2007. MS/HS. 272 pages. ISBN-10: 0061140996

In this story of star crossed lovers, blond blue-eyed Annabel is in love with Esteban, an illegal immigrant from Columbia. Prejudice is rampant in the town. Although Annabel's father, who is a contractor, hires the illegals, he doesn't want his daughter dating one of them, and Esteban's older sister calls Annabel "flour face" and thinks all white girls are loose. Will they be able to defy the odds and remain together?

Kidd, Ronald. **On Beale Street**. Simon & Schuster Children's Publishing, 2008. MS/HS. 256 pages. ISBN-13: 978-1416933878

In the summer of 1954 in Memphis, Johnny Ross, a 15-year-old white boy, discovers Beale Street, the heart of the Negro blues and music scene. He begins working at Sun Records and meets Elvis Presley who is just beginning to record there. As Johnny gets more involved with people in the music business, he discovers ties to secrets from the past and a father he never knew.

Kidd, Ronald. **The Year of the Bomb**. Simon & Schuster Children's Publishing, 2009. MS. 208 pages. ISBN-13: 978-1416958925

In 1955 Paul and his friends, who love horror movies, are ecstatic to find out *The Invasion of the Body Snatchers* is being filmed in their town. Visiting the set, they meet two FBI agents posing as extras, who are investigating people with possible Communist ties. The boys begin an investigation of their own that leads them to wonder about "doing the right thing."

Kingsley, Kaza. **Erec Rex – The Dragon's Eye**. Firelight Press, Inc., 2007. MS. 400 pages. ISBN-10: 0978655532

Erec Rex and his buddy Bethany go to rescue his mother who is being held prisoner by King Pluto in a magical kingdom below Upper Earth. When they get there, they end up in a contest that will decide the next three rulers of the three lower kingdoms. While competing, they also have to solve the mysteries of his heritage and King Piter's funk, as well as discover what evil culprits are attempting to take over the kingdoms.

Kinney, Jeff. **Diary of a Wimpy Kid: Rodrick Rules**. Amulet, 2008. MS. 224 pages. ISBN-10: 0810994739

In the second book of the series Greg, a junior high diarist, begins a new school year which is filled with pranks and disasters. The text and cartoon format chronicles the sibling rivalry between Greg and his older brother Roderick, who is a wannabe drummer in a heavy metal band, as well as Greg's school shenanigans and correspondence with his French pen pal.

Kirkbride, Tom. **Gamadin**. Emerald Book Company, 2008. MS. 446 pages. ISBN-13: 978-1934572061

Sixteen-year-olds Harlow Pylott and Matt Riverstone live to go surfing. After they rescue a famous movie star and the half-alien Leucadia Mars when their boat capsizes from a rogue wave, the boys are drawn into the adventure of a lifetime. Leucadia's mother knows that Dakadude killers are looking for Millawanda, a Gamadin spaceship which is the galaxy's most powerful weapon. She also knows that it is the surfers dudes' destiny to save Millawanda and along with her the Earth.

Klass, David. **Whirlwind**. Farrar, Straus and Giroux (BYR), 2008. MS/HS. 304 pages. ISBN-10: 0374323089

The second book in the Caretaker Trilogy finds Jack Danielson returning from his quest to save the Earth's oceans in *Firestorm* to his hometown and his girlfriend PJ, only to find she has been kidnapped by the Dark Army. He follows her to the Amazon where he must find the missing time-traveling wizard, Kidah, who will help him save the rainforests from destruction by the evil Dark Lord and in the process rescue PJ, who is his captive.

Kluger, Steve. **My Most Excellent Year: A Novel of Love, Mary Poppins, & Fenway Park**. Puffin; Reprint edition, 2009. MS/HS. 416 pages. ISBN-13: 978-0142413432

In alternating voices three Boston teens describe their most excellent year for a class assignment. T.C. is a die-hard Red Sox fan who is "the cool kid everyone wants to be." He has a crush on Alejandra, who is the daughter of an ambassador, who has political aspirations for his daughter, even though she wants to be a performer. Augie is

T.C.'s best friend, who is obsessed with Broadway musicals and a boy named Alex. Augie enlists Alejandra to perform in the school talent show which he is directing, while T.C. plays baseball and tries to make a dream come true for a deaf orphan who longs for Mary Poppins to appear and save him from his lonely life.

Koertge, Ron. **Shakespeare Makes the Playoffs**. Candlewick; 1 edition, 2010. MS. 176 pages. ISBN-13: 978-0763644352

In the sequel to *Shakespeare Bats Cleanup* Kevin Boland is experimenting with writing poetry while worrying about his baseball team making the playoffs. To complicate matters, he finds his interest in his girlfriend Mira waning, when he meets Amy at an open mike poetry night and they become "Poetry Buddies," sharing their poems through email exchanges.

Koertge, Ron. **Strays.** Candlewick, 2007. MS/HS. 176 pages. ISBN-10: 0763627054

Sixteen-year-old Ted would rather talk to animals than to humans; animals never lie and, unlike the kids at school, he understands them. When Ted's parents die in a car accident, he particularly identifies with strays because, as a foster kid, that's kind of what he is. As he bonds with his foster brothers, Ted begins to realize that he maybe able to depend on people as well as animals.

Konigsburg, E.L. **The Mysterious Edge of the Heroic World.** Ginee Seo Books, 2007. MS. 256 pages. ISBN-10: 1416949720

An unlikely friendship develops between William and Amadeo, two precocious sixth graders, who join forces to help William's mother sort through the belongings of an eccentric neighbor. Amadeo dreams of someday making an important discovery, and he thinks there are possibilities among the neighbor's belongings, particularly a piece of art by Modigliani. Amadeo's godfather is preparing an exhibit of Degenerate Art for the Sheboygan Art Center, and Amadeo believes this piece may belong in it.

Korman, Gordon. **Pop**. Balzer + Bray, 2009. MS. 272 pages. ISBN-13: 978-0061742286

Practicing in the park, preparing for football tryouts at his new school, Marcus meets Charlie, an eccentric older guy who clearly knows a lot about football. As Charlie teaches Marcus to "love the pop," the sound that comes with the perfect hit, Marcus realizes that fearlessness has been missing from his game. However, when Marcus discovers Charlie's secret, he also realizes there's a price to pay for this bravery.

Kress, Adrienne. **Alex and the Ironic Gentleman**. Weinstein Books, 2007. MS. 320 pages. ISBN-10: 160286005X

Alex, who lives with her uncle above his doorknob shop, learns that her new teacher Mr. Underwood is a descendant of a famous pirate, who has hidden a treasure map in a house run by the Daughters of the Founding Fathers' Preservation Society. Alex finds the map and escapes, only to find her uncle has been murdered and her teacher kidnapped. It is up to Alex to board a pirate ship, the *Ironic Gentleman*, and go rescue him.

Kuehnert, Stephanie. **I Wanna Be Your Joey Ramone**. MTV, 2008. HS. 352 pages. ISBN-10: 1416562699

Emily Black's mother left her, when she was four months old, supposedly to follow the punk rock music scene. Emily's dad has raised her with a passion for rock n' roll, and now she is the lead singer and guitarist in a punk rock band. Her angst is fueled by her mother's abandonment, and Emily hopes she will write the song that will ultimately bring her mother back home.

Kwok, Jean. **Girl in Translation**. Riverhead Hardcover, 2010. MS/HS. 304 pages. ISBN-13: 978-1594487569

Kimberly and Ma move to from China to Brooklyn in the 1980s to work in her aunt's clothing factory and live in a roach infested condemned apartment. Kimberly quickly realizes that education is her ticket out of the slums and works hard to excel in school. She is rewarded by getting a scholarship to a prestigious private high school and ultimately college, but her struggle to fit in socially is a bigger challenge.

Lamarche, Phil. **American Youth.** Random House, 2007. HS. 240 pages. ISBN-10: 1400066050

When ninth grader Ted LaClare is showing off his father's guns to two friends who are brothers, one of them accidentally shoots the other. Although Ted tries to anesthetize himself with booze, drugs, sex and membership in a vigilante group calling themselves American Youth, the guilt over his involvement in the accident begins to consume him.

Landy, Derek. **Skulduggery Pleasant**. HarperCollins, 2007. MS. 400 pages. ISBN-10: 0061231150

When 12-year-old Stephanie's eccentric Uncle Gordon dies and she inherits his house, she is plunged into a world of magic, intrigue and danger. She meets a friend of her uncle's, Skulduggery Pleasant, who is a skeletal magician trying to stop an evil person named Serpine from obtaining a scepter that will allow him to rule the world. Together, these two unlikely companions fend off monsters, villains and traitorous allies in an attempt to save the world.

Laser, Michael. **Cheater**. Dutton Juvenile; 1 editior, 2008. MS. 240 pages ISBN-13: 978-0525478263

Brainy nerd Karl Petrofsky is tempted to join an underground cheating ring when cool Blaine and sexy Cara ask him to help them. He tells himself that he will be striking a blow against the schools' zero tolerance cheating policy and the tyrannical vice principal Mr. Klimchock. Forsaking his nerdy friends, Karl gets involved in the clandestine world of high tech cheating tools. Then he gets caught and has to scramble to find a plan to save his college plans and restore his reputation.

Lasky, Kathryn. **The Last Girls of Pompeii**. Viking Juvenile, 2007. MS. 160 pages. ISBN-10: 0670061964

Born with a withered arm, Julia is an embarrassment to her family and is about to be sent to live in a temple. Her beautiful slave Sura is to be sold as a concubine. As they plot to escape their respective imprisonments, Vesuvius looms in the background threatening to erupt.

Law, Ingrid. **Savvy**. Dial; Reprint edition, 2008. MS. 352 pages.ISBN-13: 978-0803733060

When Mibs Beaumont turns thirteen, she expects to receive an unworldly power or "savvy" like the rest of her family has. Unfortunately, the celebration is postponed when her father is injured in an accident. Along with her brother and the preacher's kids, Mibs decides to catch a ride with a bible salesman to the hospital where she hope her new savvy will help him regain consciousness. Unfortunately, the bus heads off the wrong way and Mibs and her friends have a devil of a time getting to their final destination.

Law, Ingrid. **Scumble**. Dial, 2010. MS. 416 pages. ISBN-13: 978-0803733077

In this companion novel to *Saavy*, Ledger Kale celebrates his thirteenth birthday, only to find his saavy is the ability to "blow stuff apart without a touch." At first, he doesn't see much value in this skill, but during a summer vist to the Flying Cattleheart in Wyoming, he meets Sarah Jane Cabot, an aspiring reporter, who discovers his secret and helps him learn to harness his powers for good.

Leal, Ann Haywood. **Also Known As Harper**. Henry Holt and Co. (BYR); 1 edition, 2009. MS. 256 pages. ISBN-13: 978-0805088816

Fifth grader Harper Lee Morgan's father is gone and her mother is struggling to pay the rent and keep the family together. Harper is hoping to win the poetry contest at school, but when they get evicted, she has to stay home with her younger brother while her mother looks for work. Harper finds strength through writing poetry and new found friends.

Lecesne, James. **Absolute Brightness.** HarperTeen, 2008. HS. 480 pages. ISBN-13: 978-0061256271

When Leonard Pelkey, a flamboyant 14-year-old, arrives in Neptune, NJ to live with his cousin Phoebe's family, she is aghast and is sure he will be an outcast. Then she is surprised to find that many people, especially the clients at her mother's beauty salon. embrace his ideas for makeovers of their bodies and minds. When he is brutally murdered, Phoebe is overwhelmed and vows to get to the bottom of his senseless death.

Le Guin, Ursula K. **Powers (Annals of the Western Shore).** Harcourt Children's Books, 2007. MS/HS. 512 pages. ISBN-10: 0152057706

The third book in the Western Shore trilogy finds Gavir, a fourteen-year-old slave in the noble house of Etra, being educated to become the scholar who will teach the family's children and slaves. When his sister is raped and killed, Gavir, crazed with grief, walks away from the city on a journey to find himself and a home.

Leavitt, Lindsey. **Princess for Hire**. Hyperion Book CH, 2010. MS. 256 pages. ISBN-13: 978-1423121923

The first book of a new series introduces fifteen-year-old Desi, who finds she is qualified for the enchanted position of subbing for real prinesses, who want a vacation. Although she is only supposed to blend in until the princess returns, Desi finds herself attempting to solve their problems and getting herself into trouble. When her mentor threatens to fire her before she reaches level two, Desi must convince her that she's doing more good than harm, and in doing so Desi discovers her own worth.

Lennon, Stella. **The Amanda Project: Invisible I**. HarperTeen, 2009. MS. 304 pages. ISBN-13: 978-0061742125

The first in a proposed eight book series introduces Callie, Nia and Hal, estranged classmates who are drawn together by Amanda, a friend who plays a prank and then disappears. The three follow clues that Amanda has left and in the process form an uneasy alliance. The project also includes an interactive web site with videos, art, music and clothing for sale. Readers are encouraged to get involved in the project by adding their own ideas which may or may not be incorporated in future books.

Lester, Julius. **Cupid-A Tale of Love and Desire**. Harcourt Children's Books, 2007.
MS/HS. 208 pages. ISBN-10: 015202056X

This clever retelling of the story of Cupid and Psyche finds Cupid treading on dangerous ground between his desire for Psyche and his mother Venus's desire for revenge. Psyche, through no fault of her own has angered Venus, and Cupid is supposed to exact his mother's revenge.

Levine, Gail Carson. **Ever**. HarperCollins, 2008. MS. 256 pages. ISBN-10: 0061229628

Olus, the god of the winds, falls in love with Kezi, a gifted Hyte rug weaver, when he goes to Hyte to study the behavior of mortals. Kezi, however, is doomed to die because of an oath her father made in haste. Olus devises a plan for Kezi to become immortal so that the priest's knife cannot kill her, but will the plan succeed?

Levithan, David. **Love is the Higher Law**. Knopf Books for Young Readers, 2009. HS. 176 pages. ISBN-13: 978-0375834684

Three Manhattan teens deal with the emotional aftermath of the 9/11 attacks. Claire, who was at school, Peter, who was waiting outside Tower Records to buy the latest Dylan album, and Jasper, who was asleep when the planes hit the twin towers, are at first casual acquaintances, but they are drawn together through sharing their impressions of the tragedy. A romance between Peter and Jasper is fostered by Claire as the three struggle with their feelings about each other and the world around them.

Levithan, David and John Green. **Will Grayson, Will Grayson**. Dutton Juvenile, 2010. HS. 304 pages. ISBN-13: 978-0525421580

In alternating chapters two characters named Will Grayson tell the story of Tiny Cooper, "The world's largest person who is really, really gay." Heterosexual Will Grayson is Tiny's best friend and homosexual will grayson, who writes in lower case letters because he's clinically depressed, becomes Tiny's boyfriend. Together the tell a story of friendship, infatuation and changing to become the person you really want to be.

Liu, Cynthea. **The Great Call of China**. Puffin, 2009. MS. 224 pages.
ISBN-13: 978-0142411346

In this Students Across the Seven Seas offering, Chinese-born Cece heads off to Xi'an China to learn about anthropology, but she has an ulterior motive. Adopted by an American couple when she was two years old, Cece wants to visit the orphanage where she spent the first two years of her life and find out about her heritage.

Livingston, Lesley. **Wondrous Strange**. HarperTeen, 2008. MS. 336 pages.
ISBN-13: 978-0061575372

Kelley Winslow is practicing her lines in Central Park for her part as Titania in *A Midsummer Nights Dream* when she meets Sonny Flannery. A mortal raised by Faeries, Sonny guards the Samhain Gate, which connects the mortal world with the Faeries' Otherworld. As art and life merge, Sonny introduces Kelley to the Faery world that surrounds her and the destiny that awaits her.

Livingston, Lesley. **Darklight**. HarperTeen; 1 edition, 2009. MS. 320 page.
ISBN-13: 978-0061575402

In the sequel to *Wondrous Strange*, Sonny is in Fairie attempting to destroy the fairies in the Wild Hunt while Kelly is rehearsing her role as Shakespeare's Juliet at the Avalon theater. When sadistic leprechauns threaten her, Kelly flees to Faerie, where with the help of Fennrys Wolf and Sonny, she must battle for her life.

Lo, Malinda. **Ash**. Little, Brown Books for Young Readers; 1 edition, 2009. MS/HS. 272 pages.
ISBN-13: 978-0316040099

In this retelling of *Cinderella*, Ash, the Cinderella character, is again a beleaguered servant under her stepmother's control. However, her fairy godfather is actually an alluring fairy with whom she makes a soul sacrificing pact so that she can attend the royal ball. Although the prince meets and is attracted to Ash, she is more interested in Kaisa, the king's huntress who has enthralled Ash when they meet in the woods and Kaisa teaches Ash to hunt. Will Ash have to sacrifice all to escape her oppressive existence and find true love?

Lockhart, E. **The Disreputable History of Frankie Landau-Banks**.
Hyperion Book CH, 2008. MS. 352 pages. ISBN-13: 978-0786838189

During the summer of her freshman year, Frankie blossoms from a scrawny child into a curvaceous beauty. When she returns to Alabaster Academy, her elite boarding school, she captures they eye of a gorgeous senior. He is the leader of the Loyal Order of the Basset Hounds, an all-male secret society from which she is excluded. Determined to be more than his "arm candy," Frankie infiltrates the society, secretly masterminding all their pranks. When the guys find out, she gets a reaction she doesn't expect.

Lockhart, e. **The treasure map of boys**. Delacorte Books for Young Readers, 2009. MS.
256 pages.ISBN-13: 978-0385734264

Ruby Oliver, heroine of *The Boyfriend List* (2005) and *The Boy Book* (2006) is back, complete with panic attacks, boyfriend troubles and social ostracism from the girlfriends she alienated in the last book. As she struggles to choose between her old boyfriend Jackson and her friend Noel, her complete self absorption is both hilarious and endearing.

Lockhart, Mlynowski and Myracle. **How to Be Bad**. HarperTeen, 2008. MS/HS .
336 pages. ISBN-10: 006128422X

This road trip saga is a collaboration by three popular YA authors. Conservative Jesse uncharacteristically steals her mom's car and heads off to Miami with her best friend Vicks and Mel, their coworker at the Awful Waffle. Jesse, who is avoiding her mom's breast cancer diagnosis, is chauffeuring Vicks to see her college boyfriend whom she is afraid is dumping her. Mel is financing the trip, hoping to win the girls' friendship. Numerous detours help the girls sort out their problems.

Lore, Pittacus. **I Am Number Four**. Harper; 1 edition, 2010. MS. 448 pages.
ISBN-13: 978-0061969553

I Am Number Four, which is the first book in the Lorien Legacies series, introduces the story of nine young alien children from the planet Lorien, who escaped with their guardians in a spaceship and came to Earth after their planet was detroyed by the Mogadorians. The Mogadorians followed them to Earth, but not before the Elders put a charm in place that determines that the children can only be killed in numerical order. As the story opens, number three meets his demise, so number four and his guardian are on high alert.

Lowry, Lois. **The Willoughbys**. Houghton Mifflin/Walter Lorraine Books; 1 edition, 2008. MS. 176 pages. ISBN-13: 978-0618979745

In the tradition of Lemony Snickett the author introduces four children who are determined to become orphans like the heroes in an old-fashioned story. References to the plots of children's classics like *The Bobbsey Twins* and *Little Women* pepper the narrative and are explained in an annotated bibliography. When the children finally get rid of their parents, they are able to follow the conventions of old-fashioned children's books "stuffed with orphans, nannies and long-lost heirs."

Lupica, Mike. **Summer Ball.** Philomel, 2007. MS. 256 pages ISBN-10: 0399244875

This book, which is the sequel to *Travel Team*, continues the story of Danny Walker, the basketball-obsessed thirteen-year-old. He and his friends are heading off to summer basketball camp, where they will compete with some of the best players in the country. Danny is still the smallest boy on the court and is feeling the pressure of being number one after winning the travel team championship.

Lupica, Mike. **The Big Field.** Philomel, 2008. MS. 288 pages. ISBN-10: 0399246258

Hutch is a talented 14-year-old baseball player whose recent demotion from shortstop strains his relationship with his coach, as well as with Daryl, his replacement. As the team battles toward the Florida state championships, Hutch struggles with baseball and with his father who is determined that his son will not be disappointed by baseball the way he was when he didn't make the majors.

Lupica, Mike. **Million Dollar Throw**. Philomel, 2009. MS. 244 pages. ISBN-13: 978-0399246265

Eighth-grade football star Nate Brodie wins the opportunity to try to make a million-dollar throw on national TV during the halftime at a Patriots game. Normally, the throw would be within his capabilities, but the pressure of his family's financial woes added to his friend Abby being diagnosed with a degenerative eye disease is messing with his mojo. Will he be able to get his head back in the game in time for the team championship and his halftime challenge?

Lupica,, Mike. **Two-Minute-Drill: Mike Lupica's Comeback Kids**. Philomel, 2007. MS. 176 pages. ISBN-10: 0399247157

One of Lupica's *Comeback Kids* series, *Two-Minute Drill* tells the story of brainy Scott Parry, new kid on the block, and Chris Conlan, the coolest kid in sixth grade and quarterback of the football team. Scott and Chris are unlikely friends, but each has something to offer the other. Scott tutors the dyslexic Chris so he can stay on the team, and Chris supports Scott's attempt to play on the football team. Together they prove there's a lot to be said for the will to succeed.

Maberry, Jonathan. **Rot and Ruin**. Simon & Schuster Children's Publishing, 2010. MS/HS. 464 pages. ISBN-13: 978-1442402324

Fourteen years ago the dead start coming back to life, and now America is overrun with zombies. The living have been forced to barricade themselves in isolated communities within the "Rot and Ruin." When Benny becomes an apprectice to his older brother Tom, who is a zombie bounty hunter, he finds out the situation is more complicated than he realized. Zombies are not just monsters; they are beings who were once someone's loved ones.

Mackall, Dandie Daley. **Crazy in Love**. Dutton Juvenile, 2007. MS/HS. 192 pages. ISBN-10: 0525477802

Seventeen-year-old Mary Jane is an excellent student, who adores her mentally challenged sister and has a loving family. When she begins a flirtation with Jackson, his girlfriend Star spreads rumors that Mary Jane is easy. After she deals with a lot of unwanted attention from other boys, Mary Jane and Jackson finally get together. She thinks everything will now be perfect, but, of course, different problems arise.

Mackey, Weezie Kerr. **Throwing Like a Girl**. Marshall Cavendish Children's Books, 2007. MS. 271 pages. ISBN-10: 07614534

When Ella moves with her parents from Chicago to Dallas midyear, she resigns herself to finishing her sophomore year without friends. However, things quickly fall into place for Ella. She gets matched up with a popular senior guy for a marriage project in her Life Science class, and even though she has never played team sports, the coach recognizes her natural athletic ability and talks her into playing on the softball team.

MacCullough, Carolyn. **Once a Witch**. Clarion Books, 2009. MS. 304 pages. ISBN-13: 978-0547223995

Although it was prophesied that Tamsin would be a powerful witch, at age 17 she seems to be powerless. Then Gabriel, her childhood friend, returns and helps her travel through time, where she unwittingly discovers she can neutralize and gain for herself other witches' talents when they are used against her. Unfortunately, she has also reopened a feud that may mean the destruction of her family.

MacLachlan, Patricia. **Edward's Eyes.** Atheneum, 2007. MS. 128 pages ISBN-10: 1416927433

Jake's little brother Edward is something special. He can make anyone laugh and everyone think. That summer on the Cape, Edward becomes the only neighborhood kid who can throw a perfect knuckleball. Then a tragic accident makes Jake reevaluate everything he's ever known.

Mackler, Caroline. **Tangled**. HarperTeen; 1 edition, 2009. MS/HS. 320 pages. ISBN-13: 978-0061731044

Four vacationing teens, whose paths cross at a Caribbean resort, narrate this story which takes places over four months. Jena, a self conscious high schooler, is uncomfortable around her mother's best friend's daughter, who is a beautiful actress; but they are thrown together when their mothers decide to vacation together. Dakota, who is mourning the death of his ex-girlfriend, hooks up with the two girls at the resort. His computer geek brother Owen, who dubs himself "loser with a laptop" on his blog, rounds out the cast.

Madigan, L.K. **Flash Burnout**. Houghton Mifflin Books for Children, 2009. MS/HS. 336 pages. ISBN-13: 978-0547194899

15-year-old photographer Blake Hewson has a gorgeous girlfriend (Shannon) and a fellow photographer friend who is a girl (Marissa). The lines begin to blur when Blake takes a picture of a passed out street person whom Marissa recognizes as her meth addicted mother. As Blake begins spending more and more time dealing with Marissa's problems, he finds it hard to be an attentive boyfriend.

Magnum, Lisa. **The Hourglass Door**. Shadow Mountain, 2009. MS. 432 pages. ISBN-13: 978-1606410936

When Dante Alexander, a foreign exchange student, arrives from Italy, Abby's life changes dramatically. He claims to have been Leonardi Da Vinci's apprentice who has traveled through time to Abby's town, along with some not-so-nice friends. As the first book in a new series draws to a close, Abby uncovers a secret that threatens their lives in the future.

Maguire, Gregory. **What-the-Dickens: The Story of a Rogue Tooth Fairy**. Candlewick, 2007. MS. 304 pages. ISBN-10: 0763629618

Ten-year-old Dinah and her siblings are weathering a terrible storm by listening to their cousin Gage tell an unusual tale about a rogue tooth fairy named What-the-Dickens. He is a newly hatched creature who is trying to find his way in the world. When he meets a feisty girl, who is a skibbereen or tooth fairy, he is introduced to a tribe of skibbereen to which he would like to belong.

Malley, Gemma. **The Declaration.** Bloomsbury USA Children's Books, 2007. MS. 320 pages. ISBN-10: 1599901196

Anna is a "surplus" in a world where longevity drugs allow people to live forever. Due to over population, a law is enacted that forbids people from having children, so she lives in a facility with other forbidden children who are raised to become servants. Then Peter arrives with news from the outside world where people are beginning to realize maybe they shouldn't live forever. Peter begs Anna to escape with him, but she is unsure who to trust.

Marchetta, Melina. **Finnikin of the Rock**. Candlewick; 1 edition, 2010. MS/HS. 416 pages. ISBN-13: 978-0763643614

Assassins have murdered the royal family of Lumatere and a curse now creates a magical barrier around the kingdom to prevent those who fled from ever returning. Finnikin, exiled son of a former guard, is serving as an apprentice to Sir Topher, the murdered king's First Man. While aiding refugees, they receive a message that leads them to Evanjalin, a novice who insists Finn has been chosen to take his people home.

Marchetta, Melina. **Jellico Road**. HarperTeen, 2008. MS/HS. 432 pages. ISBN-13: 978-0061431838

Just when Taylor Markham has been chosen to lead her classmates at Jellicoe School in the annual secret war games against a camp of military kids (Cadets) and the neighboring locals (Townies), Hannah, her guardian, disappears. Then Taylor discovers an unfinished manuscript that Hannah has written about three teenaged survivors of a horrific car accident on Jellicoe Road that provides clues to Taylor's heritage. Together with the help of Cadet leader, Jonah Griggs, Taylor begins to piece together the truth about her past and make decisions about the future. (Michael L Printz Award)

Marr, Melissa. **Wicked Lovely**. HarperTeen, 2007. MS/HS. 336 pages. ISBN-10: 0061214655

Aislinn has always seen faeries that are invisible to most people, but now they are stalking her. Keenan, the faeries' Summer King, is determined that Aislinn is destined to be the Summer Queen, for whom he has been searching for nine centuries; but Aislinn does not want to sacrifice her freedom, her best friend Seth, and life as she knows it to find out.

Marr, Melissa. **Ink Exchange**. HarperTeen, 2008. MS/HS. 336 pages. ISBN-10: 006121468X

In this companion book to *Wicked Lovely*, Leslie, a friend of Aislinn's, survives a terrible trauma and wants to take control of her body by getting a tattoo. Unfortunately, the ink of the tattoo she chooses has been laced with the blood of Irial, king of the fey's Dark Court. When the tattoo is completed, Leslie will be bound to Irial. Will Niall, the fairy who is in love with Leslie, be able to save her from this dark attachment?

Marr, Melissa. **Fragile Eternity**. HarperCollins, 2009. MS. 400 pages. ISBN-13: 978-0061214714

In the sequel to *Wicked Lovely*, Aislinn is now the Fairies' Summer Queen and she is eternally bonded to Keenan, the Summer King. She is still in love with Seth, her mortal boyfriend, but she can't even touch him without burning him. Seth decides to take matters into his own hands and find a solution so that he and Aislinn can be together forever.

Marsh, Katherine. **The Night Tourist.** Hyperion, 2007. MS/HS. 240 pages. ISBN-10: 142310689X

In this modern day adaptation of Orpheus and Eurydice, Jack Perdu follows a girl named Euri into the ghostly underworld of New York City. If he does not return in three days, he will have to remain there forever. He tries to find his dead mother, as well as rescue Euri, who is actually dead but wants to return to the world of the living.

Mass, Wendy. **Finally**. Scholastic Press; 1 edition, 2010. MS. 304 pages ISBN-13: 978-0545052429

Rory Swenson can't wait until her twelfth birthday when her parents have promised her they will allow her some independence. She has a list of eagerly anticipated freedoms, like staying home alone and riding in the front seat of the car, but when the big day arrives, the catastrophes begin.

Mass, Wendy. **Heaven Looks a Lot Like a Mall.** Little, Brown Young Readers, 2007. MS/HS. 256 pages. ISBN-10: 0316058513

After an accident in gym class, sixteen-year-old Tessa finds herself in heaven, which bears a striking resemblance to her hometown mall. Taking a journey through past events in her life, while she is in a coma in the hospital, Tess reviews her memories from the time she was a toddler up until the accident. Written in verse, the story reveals a character, who is hard on herself and others and is looking for a reason to return to the living.

Mazer, Norma Fox. **The Missing Girl**. HarperTeen, 2008. MS/HS. 288 pages. ISBN-10: 0066237769.

This well-crafted psychological thriller has multiple narrators, who reveal the details of the abduction of a young girl, Autumn, by a psychopathic pedophile. The story is told from the points of view of the abductor, Autumn, and two of her sisters. Suspense builds throughout the story, as readers wait for the abduction and then finally root for Autumn as she tries to outwit the man who has imprisoned her.

McDonald, Abby. **Boys, Bears and a Serious Pair of Hiking Boots**. Candlewick; 1 edition, 2010. MS/HS. 304 pages. ISBN-13: 978-0763643829

Jenna, a teen environmental activist, is thrilled to be spending the summer with her godmother in the Canadian woods. Expecting to find like minded people, she is shocked when the local kids reject her eco-posturing and her godmother rejects her "green ideas" for her B&B remodel as too expensive. Slowly, Jenna begins to realize there are two sides to every issue and compromising your ideals may be necessary to do the right thing.

McGowan, Keith. **The Witch's Guide to Cooking with Children**. Henry Holt and Co. (BYR); 1 edition, 2009. MS. 192 pages. ISBN-13: 978-0805086683

This modern version of *Hansel and Gretel* introduces 11-year-old Sol and his 8-year-old sister Connie, who are the neighbors of an ancient witch, who loves children, well to eat them that is. When their no-so-adoring parents, give them to the witch, Sol, a science-tech whiz kid, is determined that they will be the first to escape her clutches.

McKenzie, Nancy. **Guinevere's Gift**. Knopf Books for Young Readers, 2008. MS. 336 pages. ISBN-10: 0375843450

Subtle details of the Arthurian legend are woven into this story of thirteen-year-old Guinevere, who gets involved in derailing a plot to take over the lands of Queen Alyse and King Pellinore, her aunt and uncle. When Gwen finds out their evil neighbor, Sir Darric, has been stealing their cattle and plans to wed their daughter, she enlists the help of the Old Ones to save the day.

McKinley, Robin. **Dragonhaven.** Putnam Juvenile, 2007. MS. 272 pages. ISBN-10: 0399246754

Jake Mendoza has grown up at the Smokehill National Park in the American West, which is a wilderness haven for dragons. In this alternate contemporary world, dragons are hunted by humans because the dragons are considered to be dangerous fire-breathing animals that eat livestock. Jason has inherited his scientist parents' commitment to the park's secret inhabitants. When he rescues an orphaned baby dragon, he sets in motion a series of events that may ultimately save the dragons from extinction.

McMann, Lisa. **Wake**. Simon Pulse, 2008. MS/HS. 224 pages. ISBN-13: 978-1416974475

Janie Hannagan has been inexplicably pulled into other people's dreams since she was eight years old. Through a patient at the Heather Nursing Home where she works, Janie finds out she is a dream catcher and has the ability to help others resolve their nightmares. Exhausted by being constantly pulled into the dreams of fellow students who are napping at school, Janie seeks to find a way to control the dreaming. Then she gets involved with Cabel, a former bad-boy who has hellish nightmares, and Janie realizes that her ability may be a blessing and not just a curse.

McMann, Lisa. **Fade**. Simon Pulse, 2009. MS/HS. 256 pages. ISBN-13: 978-1416953586

In the sequel to *Wake* Janie and Cabel are investigating teachers suspected of drugging and abusing students at class parties. Janie sets herself up as bait and their relationship is strained as Cabel feels unable to protect her. The physical toll her dream catching will ultimately exact is also revealed, and Janie needs to decide how much she is willing to sacrifice in order to continue her undercover job of dream catching for the police.

McMann, Lisa. **Gone**. Simon Pulse; 1 edition, 2010. 214 pages. ISBN-13: 978-1416979180

Janie discovers her long lost father is also a dream catcher. When she meets him for the first time, he is in a coma in the hospital. As Janie is pulled into his hellish nightmares, she realizes that he chose a life of isolation, rather than face the debilitating side effects of using his abilities. However, if she makes the same choice, it means abandoning her undercover work and, more importantly, Cabel, whom she loves more than life itself.

McNamee, Graham. **Bonechiller**. Wendy Lamb Books, 2008. MS/HS. 304 pages. ISBN-13: 978-0385746588

Danny and his friend Howie have been stung by a cannibalistic beast known in Indian lore as a Windingo. Now they are in a race against time before they are consumed by the beast who is stalking them in the frozen Canadian tundra. This supernatural thriller will keep readers turning pages as the boys and their friends seek a way to defeat the "bonechiller."

Mead, Richelle. **The Vampire Academy**. Razorbill, 2007. HS. 332 pages. ISBN-10: 159514174X.

This first book in a new series introduces Lissa, a vampire princess and Rose, her best friend and guardian, who is half-human/half-vampire. After two years on the run they are caught and sent back to St. Vladimir's Academy for vampires, where they face peer pressure, gossip and anonymous threats that may be lethal.

Medina, Meg. **Milagros: Girl from Away**. Henry Holt and Co. (BYR), 2008. MS. 288 pages ISBN-13: 978-08050823

Twelve-year-old Milagros, whose father is a pirate and mother is a healer with magical powers, feels like an outsider until she discovers powers of her own. When neighboring islanders attack her home, Milagros escapes in a small raft and ends up on an island between Maine and nowhere. As she finds friendship with an elderly Mexican woman, Milagros begins making magical connections that will help her on her journey to self discovery.

Meldrum, Christina. **Madapple**. Knopf Books for Young Readers, 2008. MS/HS. 416 pages.ISBN-13: 978-0375851766

Aslaug, whose lives in isolation with her eccentric mother, is devastated when her mother dies mysteriously and she is charged with murder. Aslaug seeks out her estranged cousins and aunt who is a charismatic preacher and lives with them until they, too, die under mysterious circumstances. As the narrative alternates between Aslaug's life after her mother's death and her trial for murder, the reader is drawn into a world of mysticism and intrigue.

Meyer, Carolyn. **Duchessina**. Harcourt Children's, 2007. MS. 261 pages. ISBN-10: 0152055886

This is the story of the early years of Catherine de' Medici, who becomes queen of France in the sixteenth century. Subject to political treachery, sinister court intrigues and family secrets, Catherine's early life was anything but pampered. Her childhood is spent in stark convents, as well as opulent palaces, but the challenges she faces help to create the notoriously strong willed queen.

Meyer, L.A. **Mississippi Jack: Being an Account of the Further Waterborne Adventures of Jacky Faber, Midshipman, Fine Lady, and Lily of the West.** (Bloody Jack Adventures) Harcourt Children's Books, 2007. MS. 624 pages. ISBN-10: 0152060030.

The fifth book in the series finds the intrepid Jacky Faber heading west, hoping that the British authorities won't find her in the wilds of America. There she tricks a scoundrel out of his flatboat and turns it into a floating casino-showboat. As she heads to New Orleans, she battles Indians, outlaws and British soldiers. Meanwhile, her own true love Jaimy is wandering through the wilderness, following her trail.

Meyer, Stephenie. **Breaking Dawn**. Little, Brown Young Readers, 2008. MS/HS. 768 pages. ISBN-10: 031606792X

The final book in the vampire love saga finds Bella and Edward the parents of a half human, half vampire child, whom they and the entire Cullen family must protect from the Volturi, who are determined to destroy her. Bella, who has been changed into a vampire during childbirth, must employ all of her new found powers to protect the ones she loves.

Meyer, Stephenie. **Eclipse**. Little, Brown Young Readers, 2007. MS/HS. 640 pages. ISBN-10: 0316160202

In *Eclipse*, the third book in Stephenie Meyer's vampire love saga, Bella once again finds herself surrounded by danger. In the midst of it all, she is forced to choose between her love for Edward and her friendship with Jacob. With her graduation quickly approaching, Bella has one more decision to make: life or death?

Meyer, Stephenie. **The Host**. Little, Brown and Company; 1 edition, 2008. HS. 624 pages. ISBN-13: 978-0316068048

Melanie Stryder is unwilling to relinquish her body to the Wanderer, the alien soul who invades it. Wanderer, overcome by Melanie's memories of her lover and family, seeks them out in a hidden human cell. Although the humans make it difficult for her, Wanderer comes to love Melanie's brother who accepts her and to fight her body's attraction to her lover who rejects her. As she slowly wins the humans over, Wanderer wonders if there is a way the humans and aliens can learn to live in harmony.

Mlynowski, Sarah. **Gimme a Call**. Delacorte Books for Young Readers, 2010. MS. 320 pages. ISBN-13: 978-0385735889

When she drops her cell phone in a fountain, Devi, a high school senior, finds she is able to call Frosh, her freshman self. After devoting herself exclusively to her boyfriend Bryan for four years, he has broken up with her, and Devi is determined to change her destiny by not getting involved with him. She instructs Frosh to focus on academics, activities, and female friendships instead. At first Frosh follows Devi's instructions, but she finds herself on overload and having a hard time resisting Bryan's persistent attentions.

Murdock, Catherine. **The Off Season.** Houghton Mifflin, 2007. MS/HS. 288 pages. ISBN-10: 0618686959

In this sequel to *Dairy Queen* D.J. Schwenk is playing linebacker on the high school football team, hanging out with the quarterback of the rival football team, and helping out on her family's struggling dairy farm. Her junior year has started off remarkably well. Little does she know she is in for "a whole herd of trouble."

Myers, Walter Dean. **Game**. Harper Teen, 2008. MS. 224 pages. ISBN-10: 0060582944

Like many basketball players from Harlem, Drew Larson dreams of a Division I scholarship and the NBA. Blessed with a strong family, he has managed to stay away from the street gang associations that plague many young players. Then the coach begins favoring a new white player and Drew struggles to maintain his drive to succeed.

Myers, Walter Dean. **Harlem Summer**. Scholastic Press, 2007. MS. 176 pages. ISBN-10: 043936843X

It's the summer of 1925 in Harlem, and 16-year-old Mark Purvis finds himself in serious trouble when a truckload of booze owned by mobster Dutch Schultz vanishes, when Mark is supposed to unload it. In the meantime, Mark finds a job working for W. E. B. DuBois' magazine, the *Crisis,* where he meets leading figures of the Harlem Renaissance.

Myers, Walter Dean. **Riot**. Egmont USA, 2009. MS. 192 pages. ISBN-13: 978-1606840009

The New York Draft Riots of 1863 are the subject of this novel which is written in screenplay format. 15-year-old Claire, the biracial daughter of a black man and an Irish woman, witnesses the tensions explode between the blacks in New York City and the Irish youth who are angry about the being drafted to fight for the freedom of people they see as job competition.

Myers, Walter Dean. **Sunrise Over Fallujah**. Scholastic Press, 2008. MS. 304 pages. ISBN-13: 978-0439916240

Over his parents' objections, Robin Perry leaves Harlem and joins the army instead of heading off to college. He is stationed in a Civil Affairs unit in Iraq, where he says, "We have an enemy we can't identify and friends we're not sure about." He and his comrades are assigned to win over the Iraqi people, not an easy job in the "fog of war."

Myracle, Lauren. **l8r, g8r.** Amulet, 2007. MS. 240 pages. ISBN-10: 081091266X

The third book in the "online chat" series finds Maddie, Zoe, and Angela chatting about boyfriends, college applications and getting back at a nasty classmate.

Myracle, Lauren. **Peace Love and Baby Ducks**. Dutton Juvenile, 2009. MS. 192 pages. ISBN-13: 978-0525477433

When fifteen-year-old Carly returns from summer camp, she finds her younger sister Anna has blossomed into a curvaceous beauty. Carly, who now embraces a natural eco-friendly lifestyle, is at odds with her formerly adoring sister who just wants white teeth, the perfect pastel outfit, and the guy that Carly wants. What's a sister to do?

Na, An. **The Fold**. Putnam Juvenile, 2008. MS. 192 pages. ISBN-13: 978-0399242762

Joyce Park longs to be as beautiful as her older sister so that she can capture the attention of John Ford Kang, a popular, gorgeous classmate. When Joyce's wealthy aunt offers her cosmetic surgery to add a fold to her eyelids, she is at first appalled, then tempted. She wonders if she conforms more closely to conventional standards of beauty, will she gain the self-confidence she is lacking and win JFK's heart?

Napoli, Donna Jo. **The Smile**. Dutton Juvenile, 2008. MS. 240 pages. ISBN-13: 978-0525479994

In an artful blending of fact and fiction, the author explores the mystery behind the enigmatic smile of Leonardo da Vinci's Mona Lisa. Monna Elisabetta is looking forward to her thirteenth birthday party when her mother suddenly dies. The event is cancelled and Elizabetta turns to working alongside her father in his silk business to deal with her grief. When her father's friend Leonardo introduces her to Giuliano de Medici, they develop a mutual admiration for each other. However, the Medici family's political problems and Elizabetta's father's plans for her betrothal to another man, thwart the lovers' secret plans to marry.

Nayeri, Daniel and Dina. **Another Faust**. Candlewick, 2009. MS/HS. 400 pages. ISBN-13: 978-0763637071

Five teenagers make a bargain with the devil who promises them their hearts' desires, but at a steep price. They disappear from their homes and end up in the care of a governess, Nicola Vileroy, who exploits them and their talents. As they enter an exclusive prep school in New York City, the teens are determined to find success, no matter what the cost.

Nelson, Blake. **They Came From Below.** Tor Teen, 2007. MS/HS. 304 pages. ISBN-10: 0765314231

Seventeen-year-old Emily and her best friend Reese come to Cape Cod every summer, hoping to meet cool guys. This summer they meet "Steve and Dave," two aliens who have been summoned from the depths of the ocean by a threat of global pollution. They have acquired human form and enlist the girls' help in a desperate attempt to save the ocean.

Nelson, Jandy. **The Sky Is Everywhere**. Dial; 1 edition, 2010. MS/HS. 288 pages. ISBN-13: 978-0803734951

When her older sister Bailey dies suddenly, Lennie, who has always been the companion pony to Bailey's racehorse, is devastated. She takes solace in a mutual attraction to her sister's fiancé, Toby, while at the same time falling head over heels in love with Joe, a gifted musician who is a new student at her high school. Although Joe helps her rediscover her passion for music, her relationship with Toby threatens their happiness.

Ness, Patrick. **The Knife of Never Letting Go**. Candlewick, 2009. MS/HS. 496 pages. ISBN-13: 978-0763645762

The first book of the Chaos Walking series introduces Todd Hewitt, who lives in a community on a planet where all the women are dead and the men are infected with a disease that makes all their thoughts audible. After finding a pocket of silence, Todd and his loyal dog Manchee flee and meet up with a girl whose thoughts are silent. Pursued by the town's preacher and his followers, Todd and his companions struggle to survive in an increasingly confusing world.

Newton, Robert. **Runner**. Knopf Books for Young Readers, 2007. MS. 224 pages. ISBN-10: 0375837442

Sixteen-year-old Charlie seeks solace in running after his father dies in Melbourne, Australia in 1919. He catches the eye of Squizzy Taylor, a notorious mobster, and against his mother's wishes Charlie becomes a courier for him. When the gang wars heat up and his best friend is brutally beaten, Charlie has to decide what direction his life will take.

Nix, Garth. **Lady Friday.** Scholastic Press, 2007. MS. 320 pages. ISBN-10: 0439700884

The fifth book in the series finds Arthur Penhaligon trying to find the Fifth Key and gain control of the Middle. His friend Leaf, who has been captured by Lady Friday, is being used to lure Arthur into a trap. The complex plot and witty wordplay will not disappoint fans of the series.

Norris, Shana. **Troy High**. Amulet Books, 2009. MS. 272 pages.ISBN-13: 978-0810946477

This modern day retelling of Homer's Illiad chronicles the football rivalry between the Troy High Trojans and the Lacede High Spartans. Troy High School sophomore, Cassie, who is best friends with Greg, class president at Lacede, struggles to deal with the animosity between their football player brothers. Then matters heat up when the school district changes the school boundary lines and gorgeous Elena changes schools, as well as boyfriends

O'Connell, Jenny. **The Book of Luke**. MTV, 2007. HS. 304 pages. ISBN-10: 1416520406

After Emily and her friends are rudely dumped by their respective boyfriends, the girls decide to write a caustic instruction book for the school time capsule that teaches guys the right way to treat girls. Emily is supposed to test out their tips on Luke Preston - the hottest guy in school, who just broke up with Emily's best friend by email! However, Emily soon finds out that there are two sides to every story, and she may have a few things to learn herself.

Ockler, Sarah. **Twenty Boy Summer**. Little, Brown Books for Young Readers; Reprint edition, 2010. HS. 320 pages. ISBN-13: 978-0316051583

Anna and Frankie are best friends. Anna and Frankie's brother, Matt, have finally acknowledged their mutal attraction and they are trying to find a way to tell Frankie, when Matt dies suddenly. Both girls are heart broken, but Anna continues to keep her relationship with Matt a secret. When the girls head to California with Frankie's parents, they make a pact to flirt with at least twenty boys on their beach vacation; but when Anna falls for a surfer, she feels like she is cheating on Matt's ghost.

Oliver, Lauren. **Before I Fall**. HarperCollins; 1 edition, 2010. MS/HS.480 pages. ISBN-13: 978-0061726804

After dying in a fatal car accident, mean girl Samantha wakes up the next day to find she must relive the events of the previous day again and again. At first, knowing she's already dead, she misbehaves with abandon. However, as she reawakens each morning, she begins to realize she has an opportunity to right her wrongs and live a last day that she can be proud of.

Oswald, Nancy. **Hard Face Moon**. Filter Press, 2008. MS. 204 pages. ISBN-13: 978-0865410893

Hides Inside is a young Cheyenne boy who suffers the taunts of other braves because he is unable to speak. Longing to become a warrior, he struggles to prove himself to his tribe. On November 29, 1864, his village is encamped along Sand Creek and is attacked by Colorado Territory militia in a bloody battle that is now known as the Sand Creek Massacre.

Palmer, Robin. **Cindy Ella.** Puffin, 2008. MS. 304 pages. ISBN-10: 014240392X

When Cindy writes a scathing anti-prom letter to the school newspaper, almost everyone at her private LA high school thinks she has committed social suicide. The only people who support her are her BFFs India and Malcolm, her mysterious IM pal BklynBoy, and surprisingly Adam, the most popular boy Castle Heights High. Will this fairy tale story have a happily-ever-after ending?

Palmer, Robin. **Geek Charming**. Puffin, 2009. MS. 288 pages. ISBN-13: 978-0142411223

When Dylan, the queen bee at Castle Heights High, drops her designer bag in the mall fountain, Josh comes to the rescue in exchange for Dylan's participation in his USC application film. He wants to document the "inner workings of the in crowd" at their school. As Dylan's social cache diminishes when her popular boyfriend drops her, Josh's is increasing due to a makeover orchestrated by Dylan. Will Josh give into his friends and edit the documentary to show Dylan in a negative light, or will he show the girl who has become his best friend?

Paolini, Christopher. **Brisingr**. Knopf Books for Young Readers, 2008. MS. 784 pages. ISBN-13: 978-0375826726

The third novel in Paolini's Inheritance cycle finds Eragon continuing to plan for the upcoming battle with Galbatorix. His cousin Roran rescues his fiancé from the Ra'zac and immediately begins fighting with the Varden. Meanwhile Eragon is off to encourage the Dwarves to choose a king who is sympathetic to the Varden cause. Finding out more about his lineage and searching for a replacement sword keep Eragon busy as he heads toward the epic battle in the fourth and final installment.

Park, Linda Sue. **A Long Walk to Water**. Clarion Books, 2010. MS. 128 pages. ISBN-13: 978-0547251271

In alternating chapters the stories of Salva, one of the Lost Boys of the Sudan, and Nya, a young Sudanese girl whose life revolves around an eight hour trip each day to fetch water, are revealed. Salva flees when his village is attacked and ends up in refugee camps in Ethiopia, and Kenha. After several years he is sent to Rochester New York where he starts a project that will ultimately touch the lives of many Sudanese, including Nya.

Parker, Robert B. **Chasing the Bear: A Young Spenser Novel**. Speak, 2010. MS. 176 pages. ISBN-13: 978-0142415733

Parker chronicles the teen years of his detective hero, who grew up in a household of men. Spenser is telling the story to his longtime love Susan, who listens to him reveal how his father and uncles taught him the difference between what's legal and what's right. He tells her about encountering a black bear in the woods, as well as defending his friends Jeannie, who has an abusive father, and Aurelio who is bullied by racists at their school.

Parker, Robert B. **Edenville Owls**. Puffin, 2008. MS. 208 pages. ISBN-13: 978-0142411612

In his first mystery for YA readers Parker sets his story in a small Massachusetts town in 1945. Bobby witnesses a parking lot argument between Miss Delaney, his eighth grade teacher, and a suspicious stranger. He enlists the help of his JV basketball team and Joanie, a childhood friend, to help Miss Delaney and discovers she has a troublesome past.

Parker, Robert B. **The Boxer and the Spy**. Philomel, 2008. MS/HS. 224 pages. ISBN-13: 978-0399247750

Fifteen-year-old boxer-in-training Terry Novak and his best friend Abby are determined to get to the bottom of the death of a classmate of an apparent suicide. The presence of steroids in the corpse just doesn't seem to fit what they knew about their shy nerdy friend. Their investigations pit them against the school principal, a beefy football player and a local politician, who are determined to prevent the two from learning the truth.

Patneaude, David. **Epitaph Road**. EgmontUSA, 2010. MS/HS. 272 pages. ISBN-13: 978-1606840559

This post-apocalyptic thriller takes place in 2097 after an airborne virus has wiped out 97% of the male population. Woman now rule the world and have eradicated poverty, crime, and war, but the few remaining men are not happy campers. Fourteen-year-old Kellen Dent, whose neglectful mother is on the ruling Population Apportionment Council, overhears his mother talking about an intentional resurgence of the virus. He and his friends Sunday and Tia decide to go warn Kellen's father, who is one of the rebellious men living away from female rule. In the process they discover a secret about the virus which rocks their world.

Patterson, James. **Maximum Ride – Saving the World and Other Extreme Sports**. Little, Brown Young Readers, 2007. MS. 416 pages. ISBN-10: 0316155608

In the third book of Patterson's Maximum Ride series, Max and her Flock attempt to defeat the takeover of Re-evolution, an experiment that threatens to wipe out two thirds of the world's population in order to create a superior master race. Separated into two groups, the Flock works to save the world and in the process they find out a lot about themselves.

Patterson, James. **Maximum Ride: The Final Warning**. Little, Brown and Company, 2008. MS. 272 pages. ISBN-10: 0316002860

When Max and the Flock are recruited to aid scientists who are studying the effects of global warming, they head off for Antarctica. Hoping to escape the government forces that are constantly watching them, the group doesn't realize there is also another sinister villain who is hoping to capture them and sell them to the highest bidder.

Patterson, James. **Max**. Little, Brown and Company, 2009. MS. 320 pages. ISBN-13: 978-0316002899

In the fifth book in the Maximum Ride series Max and the flock have returned from Antarctica and are performing in an air show which benefits the Coalition to Stop Madness (CSM). When they are attacked in the air, they take refuge and try to uncover who is out to stop them and destroy the CSM. Then they learn that the sea life off Hawaii's coast is dying and someone is destroying hundreds of ships. Could the two be related?

Paulsen, Gary. **Lawn Boy Returns**. Wendy Lamb Books, 2010. MS. 112 pages. ISBN-13: 978-0385746625

In the sequel to *Lawn Boy* the narrator, a twelve-year-old lawn service mogul, is now experiencing the problems that come with business expansion. In addition to tax problems and an unruly bunch of employees, he now has unwanted fame which is threatening his sanity. All he wants to do is go back to mowing lawns and being a kid, but that seems to be an impossibility.

Paulsen, Gary. **Woods Runner**. Wendy Lamb Books; 1 edition, 2010. MS. 176 pages. ISBN-13: 978-0385738842

In this depiction of the American Revolution, 13-year-old Samuel, whose parents have moved to a woodland settlement for peace and quiet, returns from hunting to find his home burned to the ground and his parents missing. He sets off to find them and along the way encounters vicious Red Coats and Hessians, as well as helpful rebels. In alternating chapters historical notes provide background information to help the reader understand the atrocities of this war.

Peacock, Shane. **Eye of the Crow: The Boy Sherlock Holmes –His First Case.** Tundra Books, 2007. MS. 264 pages. ISBN-10: 0887768504

With a highborn mother and a poor Jewish father, thirteen-year-old Sherlock Holmes is an outcast who amuses himself by piecing together the smallest details to construct histories for the people he meets. But then he attempts to solve a sensational murder and his game turns deadly. This first book in a new series introduces a boy whose powers of observation, sense of justice and sad past shed light on the eccentricities of the most famous detective in literature.

Peck, Richard. **On the Wings of Heroes.** Dial, 2007. MS. 160 pages.
ISBN-10: 0803730810

Initially, Davy Bowman's idyllic Illinois neighborhood is a place where "nobody was a stranger...Everybody played." Then World War II sends Davy's older brother into the army and depresses his dad, who is reminded of his own war experiences. Davy and his classmates begin to support the war effort and wait nervously on the home front for the outcome of the war.

Peet, Mal. **Tamar**. Candlewick 2007. MS/HS. 432 pages. ISBN-10: 0763634883

In separate narratives Tamar, a teenage girl, struggles to understand her grandfather's suicide, and the same man works with the local Nazi resistance movement in Holland during WWII. When Tamar is left a box of her grandfather's effects, she undertakes a quest to understand the mysterious contents and finds that things were not as they seemed.

Peterfreund, Diana. **Rampant**. HarperTeen, 2009. HS. 416 pages. ISBN-10: 0061490008

The first book in a new fantasy adventure series introduces Astrid Llewelyn, who is a direct descendant of Clothilde, a powerful unicorn hunter. After her boyfriend is gored by a monstrous unicorn, Astrid finally believes her mother's claim that she is destined to save humanity from a foe that was once thought to be extinct. Astrid joins fellow huntresses, who are training in the Cloisters in Rome, and learns to embrace her destiny.

Peters, Julie Anne. **By the Time You Read This, I'll Be Dead**. Hyperion Book CH, 2010. HS. 224 pages. ISBN-13: 978-1423116189

After many failed suicide attempts, Daelyn signs into an interactive website, "Through-the-Light," that guides people through the suicide process, including pain and effectiveness rating for different methods of killing oneself. She gives herself 23 days until her "Date of Determination." Then she meets Santana, a quirky cancer patient who wants nothing more than to live. Despite her hostility, he is determined to befriend her and change her view of life.

Petrucha, Stefan. **Split**. Walker Books for Young Readers, 2010. MS/HS. 272 pages.
ISBN-13: 978-0802793720

After his mother's death Wade devolves into two personalities: one a hard working computer geek who is developing a computer program to prove that the town's particle accelerator could destroy the world, the other a hard living, wise cracking musician who is in debt to the mafia. At first the two Wades dream of each other, then they meet and change places to solve each others' problems.

Pfeffer, Susan Beth. **The Dead and the Gone**. Harcourt Children's Books; 1 edition, 2008. MS. 336 pages. ISBN-13: 978-0152063115

The companion book to *Life As We Knew It* recounts the events in New York City when an asteroid knocks the moon closer to earth. Alex Morales is struggling to care for his sisters because his parents are presumed dead in the tsunamis that resulted from the catastrophe. As food supplies dwindle and the wealthy leave the city, Alex looks to his Catholic faith in order to find a way to survive.

Pierce, Meredith. **The Dark Angel.** Little, Brown Young Readers, 2007. MS/HS. 256 pages. ISBN-10: 0316067237

This book was originally published in 1982 and was an ALA Best Book for Young Adults, a New York Times Notable Children's Book, a Parent's Choice Award Superbook, and a Booklist Best Book of the Decade. With the popularity of vampire books now, the dark angel trilogy is being republished. The Dark Angel is a beautiful, but evil, vampire who can only reach his full power when he has fourteen brides. Aeriel, who has been kidnapped to serve his thirteen brides, finds some redeeming qualities in him and decides she wants to save him.

Pierce, Tamora. **Melting Stones**. Scholastic Press, 2008. MS. 320 pages. ISBN-10: 0545052645

In this print edition of the 2007 audiobook, Pierce introduces a new series about the students of the Circle Opens characters. In the first book *Melting Stones* Evvy has been training as a stone mage for four years. She accompanies her mentor to the Battle Islands to find out why plants and animals are dying there. With the help of Luvo, the living stone heart of a mountain, Evvy determines the problem and works to avert disaster.

Pike, Aprilynne. **Wings**. HarperTeen, 2009. MS. 304 pages. ISBN-13: 978-0061668036

The first book in a new series introduces Laurel Sewell, a teenage girl who is bewildered when a flower begins to bloom out of her back. With the help of her friend David, she finds out that she is a fairy which is actually a highly evolved plant. Together with Tamani, her fairy guardian, she and David try to save her family land which harbors a gate to the fairy world and will soon be in the hands of trolls.

Pike, Aprilynne. **Spells**. HarperTeen; 1 edition, 2010. MS.368 pages. ISBN-13: 978-0061668067

The sequel to *Wings* finds Laurel, who has recently discovered she's a fairy, studying at the Fairy Academy in Avalon for the summer. She is torn between her love for David, her human boyfriend, and her feelings for Tamison, the fairy who is in love with her. Realizing she must reconcile her two lives, she takes chances that threaten her safety and those she loves.

Powers, J.L. **The Confessional.** Knopf Books for Young Readers, 2007. HS. 304 pages. ISBN-10: 0375838724

When a Mexican terrorist blows up himself and a bridge in El Paso, Texas, tension between the Mexican students and white students at a Catholic boys school heats up. Then white Mac Malone beats up Bernie Martinez and ends up dead the next day. Mac's best friend Greg Gonzalez attempts to find Mac's murderer and in the process stirs up a lot of questions about loyalties, faith and personal responsibility.

Pratchett, Terry. **Nation**. HarperCollins, 2008. MS. 384 pages. ISBN-13: 978-0061433016

After a tidal wave deposits Mau, a native boy seeking manhood, and Daphne, an upper class girl sailing on an English vessel, onto the same tropical island, they find ways to communicate and try to survive. As survivors from other islands arrive at this island "nation," Mau and Daphne attempt to forge a new social order that redefines religion, justice, gender identity and formerly accepted scientific ideas. (Printz award nominee.)

Preble, Joy. **Dreaming Anastasia: A Novel of Love, Magic, and the Power of Dreams**. Sourcebooks Jabberwocky , 2009. MS. 320 pages. ISBN-13: 978-1402218170

In this supernatural romance, 16-year-old Anne Michaelson has recurring dreams involving Anastasia Romanov, who is being held captive by the witch Baba Yaga. Ethan Kozinsky, who has been searching for years to find the girl who has been predestined to save Anastasia, appears at Anne's high school to enlist her help. Anne, who is fearful of getting involved, cannot deny her attraction to Ethan and get caught up in the intrigue.

Printz, Yvonne. **The Vinyl Princess**. HarperTeen, 2009. MS/HS. 320 pages. ISBN-13: 978-0061715839

Allie, a sixteen-year-old audiophile, champions vinyl records in the age of downloads. She works at Bob & Bob's Records in Berkeley and starts a music blog that attracts international followers. Over the summer of her sophomore year she navigates her divorced parents' new relationships, crushes on a mysterious stranger and helps her best friend Kit spy on her cheating rocker boyfriend. Of course, she finds prince charming where she least expects him

Prose, Francine. **Bullyville.** HarperTeen, 2007. MS/HS. 272 pages. ISBN-10: 0060574976

Fortunately, Bart has the flu on September 11, 2001, and his mother has to stay home from work in New York City's twin towers. Unfortunately, his estranged father, who also works there, is killed. Bart is now known as the "miracle boy," and the attention earns him a scholarship to private prep school in town, known for its intense hazing. How long will Bart put up with the bullying before he retaliates?

Pullman, Phillip. **Once Upon A Time in the North**. Knopf Books for Young Readers, 2008. MS. 112 pages. ISBN-10: 0375845100.

This prequel to Pullman's Dark Materials trilogy finds Lee Scoresby and his jackrabbit daemon uniting with armored bear Iorek Byrnison to help a sea captain whose cargo has been impounded by a corrupt politician. There is a pullout board game Peril of the Pole to compliment the story.

Quinn, Spencer. **Dog On It: A Chet and Bernie Mystery**. Atria, 2009. MS/HS. 336 pages. ISBN-13: 978-1416585848

The first book in a new mystery series introduces Private Investigator Bernie Little and his canine partner Chet, who narrates the story. A wealthy divorcee hires them to find her missing 15-year-old daughter, Madison. Madison's shady land developer father tries to convince them she's a runaway, but Chet and Bernie are not buying it and set out on a dangerously wild adventure to find her.

Rapp, Adam. **Punkzilla**. Candlewick, 2009. HS. 256 pages. ISBN-13: 978-0763630317

Fourteen-year-old street urchin Jamie, aka Punkzilla, is hitchhiking from Portland to Memphis to see his gay playwright brother who is dying of cancer. Along the way he meets a variety of disenfranchised characters who help him in one way or another. Told through a series of letters to his brother, Punkzilla's story is one of despair and heartbreak, which is tempered by tenderness and hope.

Rees, Celia. **Savoy**. Bloomsbury USA Children's Books; 1st edition, 2008. 416 pages. ISBN-13: 978-1599902036

During the French Revolution 17-year-old Sovay disguises herself as "Captain Blaze," a highway robber, to test her fiancée's loyalty. She finds it so exhilarating that she continues to hold up carriages and ultimately uses the disguise to find her missing brother and father, who have been condemned for supporting the Revolution.

Reeve, Philip. **Here Lies Arthur**. Scholastic Press, 2008. MS. 352 pages. ISBN-13: 978-0545093347

The story of King Arthur is told from the point of view of Gwyna, a young girl who is taken in by Myddrin, the king's bard, who weaves tales of his heroic prowess. Myddrin disguises her as Gwyn, his servant boy, and has her help him create the myth of the once and future king. The well-known supernatural elements of the story are explained as conjuring tricks that Gwyna and Myddrin create and exaggerations of the truth that Myddrin spins to turn Arthur into a legendary hero.

Reinhardt, Dana. **Harmless**. Wendy Lamb Books, 2007. MS/HS. 240 pages. ISBN-10: 0385746997

When freshmen Anna and Emma and Mariah, almost get caught going to a sleepover at a senior boy's house, they make up a story about being attacked in the park. When a man is arrested for this alleged attack, the girls' lies spiral out of control. Told from the girls' alternating points of view, the story explores their differing sensibilities about the devastating consequences of their dishonesty.

Reinhardt, Dana. **How to Build a House: a novel**. Wendy Lamb Books, 2008. MS/HS. 240 pages. ISBN-13: 978-0375844539

Seventeen-year-old Harper is heading to Bailey, Tennessee to help a family rebuild their house which has been destroyed by a tornado. Harper is escaping from her own home in LA which has fallen apart when her stepmother and siblings move out as a result of her father's infidelity. When Harper meets Teddy, the son of the homeless Tennessee family, he helps her rebuild her family relationships, as she helps him rebuild his home.

Rennison, Louise. **Love is a Many Trousered Thing (Confessions of Georgia Nicolson)**. HarperTeen, 2007. MS. 271 pages. ISBN-10: 0060853875

This is the eighth book in the popular Georgia Nicolson series which is again written in diary format and has a glossary for the British slang. Georgia finds herself trying to decide between Masimo, her Italian one and only, and Robbie, the original sex god.

Reynolds, Phyllis Naylor. **Almost Alice**. Atheneum , 2008. MS/HS. 288 pages. ISBN-13: 978-0689870965

The most recent book in the Alice series finds Alice questioning who she is. Patrick, her former boyfriend, has asked her to the prom, but still doesn't seem to have much time for her. But then one of her friends gets pregnant and Alice's problems seem to pale in comparison.

Rhodes-Courter, Ashley. **Three Little Words**. Atheneum, 2008. MS/HS. 320 pages. ISBN-10: 1416948066

Ashley was three years old when she and her brother were removed from their mother. In the next nine years she endured fourteen different foster placements. When finally finds a home and accepts that her mother's an unfit parent, Ashley with the help of her adoptive parents begins to fight the abuse in the state's foster-care system.

Rinaldi, Ann. **Juliet's Moon**. Harcourt Children's Books, 2008. MS. 256 pages. ISBN-10: 0152061703
Juliet's brother Seth is a member of William Quantrill's renegade Confederate brigade. When she, his fiancé and other female relatives of its members are arrested as spies, they are imprisoned in a dilapidated house that collapses, killing many of the girls inside. As Juliet struggles to deal with continued confrontation, her brother's devotion and her relationship with Sue Mundy, a man masquerading as a woman, help her deal with the trauma of war.

Riordan, Rick. **The Battle of the Labyrinth**. Hyperion, 2008. MS. 368 pages. ISBN-10: 1423101464
In the fourth book in the Percy Jackson and the Olympians series the war between the Olympians and the evil Titan Kronos is near. Percy and his friends are at Camp Half-Blood and Luke the former camp counselor is up to no good. They must enter Daedalus's labyrinth to find a way to stop him.

Riordan, Rick. **The Last Olympian**. Disney Hyperion Books for Children, 2009. MS. 400 pages. ISBN-13: 978-1423101475

In the final book of the Percy Jackson Saga, the battle between the Olympians and the Titan Kronos, who is inhabiting the body of the demigod Luke, is resolved. Morpheus puts New York City inhabitants to sleep so that the conflict between Kronos's monster forces and the league of gods and demigods can take place. Percy dips himself in the Styx so that he is nearly invincible, as he masterminds the epic conflict to save Olympus, which is now at the top of the Empire State Building.

Roberts, Judson. **Dragons from the Sea(The Strongbow Saga –Book Two).** HarperTeen, 2007. MS/HS. 352 pages. ISBN-10: 0060813008
The second book in the Strongbow Saga finds Halfdan Hrorikson fighting with the Danes against the Franks. He has joined the crew of Jarl Hastein on *The Gull* and gets involved in the fray when they decide to attack the Franks. The world of the Vikings is accurately depicted in this tale of battle and revenge.

Roberts, Judson. **The Road to Vengeance (The Strongbow Saga: Book 3).** HarperTeen , 2008. MS/HS. 352 pages. ISBN-10: 0060813040
The third book in the Strongbow Saga chronicles the Danish campaign against the Franks. Halfdan still has Genevieve prisoner and is hoping to ransom her. She fears that her father who has banished her to a monastery will refuse. As Halfdan and Genevieve continue to grow closer, Halfdan realizes that he must put his vow for vengeance first and avenge his brother's death.

Rosoff, Meg. **What I Was**. Viking Adult, 2008. MS/HS. 224 pages. ISBN-10: 0670018449
The narrator, who is entering his third prep school in as many years, becomes obsessed with Finn, an orphan who is living alone in a hut on the beach near school. He sneaks out to visit Finn every change he gets. Unfortunately, he exposes Finn to a virulent fever, and his attempts to nurse him back to health have disastrous results.

Rothfuss, Patrick. **The Name of the Wind**. DAW, 2008. MS/HS. 736 pages. ISBN-13: 978-0756404741

The first book in The Kingkiller Chronicles trilogy introduces Kvothe, who is telling the tale of his life to a biographer called Chronicler. Kvothe's story begins with his boyhood, which was spent with his parents in an acting troop. When the demon Chandrians kill the whole troop while Kvothe is away, he vows revenge. He spends three years as a feral child on the streets of Tarbean, then makes his way to the University where he hopes to find out as much as possible about the Chandrian and learn the magic of naming to further his quest.

Rowling, J.K. **Harry Potter and the Deathly Hallows**. Arthur A. Levine Books, 2007. MS. 759 pages. ISBN-10: 0545010225

The seventh and final book in the Harry Potter series does not disappoint. Harry, Hermoine, and Ron must attempt to defeat Voldemort by finding and destroying Horcruxes he has created. The quest includes challenges, traps, twists, romance and, of course, the final showdown.

Russon, Penni. **Breathe**. HarperTeen, 2007. MS/HS. 368 pages. ISBN-10: 0060793937

In this sequel to *Undine* the title character has promised her mother not to use her magical powers which she discovered in the first novel. However, when Undine travels to Corfu to explore her roots with her long-absent father, and her best friend Trout struggles to find out about the nature of her dangerous magical powers, the promise is hard to keep.

Ryan, Carrie. **The Forest of Hands and Teeth**. Delacorte Books for Young Readers, 2009. MS/HS. 320 pages. ISBN-13: 978-0385736817

In this futuristic zombie novel, Mary lives in a village which is governed by a religious Sisterhood, whose job it is to protect the villagers from the zombies who live in the forest which surrounds the town. Her life is mind numbingly structured and preordained. She yearns to marry Travis, the man she loves, rather than his brother to whom she is betrothed, and to break free of the rigid traditions that enslave them. Hoping to find the ocean that her deceased mother told her about, she and six others escape only to be confronted by horrors she never could have imagined.

Ryan, Pam Munoz. **Paint the Wind.** Scholastic Press, 2007. MS. 336 pages. ISBN-10: 0439873622

Alternating stories between Artemisia, the dam who has just given birth to Klee, and Maya, the eleven-year-old girl who moves from her strict grandmother's home to a ranch in Wyoming, *Paint the Wind* is a horse lover's dream. When her grandmother dies of a stroke, Maya is sent to live with her maternal grandfather, great uncle and great aunt Vi. She spends the summer with Vi at her field camp in the mountains, where she becomes acquainted with Artemisia, her mother's horse who has returned to the wild.

Ryan, Sara. **The Rules for Hearts.** Viking Juvenile, 2007. HS. 272 pages. ISBN-10: 0670059064

In this sequel to *Empress of the World* Battle Hall Davies joins her brother in Portland, Oregon for the summer before her first year of college. Her rocky reunion with her runaway brother, whom she hasn't seen for four years, is complicated by her crush on a woman, who lives with them in a house full of quirky actors.

Sachar, Louis. **The Cardturner**. Delacorte Books for Young Readers, 2010. MS. 352 pages. ISBN-13: 978-0385736626

When Alton Richards' mother insists he become his blind great-uncle's chauffeur and cardturner at local bridge tournaments, he thinks he's in for the most boring summer ever. He knows nothing about bridge and his rich grumpy uncle is not much fun to be around. However, when Alton meets cute Toni Castaneda, another inheritance seeking relative, and begins playing the game with her, he gains a new appreciation for his uncle, as well as the game that gives him a reason to live.

Sachs, Marilyn. **The Fat Girl**. Flux, 2007. MS. 226 pages. ISBN-10: 0738710008

In this dark retelling of Pygmalion, Jeff Lyons feels remorse when he cruelly remarks on Ellen de Lucas's obesity, so he undertakes her "makeover." Intoxicated by the feeling of control he has over her, he confuses it with love.

Saenez, Benjamin Alire. **Last Night I Sang to the Monster**. Cinco Puntos Press; 1 edition, 2009. HS. 304 pages. ISBN-13: 978-1933693583

Eighteen year old Zach, who is in a rehab facility, cannot remember much of his past life, especially what landed him in rehab. He feels like there is a monster inside him that has taken control. Fortunately, Adam, his therapist, and Rafael, his roommate and fellow alcoholic are there to help Zach with the healing process.

Sage, Angie. **Physik**. Katherine Tegen Books, 2007. MS. 560 pages. ISBN-10: 0060577371

The third book in the Septimus Heap series find Septimus battling with a new villain, a former queen whose evil spirit has been released from an enchanted portrait. When Septimus is forcibly apprenticed to an alchemist who lived many centuries earlier, the entire Heap family is involved in the rescue and finding a cure for a deadly plague that threatens the kingdom.

Sage, Angie. **Queste**. Katherine Tegen Books, 2008. MS. 608 pages. ISBN-10: 0060882077

The fourth in the Septimus Heap series introduces more trouble for Septimus when a ghost named Tertius Fume, sends him on a deadly Queste. Along with his sister Jenna and friend Beetle, Septimus decides to use the opportunity to rescue his brother Nicko who is trapped in time in the House of Foryx. The book comes with a Magykal CD and ends with a series of vignettes entitled "Endings and Beginnings."

Sandell, Lisa Ann. **Song of the Sparrow**. Scholastic Press, 2007. MS/HS. 416 pages. ISBN-10: 0439918480

In 490 A.D. 16-year-old Elaine of Ascolat lives with her father in King Arthur's base camp. The only girl in a world of men, Elaine is thrilled when Gwynivere arrives; however, conflict ensues when they find themselves jealous rivals, rather than comrades.

Sanderson, Brandon. **Alcatraz versus the Evil Librarians**. Scholastic Press, 2007. MS. 320 pages. ISBN-10: 0439925509

Thirteen-year-old Alcatraz Smedry receives a bag of sand for his birthday, which begins his involvement in the fight between the Free Kingdoms and the world we know, which is controlled by a conspiracy of Evil Librarians. He is actually part of a family that has talents that seem like liabilities. Alcatraz breaks things. When the evil librarians steal the bag of sand, Alcatraz and his compatriots must get it back at all costs.

Schlitz, Laura Amy. **Good masters! Sweet Ladies! Voices from a Medieval Village**. Candlewick, 2007. MS. 96 pages. ISBN-10: 0763615781

This Newbery award winning novel-in-verse includes 22 brief monologues which bring to life a prototypical English village in 1255. Robert Byrd's watercolors enhance the interconnected stories, and background text is provided to explain the factual information and Old English terminology.

Schmidt, Gary. **The Wednesday Wars**. Clarion Books, 2007. MS. 272 pages. ISBN-10: 0618724834

While the rest of the seventh-grade students attend religious instruction, much to his chagrin, Holling Hoodhood spends Wednesday afternoons reading Shakespeare with his teacher. Little does he know it will help him with many of the problems that plague him over the course of the 1967-68 school year.

Schneider, Robyn. **Better Than Yesterday**. Delacorte Books for Young Readers, 2007. HS. 240 pages. ISBN-10: 0385733453

Summer school at Hilliard Preparatory School, finds four friends dealing with overwhelming pressure to excel in a variety of ways. When self destructive Blake disappears, his friends jeopardize their class rank and take off to Manhattan to find him.

Schrefer, Eliot. **The School for Dangerous Girls**. Scholastic Press, 2009. MS/HS. 256 pages. ISBN-13: 978-0545035286

After being implicated in her grandfather's death, Angela Cardenas is sent to Hidden Oak, a school of last resort for rehabilitating dangerous girls. The first month the girls are isolated from the rest of the school as they are sorted into those who are redeemable and those who are lost causes, who then disappear. When some of her friends end up in the second group, Angela vows to outwit the faculty to save her friends and expose the horrific practices of this unconventional school.

Schreiber, Mark. **Star Crossed.** Flux, 2007. MS/HS. 305 pages ISBN-10: 0738710016

Christy Marlowe goes to a plastic surgeon's office to have the name of her ex-boyfriend Benjamin removed and meets Ben Penrose, who is there to have a Christy tattoo erased. Her love of astrology and his love of astronomy bring these two star crossed lovers together, but their secrets and lies may tear them apart.

Schroeder, Lisa. **Chasing Brooklyn**. Simon Pulse; 1 edition, 2010. MS/HS. 432 pages ISBN-13: 978-1416991687

This novel in verse chronicles the year after Brooklyn's boyfriend Lucca is killed in a car accident and Gabe, the boy who was driving, commits suicide. Gabe is haunting Brooklyn's dreams and Lucca is haunting his brother Nico, instructing him to help Brooklyn deal with her grief. As Nico and Brooklyn begin to train for a triathlon, they attempt to redefine their lives which have been shattered by loss.

Schroeder, Lisa. **Far from You**. Simon Pulse; 1 edition, 2010. MS/HS. 384 pages. ISBN-13: 978-1416975076

Four days in a snowbound car with her stepmother and baby stepsister Ivy, give Alice time to reflect on the bitterness she feels about her mother's death from cancer and her father's new family, as well as her confusion about her relationships with her rebel boyfriend Blaze, who is pressuring her to sleep with him, and her best friend Claire, who is ready for Alice to move on from her ceaseless grief.

Schroeder, Lisa. **I Heart You, You Haunt Me**. Simon Pulse, 2008. MS/HS. 240 pages. ISBN-10: 1416955208

This novel-in-verse chronicles a year in the life of fifteen-year-old Ava, following the death of her boyfriend in a tragic accident. Overwhelmed with guilt, Ava feels his presence in her house, and she spends all of her time there with his spirit. As her friends and family beg her to move on, she struggles with the decision, knowing that she can never live a normal life if she does not let him go.

Scott, Elaine. **Secrets of the Cirque Medrano**. Charlesbridge Publishing, 2008. 216 pages. ISBN-13: 978-1570917127

This story behind Picasso's Family of Saltambiques, as imagined by the author, involves 14-year-old Brigitte, who works in her aunt's Montmartre café, frequented by Pablo Picasso, Russian diplomats and circus performers. Thrilled by the attentions of a young acrobat, she is fascinated by the Cirque Medrano and dreams of leaving the drudgery of serving food to join the circus. Brigitte's attempt to solve the disappearance of one of the circus performers leads her into a world of revolutionaries, secret police and intrigue.

Scott, Elizabeth. **Living Dead Girl**. Simon Pulse, 2008. HS. 176 pages. ISBN-13: 978-1416960591

Alice, once known as Kyla, was kidnapped and raped by Ray when she was 10 years old and has been his captive sex slave for the last five years. But Ray likes little girls and now he has Alice searching for her successor. She sees choosing Ray's next victim as the only way out of this horror story that is her life. In the process, however, she meets a needy teenage boy and a police officer that suspect she is in trouble. Will they be able to help her before it's too late?

Scott, Elizabeth. **Perfect You**. Simon Pulse, 2008. MS. 304 pages. ISBN-10: 1416953558

When Kate Brown's father quits his job to sell infomercial vitamins at the mall and she is forced to work with him, she's sure things couldn't get any worse. Then her best friend dumps her and her annoying grandmother moves in with her family. When gorgeous, unattainable Will starts flirting with her, she's sure he's just looking for another conquest. Isolating herself seems to be the only answer, or is it?

Scott, Elizabeth. **Something Maybe**. Simon Pulse, 2009. MS. 217 pages. ISBN-13: 978-1608477531

Hannah, whose mother is a Web-chat hostess and father is an elderly celebrity playboy, tries to avoid entanglements by keeping a low profile, working at a drive-through burger place. She has a crush on Josh, a co-worker who seems to be Mr. Perfect, but is also drawn to the annoying Finn, who keeps up a running sarcastic commentary on her every awkward interaction with Josh. As she is struggling with her love life, she is also navigating the troubled waters of celebrity parents who won't behave.

Scott, Elizabeth. **Stealing Heaven**. HarperTeen , 2008. MS. 320 pages. ISBN-10: 0061122807

Dani has been her mother's accomplice in stealing from wealthy homes since she can remember. They move from town to town where her mother makes temporary connections with men to get information about the town's wealthiest homes and then robs them. Dani has no friends, no school, no home, until they move to Heaven, where she not only makes a friend, but also starts a flirtatious relationship with a young cop. Will she get the courage to leave her mother's life of crime behind and follow her own dreams?

Scott, Michael. **The Alchemyst – The Secrets of the Immortal Nicholas Flamel.** Delacorte Books for Young Readers, 2007. MS. 400 pages. ISBN-10: 0385733577.

Fifteen-year-old twins, Josh and Sophie, find out not only are they working for Nicholas Flamel, famed 14th century alchemist, but they themselves are potentially powerful magicians. When the evil Dr. Dee steals the Codex, the book with the formula for immortality, it is up to them to recover it.

Selfors, Suzanne. **Coffeehouse Angel.** Walker Books for Young Readers, 2009. MS/HS. 288 pages. ISBN-13: 978-0802798121

16-year-old Katrina Svenson brings coffee and a Danish to a vagrant who is sleeping in the alley behind her grandma's coffee shop, and later finds out he's an angel who is a messenger from Heaven. For her kindness he must grant her heart's desire. But what does she want – love, fame, or fortune? While Katrina is busy trying to decide, her grandma's coffeehouse is failing, her best guy friend is dating her nemesis, and her cat becomes famous for killing a giant rat in the coffeehouse. To complicate matters she is attracted to the angel and would like for him to stick around.

Selfors, Suzanne. **Saving Juliet.** Walker Books for Young Reader, 2008. MS/HS. 256 pages. ISBN-10: 0802797407

17-year-old Mimi Wallingford is starring as Juliet opposite Troy Summers, a vapid teen pop star. It is hoped that his popularity will boost ticket sales at her family's debt-ridden theater. Then Mimi breaks a vial which supposedly contains ashes from Shakespeare's quill. She and Troy inhale the ashes and are transported to 16th century Verona, where they meet the real Romeo and Juliet. Mimi is determined to save Juliet from her fate, but Mimi's actions have dire consequences.

Selznik, Brian. **The Invention of Hugo Cabret.** Scholastic Press, 2007. MS. 533 pages. ISBN-10: 0439813786

Hugo, a twelve-year-old orphan, lives in the walls of a Paris train station at the turn of the 20th century, where he maintains the clocks and steals what he needs to live. He is working to restore an automaton he and his father found in the remains of a museum fire. The author blends narrative, illustrations, and cinematic technique to create this truly unique tale of a boy struggling to do more than just survive.

Sensel, Joni. **The Humming of Numbers**. Henry Holt and Co. (BYR), 2008. MS/HS. 256 pages. ISBN-13: 978-0805083279

Aiden is a novice monk in 10th century Ireland, who hopes to take monastic vows in order to learn to copy manuscripts. He has the unusual power to sense the energy given off by living things, which he feels as the humming of numbers. When he meets Lana, the illegitimate daughter of the local lord, he finds she is able to use wood to work magic. After marauding Vikings attack their village, the two must use their magical skills to devise a plan to cast out the invaders and save the remaining villagers.

Sharenow, Robert. **My Mother the Cheerleader.** Laura Geringer Books, 2007. HS. 297 pages. ISBN-10: 061148972

Louise Collins lives with her mother in their New Orleans boardinghouse called Rooms on Desire. Life seems pretty uneventful until desegregation begins and six-year-old African-American Ruby Bridges enrolls at Louise's school. Louise's mother pulls her out of school and joins the Cheerleaders, who gather every morning to heckle Ruby as she enters the building. When a mysterious man from New York arrives at the boardinghouse, Louise begins to question her world and her values.

Sherry, Maureen. **Walls Within Walls**. Katherine Tegen Books; 1 edition, 2010. MS. 368 pages. ISBN-13: 978-0061767005

The first book in a new mystery series introduces CJ, Brid, and Patrick, who move into a Fifth Avenue apartment previously owned by the Post family and stumble upon a puzzle filled with codes and clues that lead them to a fortune Mr. Post left his children. Following clues to various locations throughout Manhattan, the kids discover fascinating historical information in this architectural treasure hunt.

Sheth, Kashmira. **Boys without Names**. Balzer + Bray, 2010. MS. 316 pages. ISBN-13: 978-0-06-185760-7

11-year-old Gopal and his family must move to his uncle's house in Mumbai when they loses their farm. Separated from his father, Gopal guides his mother and siblings to Mumbai. Hoping to help his family, he takes what he thinks will be a day job at a factory, but is instead held prisoner with five other boys in a sweatshop where they are abused and forced to do tedious bead work. While Gopal dreams of escape, he slowly builds friendships with the other boys by telling them stories and encouraging them to share theirs.

Shulman, Polly. **The Grimm Legacy**. Putnam Juvenile, 2010. MS. 336 pages. ISBN-13: 978-0399250965

Elizabeth, who is a lonely new student at a Manhattan prep school, is thrill when she is recommended by her favorite teacher for a job at the New York Circulating Material Repository, a library for objects rather than books. As she is befriended by the other pages, she learns that the repository's Grimm collection is filled with magical objects from fairy tales. When some of the objects begin to disappear, it is up to the pages to find the thief.

Shusterman, Neal. **Antsy Does Time**. Dutton Juvenile, 2008. MS. 256 pages. ISBN-10: 0525478256

This companion book to *The Schwa Was Here,* finds Antsy Bonano enlisting people to "sign over" a month of their life to his "dying" friend Gunnar. Then a family member has a heart attack after signing over two years of his life, and the donors begin to wonder if there was more than symbolism to their gesture.

Shusterman, Neal. **Unwind**. Simon & Schuster Children's Publishing, 2007. MS/HS. 352 pages. ISBN-10: 1416912045

After the Heartland Wars, laws have been enacted forbidding abortion, but allowing unwanted teenage children to be sold for body parts or "unwound." Connor, a troublemaker, Risa, an orphan, and Lev, a religious "tithe," are all scheduled to be unwound. However, they are brought together by chance, and manage to escape. If they can survive until their eighteenth birthday, they can't be harmed. In a harrowing cross-country journey, they are literally running for their lives.

Skovron, Jon. **Struts and Frets**. Amulet Books, 2009. MS/HS. 304 ISBN-13: 978-0810941748
17-year-old Sammy wants nothing more than fame and fortune as a rock star. However, his band's lead singer is a loose cannon, his jazz musician grandfather is suffering from dementia and his best girl friend is becoming more than a friend. Struggling to become a legitimate musician amidst the chaos that is his life may be more than he can handle.

Slayton, Fran Cannon. **When the Whistle Blows**. Philomel, 2009. MS. 160 pages. ISBN-10: 0399251898

In a series of short stories involving seven consecutive Halloweens, the life of Jimmy Cannon plays out in West Virginia during the 1940s. Starting out as a twelve-year-old, Jimmy matures from an adventuresome child into a young man.

Sleator, William. **Test**. Amulet, 2008. MS/HS. 240 pages. ISBN-10: 0810993562

Ann is a teenage girl living in an elitist, security-obsessed society in the United States in the near future. When she is harassed on her way home from school by a thug on a black motorcycle, she and a friend begin an investigation that uncovers a conspiracy involving the greedy owner of a school testing company. Students who pass this test have bright futures; those who fail disappear or worse.

Smith, Charles R. **Chameleon**. Candlewick; 1 edition, 2008. MS/HS. 384 pages. ISBN-13: 978-0763630850

Fourteen-year-old Shawn, whose parents are divorced, spends most of his time in his mom's Los Angeles inner-city neighborhood, where he and his homeboys hang out playing basketball and trying to avoid getting harassed by warring gang members. He flirts with Marisol, a beautiful Mexican classmate, and struggles with the decision about attending high school with his friends or transferring to the safer, more academic high school near his dad's home.

Smith, Cynthia Leitich. **Tantalize**. Candlewick, 2007. MS/HS. 336 pages. ISBN-10: 0763627917

Seventeen-year-old Quince Morris, who was orphaned at 13, has been living with her uncle and managing the family's restaurant. Kieran, her best friend and the love of her life, is a werewolf in training who can not return her affection because he's not fully in control of his shape shifting. Right before the grand reopening of the new vampire-themed restaurant, the chef is brutally murdered werewolf style. Quince has a month to train the newly hired chef, who is coming on to her, and at the same time deal with the fact that Kieran is abandoning her to join his own wolf pack.

Smith, Cynthia Leitich. **Eternal**. Candlewick, 2009. MS/HS. 320 pages. ISBN-13: 978-0763635732

In this companion novel set in the same alternate world as *Tantalize*, Miranda is saved from death by her guardian angel Zachary, only to be turned into a vampire princess. In order to redeem himself Zachary infiltrates the house of Dracl as Miranda's personal assistant. He awakens the last vestige of Miranda's humanity and together they attempt to wage a supernatural battle against the undead.

Smith, Sherri L. **Flygirl**. Putnam Juvenile, 2009. MS. 256 pages. ISBN-13: 978-0399247095

In 1941 African American Ida Mae Jones, whose father taught her to fly his crop dusting plane, applies for the Women Airforce Service Program to help with the war effort at home. However, in order to do so, she has to leave her family and friends and pass as white. She completes a rigorous training program and flies dangerous missions, all the while guarding the secret that would put an end to her military career.

Smith, Tara Bray. **Betwixt.** Little, Brown Young Readers, 2007. MS/HS. 496 pages. ISBN-10: 031606033X

In this paranormal thriller, artistic Ondine Mason, her friend Morgan D'Amici, and Nix Saint-Michael, an Alaskan runaway, become involved in the world of the Fay, when they attend a secret rave in the woods around Mt. Hood. In a ritual known as the Ring of Fire, their true natures are revealed. This is the beginning of a series in which the three teenagers will have critical roles in a deadly conflict in another world.

Soesbee, Ree. **Pillar of Flame**. Mirrorstone, 2007. MS. 256 pages. ISBN-10: 0786942487

Volume one in the Elements Series, which is part of the popular Dragonlance Series, introduces the quest to destroy the Crescent Cabal, which is trying to seize control over all the wizards and pillars of the earth. Nearra and her sister Jirah have to restore the magic fire to Krynn, which involves destroying the pillar of flame.

Somper, Justin. **Vampirates 3: Blood Captain**. Little, Brown Young Readers, 2008. MS. 576 pages. ISBN-13: 978-0316020855

The third book in the Vampirates series finds Grace accompanying her blind vampire friend Lorcan to the Sanctuary where vampires go for healing. In an alternating narrative her twin brother Connor is dealing with the conflict he feels after his first kill as a pirate. Meanwhile, his friend Jez has joined forces with the evil Sidorian, who is determined to recruit a battalion of vampires who do not resist their blood thirsty yearnings. The non-stop action continues as Grace and Connor each struggle with decisions about the future.

Sones, Sonya. **What my girlfriend doesn't know**. Simon & Schuster Children's Publishing, 2007. MS/HS. 304 pages. ISBN-10: 0689876025

In this sequel to *what my mother doesn't know,* Sophie and Robin are still together and are being ostracized by the whole school. Sophie seems to enjoy being a renegade, but Robin is distressed that the once popular Sophie is now a pariah. When he is invited to take an art course at Harvard and he finds acceptance he has never known, he wonders if Sophie would be better off without him.

Sonnenblick, Jordan. **Zen and the art of faking it**. Scholastic Press, 2007. MS. 272 pages. ISBN-13: 978-0439837071

After his father goes to jail for fraud, San Lee and his mother move to Pennsylvania and San sees the opportunity to reinvent himself. When he becomes the resident expert on Buddhism in social studies class, he decides take on a Zen master persona to impress the other students and in particular a folk singing girl named Woody. He offers spiritual advice and begins to make a difference in people's lives. However, as the lies mount up, he begins to remind himself of his fast talking dad, and he wonders if he's doing more harm than good.

Soto, Gary. **Mercy on these Teenage Chimps**. Harcourt Children's Books, 2007. MS. 160 pages. ISBN-10: 0152060227

Ronnie Gonzalez and Joey Rios hit puberty, and they are so awkward that they feel like they've turned into teenage chimps. When Joey gets a crush on a champion gymnast and the wrestling coach embarrasses him in front of her, Joey climbs up a tree and refuses to come down. Ronnie struggles to find a way to save his friend's reputation and get him out of the tree.

Spinelli, Jerry. **Eggs**. Little, Brown Young Readers , 2007. MS. 224 pages. ISBN-10: 0316166464

Nine-year-old David lives with his grandmother, because his mother has recently died and his father travels. 13-year-old Primrose, who has an absentee father and a childlike, fortuneteller mother, meets David when she moves into a nearby abandoned van. Despite their differences Primrose and David develop a supportive yet rocky relationship, which helps them deal with what is missing in their lives.

Spinelli, Jerry. **Love, Stargirl.** Knopf Books for Young Readers, 2007. MS/HS 288 pages. ISBN-10: 0375813756

This sequel to *Stargirl* finds Stargirl in Pennsylvania, writing "the world's longest letter" to Leo, the boy who dumped her in the earlier novel. As Stargirl longs for Leo, she begins to meet people in her new community. In a diary format she details her adventures with Dootsie, a five-year-old neighbor, Betty Lou, an agoraphobic divorcee, and Perry Delloplane, a charismatic thief.

Spinelli, Jerry. **Smiles to Go.** Joanna Cotler, 2008. MS. 256 pages. ISBN-10: 0060281332

Will Tuppence is an obsessive, science loving, chess playing ninth grader whose precocious little sister is driving him crazy. When he sees his best friends Mi-Su and BT kissing, he freaks out and decides he is in love with Mi-Su himself. To add to his misery he has just found out that scientists have substantiated proton decay and he wonders if anything really matters, if everything in the universe is impermanent.

Springer, Nancy. **The Case of the Left-Handed Lady: An Enola Holmes Mystery**. Philomel , 2007. MS. 192 pages. ISBN-10: 0399245170

This is the second installment in a series about Sherlock Holmes's younger sister Enola, who starts her own detective agency in London. She is on the run from her brothers, who want her to become a proper lady. While Sherlock is looking for Enola, she is looking for Lady Cecily, a privileged girl her own age who has disappeared.

Springer, Nancy. **The Case of the Bizarre Bouquets: An Enola Holmes Mystery**. Philomel, 2008. MS. 176 pages. ISBN-10: 0399245189

In the third book in the series Enola, the younger sister of Sherlock Holmes, is trying to find the missing Dr. Watson by discovering who is sending bizarre bouquets to his wife. Decoding messages left in the newspaper, Enola tracks the clues to his disappearance through the seamy side of Victorian London.

St. James, James. **Freak Show**. Dutton Juvenile, 2007. HS. 224 pages.
ISBN-10: 0525477993

Billy Bloom, teenage drag queen, arrives at conservative Eisenhower Academy in his full regalia and is soon beaten to a bloody pulp. When the quarterback on the football team comes to his defense, Billy is smitten. This familiar outcast runs for homecoming queen story has an unusual twist, because this time a "queen" wants to be Queen.

Staples, Suzanne Fisher. **The House of Djinn**. Farrar, Straus and Giroux, 2008. MS. 224 pages. ISBN-10: 0374399360

In this sequel to *Shabanu* and *Haveli,* Shabanu is in hiding and her daughter Mumtaz is being raised by Shabanu's resentful half-sister. Mumtaz's American cousin Jameel, who is like a brother, and Baba, the beloved family patriarch, are the only ones who understand her. When Baba dies and Jameel is named as the Amirzai tribal leader, Mumtaz finds out she is to marry Jameel. If they adhere to traditional Islamic values and fulfill their duty to the family, they will both have to give up the dreams they have for the future.

Strasser, Todd. **Boot Camp.** Simon & Schuster Children's Publishing, 2007. HS. 256 pages. ISBN-10: 141690848X

Garrett's parents are disgusted by his noncompliant behavior and pay to have him abducted and taken to boot camp, a stealth prison system where any teenager under the age of eighteen can be imprisoned at his parents' whim. After six months of beatings and abuse, his spirits are so low that he decides to go along with a risky escape plan that could cost him his life.

Staub, Wendy Corsi. **Lily Dale: Awakening.** Walker Books for Young Readers, 2007. MS. 240 pages. ISBN-10: 0802796540

After her mom dies, Calla goes to live with her grandmother in Lily Dale, a town full of psychics. The longer Calla stays in town, the stranger things become. She begins to wonder if she, too, has the gift and if her mother's death was really an accident. This book is the first in a new paranormal thriller series.

Staub, Wendy Corsi. **Lily Dale: Believing.** Walker Books for Young Readers, 2008. MS. 256 pages. ISBN-10: 0802796567

In the sequel Calla continues to mourn her mother and receives messages from beyond regarding a serial killer who is abducting young girls. Calla is also still struggling with her attraction to two very different boys and her father's desire to move her to California and away from the clues that may help her get to the bottom of her mother's death.

Staub, Wendy Corsi. **Lily Dale: Connecting**. Walker Books for Young Readers, 2008. MS. 304 pages. ISBN-13: 978-0802797858

The third installment in the Lily Dale paranormal thriller series finds Calla getting closer to finding out who murdered her mother. As she and Jacy sift through the clues, Calla is stalked by the spirit of her mother's high school boyfriend. When Calla heads to Florida to get her mother's laptop and see her old friends, many issues are resolved, but others are left to be explored in *Lily Dale: Discovering*, the next installment in the series.

Stead, Rebecca. **When You Reach Me**. Wendy Lamb Books; 9th Printing of First Edition edition, 2009. MS.208 pages. ISBN-13: 978-0385737425

In this Newberry winning book, sixth-grader Miranda struggles to understand a series of time bending anonymous notes that begin with one that states. "I am coming to save your friend's life, and my own . . . you must write me a letter." As she attempts to unravel the mystery, she is also helping her mother prepare for being a contestant on $20,000 Pyramid and working to expand her friendships after her best friend Sal for reasons unknown dumps her.

Stiefvater, Maggie. **Shiver**. Scholastic Press; 1 edition, 2009. 400 pages. MS/HS. ISBN-13: 978-0545123266

The first book in a proposed trilogy introduces Grace who has always been enthralled by the wolves who live in the woods behind her house. Attacked by the wolves when she was a child, Grace remembers little of her rescue by Sam, a pack member who is actually a werewolf. Sam was bitten by a werewolf as a young boy and now spends the cold months of the year as a wolf. The two finally meet and fall deeply in love, but their romance is threatened by many challenges, including the fact that Sam will soon lose the ability to become human.

Stiefvater, Maggie. **Linger**. Scholastic Press, 2010. MS/HS. 368 pages. ISBN-13: 978-0545123280

The sequel to *Shiver* finds Sam struggling to take care of the werewolf pack and worrying about Grace whose health is deteriorating. Cole, a thrill seeking rock star who recently became a werewolf, creates problems for Sam and entices Isabel, who is still reeling from her brother's death. In four alternating voices this bridge book for the trilogy ramps up the excitement leaves readers longing for the next installment

Stone, Phoebe. **Deep Down Popular**. Scholastic Paperbacks, 2008. MS. 288 pages. ISBN-10: 0439802458

When popular sixth-grade classmate Conrad, Jessie Lou's secret crush, injures his leg and has to wear a leg brace, his popularity plummets. Insecure tomboy Jessie Lou is enlisted to help him around, and soon they and a quirky fourth-grader named Quentin Duster are embroiled in a battle against a Big Box store that threatens the existence of a beloved local hardware store. As Conrad seeks an experimental surgery that will restore him to his former athletic prowess, Jessie Lou finds herself dreading his return to popularity.

Sullivan, Jaqueline Levering. **Annie's War.** Eerdmans Books for Young Readers, 2007. MS. 183 pages. ISBN-10: 0802853250

World War II is over, but Annie's father is missing in action and her uncle returns from the war a raging bully. Annie moves in with her grandmother and uncle for the summer. When Grandma takes in Miss Gloria as a lodger and bookkeeper, the town's racists, including Uncle Billy, burn a cross in her yard. Annie befriends Miss Gloria, which aggravates Uncle Billy even more. Annie's seeks advice from her imaginary friend, President Truman, who counsels her on courage in the face of adversity.

Supplee, Suzanne. **Somebody Everybody Listens To**. Dutton Juvenile; 1 edition, 2010. MS. 304 pages. ISBN-13: 978-0525422426

Retta Lee Jones heads to Nashville after high school graduation to pursue her dreams of becoming a country music star. Borrowing her great aunt's car, she ends up living in it as one catastrophe after another occurs. Even more difficult are the pulls from home where her parents' marriage is dissolving. Inspired by the hard knock lives of successful country singers, whose biographies are included at the beginning of each chapter, Retta perseveres in looking for that first break to ignite her career.

Supplee, Suzanne. **When Irish Guys Are Smiling**. Puffin, 2008. MS. 224 pages. ISBN-10: 0142410160.

In the latest offering from the Students Across the Seven Seas series, Delk Sinclair is studying in Ireland where she hopes to escape from her pregnant stepmother's redecorating plans and the grief she feels over her mother's death. When she falls for a handsome Irishman, she begins to recover and revel in all things Irish.

Tashjian, Janet. **Larry and the Meaning of Life**. Henry Holt and Co. (BYR), 2008. MS. 224 pages. ISBN-13: 978-0805077353

The third book in the series finds Josh Swenson, aka Larry, depressed and looking for meaning in his life. Following a guru named Gus, Josh gets involved with a cult that includes his former girlfriend Janine. The resulting adventures include kidney donation, a decapitated dog, land mines at Walden Pond, and the possibility of finding the father he never knew.

Taylor, Greg. **Killer Pizza**. Feiwel & Friends, 2009. MS. 352 pages. ISBN-13: 978-0312373795

Who would suspect that the Killer Pizza restaurant is actually a front for zombie hunters? Guttata, shape-shifting zombies, are threatening the populace, so Toby and his co-workers train to hunt them down and kill them. A reluctant zombie hunter, Toby would actually like to become a famous chef, but he realizes no one is safe until the Guttata are eliminated.

Taylor, Laini. **The Faeries of Dreamdark: Blackbringer.** Putnam Juvenile, 2007. MS/HS. 437 pages. ISBN-10: 0399246304

This first book in a new faerie series focuses on Magpie, the granddaughter of the West Wind. She and her band of cigar-smoking crows must hunt down devils that humans are setting loose in the world. Along the way she meets, dragons, her ancient heroine Bellatrix and a princeling, who needs to find a way to remake his malformed wings. The tapestry of the world needs reweaving and Magpie is the key.

Testa, Dom. **The Comet's Curse**. Tor Teen, 2009. MS. 240 pages. ISBN-13: 978-0765321077

The first book in The Galahad series finds 251 teens hurtling into space on board a spaceship named the Galahad. After an encounter with Comet Bhaktul, a mysterious illness is plaguing all the adults on earth. The teens' mission is to find a habitable planet and preserve humanity. Unfortuantely, there is a stowaway onboard who is determined to thwart their plans.

Tharp, Tim. **The Spectacular Now**. Knopf Books for Young Readers, 2008. HS. 304 pages. ISBN-13: 978-0375851797

In this National Book Award Nominee Sutter Keely is everybody's favorite party animal and an alcoholic. He wonders why his girlfriends never last long, but doesn't stop to take a good look at himself. When he introduces his drinking habits to his new girlfriend, there are disastrous results and he begins a journey to self discovery that will change the way he navigates the world.

Thompson, Kate. **The New Policeman**. HarperTeen, 2007. MS. 448 pages. ISBN-10: 0061174270

When J.J. Liddy's mother asks for more time as her birthday gift, the fifteen-year-old sets out to find out where the time has gone. This search leads him into the heart of Tír na n'Óg, the land of eternal youth, where he uncovers a time leak, as well as the truth about some family secrets and the identity of the new town policeman.

Tracy, Kristen. **Lost it**. Simon Pulse, 2007. HS. 288 pages. ISBN-10: 1416934758

It's Tess's junior year in high school and everyone around her seems to be losing it. Her born again parents head off to survival camp and leave her with her wacky grandmother, and her best friend Zena, whose parents are having marital difficulties, is building a bomb to blow up a poodle. Then Tess falls head over heels in love with Ben. But when they begin to have problems, she realizes that "you can't depend on another person to provide your own balance."

Trigiani, Adrianna. **Viola in Reel Life**. HarperTeen, 2009. MS. 288 pages. ISBN-13: 978-0061451027

Brooklyn native Viola Chesterton ends up at boarding school in South Bend, Indiana when her parents head off to Afghanistan to make a documentary. Leaving her best friend Andrew behind, Vi expects to be miserable, but her three roommates help her adjust to her new life. Chronicling her adventures in a video journal, Vi tells the story of finding new friends, meeting a hot fellow filmmaker who becomes her boyfriend, and entering a film competition that may just make her dreams come true.

Trueman, Terry. **7 Days at the Hot Corner**. HarperTeen, 2007. MS/HS. 160 pages. ISBN-10: 0060574941

A baseball fanatic who plays third base for his high school's team, Scott Latimer is thrown for a loop when his best friend, Travis, reveals that he's gay. This happens during the citywide baseball tournament. Now, in addition to worrying about playing well in the seven-day tournament, Scott anxiously awaits the results of an HIV test that he gets in secret. He fears he may have contracted AIDS after a batting cage incident, in which he wound up with Travis's blood on his hands.

Trueman, Terry. **Hurricane**. HarperCollins, 2008. MS. 144 pages. ISBN-13: 978-0060000189

Hurricane Mitch hits a tiny Honduran village in 1998 and a mudslide wipes out most of the homes and population. 13-year-old Jose, whose father and older siblings are away, struggles to become the man of the family and find the strength to help his remaining family and neighbors recover from the devastation and begin to rebuild their lives.

Turnball, Ann. **Forged in the Fire**. Candlewick, 2007. MS/HS. 320 pages.
ISBN-10: 0763631442

This sequel to *No Shame, No Fear*, finds Susanna and Will eagerly looking forward to their upcoming marriage, after three years of separation; then, Will is imprisoned for protesting the persecution of fellow Quakers. With no word from Will, Susanna travels to London, where minor misunderstandings, as well as disastrous problems, threaten to keep them apart.

Turner, Max. **Night Runner**. St. Martin's Griffin; 1 Original edition, 2009. MS.272 Pages.
ISBN-13: 978-0312592288

Orphaned Zack Thompson has spent the last eight years in a mental ward which was the only place that seemed to be able to deal with his strange medical condition. He's allergic to the sun, can't sleep at night, and can't digest anything but blood. He has adjusted to his odd routine, until one night a guy on a motorcycle crashes into the ward and liberates him, only to leave him running for his life.

Underdahl, S. T. **The Other Sister**. Flux, 2007. MS/HS. 256 pages. ISBN-10: 0738709336

The parents of sixteen-year-old Josey are overjoyed when the daughter they were forced to give up as unwed teenagers contacts them. Josey is not so sure she's excited about no longer being the only daughter and the "smart one" in the family. Her friends, brothers, and parents, however, expect her to be ecstatic. How will she deal with her new 25-year-old sister who threatens her status in the family?

van de Ruit, John. **Spud.** Razorbill, 2007. MS/HS. 352 pages. ISBN-10: 1595141707

Spud Milton, a thirteen-year-old choirboy, is starting his first year at an elite South African boarding school. Leaving his embarrassingly dysfunctional parents, senile granny, and depressed girlfriend behind, Spud attempts to adapt to his new world, where he deals with his classmates' shenanigans, his adolescent hormones, and starring in the school musical.

van de Ruit, John. **Spud – The Madness Continues…** Razorbill, 2008. MS/HS. 304 pages. ISBN-13: 978-1595141903

This sequel to the author's autobiographical novel *Spud* finds the protagonist, who is a student at an elite boarding school in South Africa, continuing to catalogue his adventures in his diary. Spud, so named because he hadn't yet reached puberty, finds that his body and voice are changing. Not only is he displaced from his positions as soprano in the choir and boarding school pawn, but he also has to deal with his senile grandmother, his beer-drinking racist father, his mother, who is longing to go back to England and his girlfriend, who has dumped him.

Van Draanen, Wendelin. **Confessions of a Serial Kisser**. Knopf Books for Young Readers, 2008. MS. 304 pages. ISBN-13: 978-0375842481

When sixteen-year-old Evangeline, who is struggling with her parents' separation, finds a stash of romance novels under her mother's bed, she becomes obsessed with one called *The Crimson Kiss*. Searching for a crimson kiss of her own, she begins randomly kissing boys at school, as well as strangers. Her reputation takes a nose dive, as well as her relationship with her best friend.

Vaught, Susan. **Big Fat Manifesto**. Bloomsbury USA Children's Books, 2007. MS/HS. 320 pages. ISBN-10: 1599902060

Pursuing a journalism scholarship, Jamie, who is an obese high school senior, decides to write a controversial column, "Fat Girl Manifesto," for her school newspaper. Her articles include scathing tirades about the discrimination fat people experience. When her linebacker boyfriend decides to undergo bariatric surgery, Jamie's world is turned upside-down.

Vega, Denise. **Fact of Life #31**. Knopf Books for Young Readers, 2008. HS. 384 pages. ISBN-13: 978-0375848193

Kat Flynn, also known as Weird Yoga Girl, helps her mom in her home birthing center, trains for triathlons and pines for "hot" Manny Cruz. When they meet on a running trail and begin hanging out, Kat accepts the fact that Manny wants to keep their relationship a secret. Then Libby Giles, the queen bee who barely notices Kat, shows up at the birthing center and Kat begins to realize that life in the in-crowd may not be as wonderful as it seems.

Venkatraman, Padma. **Climbing the Stairs**. Speak, 2010. MS. 272 pages. ISBN-13: 978-0142414903

In 1941 Bombay 15-year-old Vidya hopes to attend college, even though most girls her age are preparing for marriage. When her father is seriously brain damaged from a beating by British colonial troops, Vidya, her parents and older brother must move to her grandfather's traditional household in Madras. Vidya's only respites from a life of servitude are her grandfather's upstairs library and a young man she meet there.

Vivian, Siobhan. **Same Difference**. Push, 2009. MS. 304 pages. ISBN-13: 978-0545004077

When her best friend Meg settles down with a boyfriend, Emily decides to enroll in a summer art institute program in Philadelphia, where she meets a motley crew of classmates and an intriguing teaching assistant named Yates. Struggling to define who she is, Emily vacillates between her shy suburban preppy image and a bold new look encouraged by Fiona, a bold punk inspired artist who befriends her.

Voelkel, J & P. **Middleworld.** Smith & Sons, Imprint of Smith and Kraus Pub. Inc., 2007. MS. 400 pages. ISBN-10: 1575255618

In the first book of The Jaguar Stones Trilogy, Max Murphy, a fourteen-year-old video game loving kid from Boston, finds himself battling the Ancient Maya Lords of Death. His parents are archeologists who accidentally unleash forces of destruction when they travel to Central America on an archeological dig. It is up to Max, the Maya chosen one, to sort out the mess.

Waters, Daniel. **Generation Dead**. Hyperion Book CH, 2008. MS/HS. 400 pages. ISBN-13: 978-1423109211

When dead teenagers start coming back to life, prejudice against these "living impaired" kids is rampant at Oakvale High. Phoebe, who is a Goth girl, finds herself attracted to Tommy, the leader of the undead. She and her best friends Adam and Margi join the Undead Studies group to see if they can begin to understand the phenomenon and bridge the rift in the student body that prejudice has created.

Waters, Daniel. **Kiss of Life**. Hyperion Book CH, 2009. MS/HS. 416 pages.
ISBN-13: 978-1423109235

In the sequel to *Generation Dead* Adam, who is now "differently biotic" after dying to save Phoebe's life, is struggling with the transformation. Phoebe is devotedly attentive to him, but he wonders if it is out of love or guilt. Her former zombie crush, Tommy, is on the road trying to further the cause of zombie awareness, while a string of local crimes is blamed on the undead teen population.

Watson, Sasha. **Vidalia in Paris**. Viking Juvenile, 2008. MS/HS. 288 pages.
ISBN-13: 978-0670010943

While studying art in Paris for the summer, Vidalia Sloane is draw into the world of art heists when she gets involved with Marcus, a Parisian bad boy. Struggling with an agoraphobic mother at home, a host family who ignores her and a suicidal friend, Vidalia finds Marcus and his glamorous life a great escape. However, as she gets further involved in criminal behavior, she begins to suffer pangs of guilt and wonders how she can redeem herself.

Weaver, Will. **Saturday Night Dirt**. Puffin, 2008. MS. 272 pages.
ISBN-10: 014240392X

The first book in Weaver's new Motor Series introduces ten characters of varying ages and ethnicities who all are involved in the world of car racing. Headwaters Speedway is a small dirt stock-car track in northern Minnesota struggling to stay in business. One Saturday night, when rainstorms at other tracks force cancellations at other tracks, big name racers join the local kids at Headwaters for a night they'll all remember.

Weaver, Will. **Super Stock Rookie**. Farrar, Straus and Giroux (BYR); 1 edition, 2009. MS. 208 pages. ISBN-13: 978-0374350611

Trace Bonham, a teenage stock-car racer, is chosen as the face of Team Blu and now has a hot stock car and his own racing team. However, he has to leave home and everything he knows behind. As he questions the legality of his engine and the way his team operates and he is told to just worry about the driving and looking good, he begins to wonder if he made the right choice.

Weaver, Will. **Checkered Flag Cheater**. Farrar, Straus and Giroux (BYR); 1 edition, 2010. MS/HS. 208 pages. ISBN-13: 978-0374350628

The third book in the Motor Series finds Trace Bonham racing on the super-stock circuit for Team Blu. His face graces billboards advertising his corporate sponsor's sports energy drink, and he is the next boy wonder on the track. When Trace begins to suspect that his mechanic is illegally juicing his car, he struggles with whether to quit or continue to win no matter what the cost.

Weinheimer, Beckie. **Converting Kate**. Viking Juvenile, 2007. MS/HS. 288 pages.
ISBN-10: 0670061522

Having moved to Maine with her mother, to live and work at her Great-Aunt Katherine's B & B, 16-year-old Kate has, in her own mind, already left the Church of the Holy Divine. Kate's disgust with her mother's rigid religious beliefs begins when her mother refuses to have a funeral for her ex-husband, Kate's dad, who is a non-believer, and escalates as she realizes how uncharitable her mother is to anyone not of her faith.

Kate's search for something to believe in requires courage, strength, and the support of her new found friends in Maine.

Westerfeld, Scott. **Extras.** Simon Pulse, 2007. MS/HS. 432 pages. ISBN-10: 1416951172
Aya is an "extra" in a society run on a "reputation economy." Each person's fame determines his wealth. She is hoping to achieve fame as a "kicker" by exposing an incognito clique which performs death defying tricks. When she infiltrates the group, she finds more than she bargains for.

Westerfeld, Scott and Keith Thompson. **Leviathan**. Simon Pulse; Reprint edition, 2010. MS. 464 pages. ISBN-13: 978-1416971740
The first book in a new steampunk series introduces Deryn Sharp, a girl who disguises herself as a boy so that she can join the crew of the Leviathan, a flying whale-ship, and Prince Alek, the son of Archduke Ferdinand, who is on the run after his father's murder. He and his entourage are in a walking Clanker tank in the Swiss Alps when the Leviathan crashes in the near vicinity. The two groups must cooperate to get the Leviathan airborn, before they are all killed by the encroaching German army. Thompson's illustrations bring the story to life.

Whitcomb, Laura. **The Fetch**. Houghton Mifflin Books for Children; 1 edition, 2009. MS/HS. 384 pages. ISBN-13: 978-0618891313

Calder has been a Fetch, an escort of souls to heaven, since his death at 19. He falls in love with the mother of Alexi and Anastasia Romanov when he sees her struggling to keep her son alive. He breaks his vow not to interfere with a soul's choice to live or die when he wills Alexi to stay on earth. Calder is then cast out of heaven and must redeem himself so that he can one again shepherd souls to the afterlife.

White. Ruth. **Way Down Deep**. Farrar, Straus and Giroux, 2007. MS. 208 pages. ISBN-10: 0374382514
Red-headed Ruby June has lived a happy comfortable life for ten years with her adoptive mother Miss Arbutus Ward, the owner of the local boardinghouse in Way Down Deep, WV. Then a new family moves to town and suggests Ruby June might be a child who was abducted from a mountain top family. As Ruby unravels the mystery of her past, she learns what is important "way down deep."

Whitman, Emily. **Radiant Darkness**. HarperTeen; 1 edition, 2009. 288 pages. ISBN-13: 978-0061724497

This retelling of the Greek myth, The Rape of Persephone, finds Persephone a willing accomplice in her abduction by Hades. The Underworld is surprisingly mundane and she spends her time gardening and working on a greeting process for the new arrived dead. Then she finds out that her mother Demeter is furious and is causing drought and famine on earth. It's up to Persephone to stand up to the gods and forge a compromise which will appease her mother and allow Persephone to stay with her beloved husband, Hades.

Wiess, Laura. **Such a Pretty Girl.** Pocket Books, 2007. HS. 224 pages. ISBN-10: 1847390382
When her father, who has been imprisoned for abusing her and other children, is released for good behavior, Meredith doesn't know where to turn. Her paraplegic friend

Andy, who has also been abused by Meredith's father, is heading to Iowa for a religious healing, and her mother wants to ignore her husband's "mistake" and resume a normal family life. Nigel, the cop who arrested Meredith's father, convinces her she must take matters into her own hands and put her dad behind bars forever.

Wiess, Laura. **Leftovers.** MTV, 2008. HS. 256 pages. ISBN-13: 978-1416546627

Although they come from different socio-economic groups, Ardith and Blair are kindred spirits. Ardith's substance abusing parents ignore the behavior of her brother who is a sexual predator, and Blair's parents ignore her aside from making her appear to be the loving daughter at her mother's political events. When a police officer gets involved in their messy lives, the girls plan to exact revenge against all those who have harmed them.

Wiles, Deborah. **The Aurora County All-Stars.** Harcourt Children's Books, 2007. MS. 256 pages. ISBN-10: 0152060685

The third book in the Aurora County series finds twelve-year-old House Jackson back to playing baseball, as star pitcher and captain of the Aurora County All-Stars. After being out for a season with a broken elbow, House is dismayed to find their only game is scheduled for the same day as Aurora County's 200th anniversary pageant, an event directed by the annoying Frances Shotz, the girl who broke House's elbow. With inspiration from Sandy Koufax and Walt Whitman, House struggles to find a way to make everybody happy.

Wilhem. Doug. **Falling.** Farrar, Straus and Giroux, 2007. MS/HS. 256 pages ISBN-10: 0374322511

Matt Shaw should have been the star of his ninth grade basketball team. Instead he is wandering the streets of his Vermont home town, listening to music on his I-pod and talking to no one. When he and Katie meet in a chat room, she figures out who he is and sets out to find out what's bothering him. Matt feels a connection with Katie, but can't bring himself to share his secret. Then the police start closing in.

Wiseman, Rosalind. **Boys, Girls, and Other Hazardous Materials**. Putnam; 1 edition, 2010. 288 pages. ISBN-13: 978-0399247965

Charlie has enrolled at Harmony Falls High, a neighboring high school, hoping to escape from the "frenemies" she made in middle school. In addition to befriending smart beautiful Sydney and reconciling with Nidhi, a girl she wronged in middle school, Charlie reconnects with Will, her childhood best friend who has returned to the neighborhood and is hot! Unfortunately, no school is devoid of problems and Charlie must navigate many of them during her freshman year.

Wittlinger, Ellen. **Parrotfish.** Simon & Schuster Children's Publishing, 2007. HS. 304 pages. ISBN-10: 1416916229

Angela, a transgendered high-school junior, *knows* that she's a boy trapped in a girl's body, so cuts her hair short, buys boys' clothing, and announces that her name is now Grady. Beginning a new life as a boy, of course, is fraught with problems. Grady encounters reactions ranging from outright hostility to loving support during his turbulent year of transition.

Wolf, Allan. **Zane's Trace.** Candlewick, 2007. MS/HS. 208 pages. ISBN-10: 0763628581

After his grandfather dies, Zane Guesswind steals his absentee father's 1969 Plymouth Barrucuda and heads for Zanesville, Ohio, where he is going to kill himself on his mother's grave. Along the way he meets Libba, a hitchhiker, who is also headed to Zanesville, and other mysterious characters who seem related to his ancestry. With every mile he travels, he gets closer to figuring out who he really is.

Wolff, Virginia Euwer. **This Full House**. HarperTeen, 2009. MS/HS. 496 pages. ISBN-13: 978-0061583049

The third novel-in-verse in the Make Lemonade Trilogy finds LaVaughn continuing to help Jolly raise her children while pursuing a nursing career. When LaVaughn is accepted into the prestigious WIMS (Women in Medical Science) after school science program, she develops a relationship with Dr. Moore, the program's founder, which she thinks will help her in her goal to go to college and leave the projects. Then LaVaughn uncovers a secret that threatens to undermine all her aspirations for the future.

Wooding, Chris. **Malice**. Scholastic Press, 2009. MS. 384 pages. ISBN-13: 978-0545160438

The first book of this new novel/comic book series introduces the world of Malice, where teens who have been abducted by Tall Jake battle clockwork monsters and other hazards. When Seth and Kady's friend Luke disappears, they notice that he appears in the next issue of *Malice*, a comic book, where he is devoured by monsters. Seth follows Luke into the dark realm, while Kady conducts an investigation of her own leading to dire consequences.

Woodson, Jacqueline. **After Tupac & D Foster**. Putnam Young Adult, 2008. MS. 160 pages. ISBN-13: 978-0399246548

Three friends weather the years from ages 11 to 13 while listening to Tupac Shakur's music and worrying about his legal troubles and shootings. They call themselves Three the Hard Way and are impacted by the truth of Tupac's lyrics. D. Foster, who has grown up with multiple foster families, particularly identifies with his struggles and draws her friends into her obsession with his life.

Woodson, Jacqueline. **Feathers**. Putnam Juvenile, 2007. MS. 208 pages. ISBN-10: 0399239898

A white student joins Frannie's all-black sixth-grade classroom and the class bully begins to call him Jesus Boy. Witnessing the boy's calm and its effect on the class, Frannie and her best friend Samantha, begin to wonder if he really is Jesus returned to save the world.

Woodson, Jacqueline. **Peace, Locomotion**. Putnam Juvenile, 2009. MS. 144 pages. ISBN-13: 978-0399246555

This sequel Woodson's novel-in-verse, *Locomotion*, find Lonnie Collins Motion writing letters to his sister Lili who is living with a separate foster family after their parents die in a fire. Lonnie is coming to turns with his living situation with Ms. Edna and worries with her about Jenkins, her grown son who is "over there fighting in the war." When Jenkins returns with physical and emotional problems, Lonnie begins longing for peace for his new family, his community and the world.

Wright, Rachel. **You've Got Blackmail**. Putnam Juvenile, 2009. MS. 208 pages. ISBN-13: 978-0399250941

Lozzie Cracknell's life involves one disaster after another. After accidentally hitting "reply all" with a snarky email about Tonya, the school bully, she is in constant fear of Tonya's retaliation. Then her parents separate and Dad moves into Tonya's building and Lozzie fears that Mom is dating Lozzie's most "unreasonableest" teacher, who she discovers is being blackmailed. When Lozzie's room is ransacked and her diary is stolen, she and her best friend Dex decide they need to take matters into their own hands and solve the mystery.

Yancy, Rick. **Alfred Kropp – The Seal of Solomon.** Bloomsbury USA Children's Books, 2007. MS. 336 pages ISBN-10: 1599900459

When the ancient ring of Solomon is stolen and fallen angels are released and wreak havoc on the earth, it is up to Alfred Kropp to once again save the world. In this second book in the series the last surviving heir of Lancelot drives the world's fastest car, shoots bullets laced with his own blood, and performs death defying feats in his own bumbling wise cracking style to overcome the forces of evil.

Yancy, Rick. **Monstrumologist**. Simon & Schuster Children's Publishing; 1St Edition edition, 2009. MS/HS. 448 pages. ISBN-13: 978-1416984481

Anthropophagi, beasts originally from Africa, have been attacking a New England village, and 12-year-old orphan William James Henry is assisting Dr. Warthrop, who studies them. When they hire a monster hunter to help them eradicate the beasts, blood and guts begin to fly.

Yeomans, Ellen. **Rubber Houses.** Little, Brown Young Readers, 2007. MS. 160 pages. ISBN-10: 031610647X

This novel-in-verse finds sixteen-year-old Kit facing the death of her younger brother from leukemia. Buddy's passion for baseball creates a structure for the book when he announces at the end of his tragic decline, "I'm calling the game." The baseball year continues with postseason grief and spring training for a family struggling to recover from a losing season.

Yoo, David. **Stop Me If You've Heard This One Before**. Hyperion Book CH, 2008. MS/HS. 384 pages. ISBN-13: 978-1423109075

Korean-American Albert Kim has decided to be an "intentional loser" at his new high school, until he gets involved with Mia Stone when they are both working at the local inn for the summer. Mia has recently broken up with her super jock boyfriend Ryan and is using the job as a distraction. Just as Albert and Mia's relationship is heating up, Ryan is diagnosed with cancer and Mia spends most of her time trying to help him. Albert is frustrated and confused as he tries to navigate the stormy seas of first love.

Young, E.L. **Storm: The Infinity Code**. Dial, 2008. MS. 336 pages.
ISBN-10: 0803732651.

    The first book in a new series finds Will, who is an ingenious teen who invents spy gadgets, has been recruited by STORM (Science and Technology to Over-Rule Misery) to help fight the forces of evil. Caspian, a fellow member, heads to St. Petersburg to rescue his scientist father, who has been abducted along with his plans for an invention which can eat the earth, if activated. Will, Andrew, the brilliant, but impractical founder of STORM, and Gaia, another teen genius, follow Caspian, hoping to save the world from destruction.

Young, E.L. **Storm: The Ghost Machine**. Dial, 2008. MS. 320 pages.
ISBN-13: 978-0803732674

    In this sequel to *STORM: The Infinity Code,* Will, Gaia and Andrew must travel to Venice to help a girl whose home has been burgled by a ghost. When they arrive in Venice, the girl is missing, and they find more is at stake than her missing family heirlooms. With an assortment of new gadgets, the trio discovers the ghosts are technology based and the team must find a way to save not only the girl, but also the intelligence chiefs of the Western World whose annual summit is about to be attacked.

Young, Janet Ruth. **The Opposite of Music.** Atheneum, 2007. MS/HS.
352 pages. ISBN-10: 1416900403

    When conventional therapies don't help his clinically depressed father, Billy and his family decide to cure him themselves. Billy's social life takes a backseat to his responsibility for his father, and as his father becomes suicidal, the situation becomes more and more desperate.

Zadoff, Allen. **Food, Girls and Other Things I Can't Have.** Egmont USA, 2009. MS/HS. 320 pages. ISBN-13: 978-1606840047

    At 306 pounds, sophomore Andy Zansky is a target for bullies, until the quarterback of the football team recruits him as a lineman. Overnight he is transformed from a Model UN geek to a popular football player. For the first time in his life he is a member of the in-crowd, but it comes with a price.

Zalben, Jane Breskin. **Leap.** Knopf Books for Young Readers, 2007. MS. 272 pages.
ISBN-10: 0375838716

    Daniel is left partially paralyzed after having an allergic reaction to anesthesia during a dental procedure. Krista, who used to be his best friend, is now preoccupied with Daniel's best friend, Bobby. Once a champion swimmer, Daniel is frustrated with his slow recovery and distraught by his parents' bitterness towards Bobby's father, the dentist "responsible" for Daniel's paralysis. When Daniel's mother leaves the family to pursue her music dreams, Daniel and Krista find themselves drawn together.

Zarr, Sara. **Once Was Lost**. Little, Brown Books for Young Readers, 2009. MS/HS. 224 pages. ISBN-13: 978-0316036047

Fifteen-year-old Samara Taylor narrates the story of the abduction of 13-year-old Jody Shaw which devastates their small community. Samara's mother is in rehab and her pastor father refuses to focus on his own family's problems, as he tends to the needs of the church community during the crisis. Samara finds herself questioning her faith in God and her parents as the kidnapping drama unfolds.

Zarr, Sara. **Story of a Girl**. Little, Brown Young Readers, 2007. HS. 208 pages. ISBN-10: 0316014532

When thirteen-year-old Deanna is caught by her dad, having sex with seventeen-year-old Tommy, her life is drastically changed. Tommy brags about the incident, and she is branded as the school slut. This is the heartbreaking story of a girl who is searching for redemption in a seemingly hostile world.

Zarr, Sara. **Sweethearts**. Little, Brown Young Readers, 2008. MS/HS. 224 pages. ISBN-10: 0316014559.

Thin popular Jenna remembers a time when she was fat Jennifer, whose only friend was an abused boy named Cameron. When he moves away, Jenna is led to believe he died. Then he miraculously reappears during her senior year, and they begin to rediscover the bond they had and work through a mutual experience of abuse that threatens to scar them forever.

Zenatti, Valerie. **A Bottle in the Gaza Sea**. Bloomsbury USA Children's Books; 1st edition, 2008. MS/HS. 160 pages. ISBN-13: 978-1599902005

When Naim, a Palestinian boy, finds a note in bottle on the beach, he begins communicating with Tal, the Israeli girl who wrote the note and had her brother throw it into the sea in Gaza. Through their email correspondence they develop a relationship that bridges the political chasm between their two countries.

Zevin, Gabrielle. **Memoirs of a Teenage Amnesiac.** Farrar, Straus and Giroux, 2007. MS/HS. 288 pages. ISBN-10: 0374349460

After a nasty head injury, high school junior Naomi cannot remember anything that happened after sixth grade; not her boyfriend Ace, her parents' divorce, or her current relationship with her best friend and co-editor of the yearbook, Will. Feeling like a different person, she alienates her former friends and enters into a relationship with the mentally unstable boy who rescued her after her accident. Readers will find themselves wondering, if their past were a blank slate, what would they do?

Ziegler, Jennifer. **How to Not Be Popular**. Delacorte Books for Young Readers, 2008. MS. 352 pages. ISBN-13: 978-0385734653

After moving to Austin, Texas, with her vagabond parents, Sugar Magnolia "Maggie" Dempsey, decides she is going to avoid making friends so she doesn't have to feel the pain of separation next time they move. Dressing in bizarre outfits she finds in her parents' thrift shop, she sets out to become an outcast, but becomes a "trend setter" instead, and she finds Operation Avoid Friends is harder to implement than she expected

Zimmer, Tracie Vaughn. **Reaching for Sun.** Bloomsbury USA Children's Books, 2007.
MS. 144 pages. ISBN-10: 1599900378

Josie, a lonely seventh grader with cerebral palsy, finds friendship with Jordan, her new neighbor who is neglected by his wealthy workaholic father. They bond over their shared love of nature and science experiments. Botanical images integrated into the author's free verse poetry will delight a variety of readers.

Zimmer, Tracie Vaughn. **42 Miles**. Clarion Books; 1 edition, 2008. MS. 80 pages
ISBN-13: 978-0618618675

This novel-in-verse- tells the story of Jo Ellen, a girl who lives in two different worlds. During the week she lives with her mom in the city and on weekends she goes to her dad's farm. She even has two different names – Ellen in the city and Joey on the farm. As she struggles to define herself, she realizes that she is the one who is going to have to bridge the 42 miles that separate her homes. Black and white composite illustrations enhance the poems that detail Jo Ellen's life.

Zink, Michelle. **The Prophecy of the Sisters**. Little, Brown Books for Young Readers;
1 edition, 2010. MS. 368 pages. ISBN-13: 978-0316027410

The first book in a new trilogy introduces Lia and Alice Milthorpe, twins who are prophesied to determine the fate of lost souls led by Samael, an evil fallen angel. One is the guardian, who will try to thwart his plans; the other is the Gate, who will attempt to help him bring about the end of the known world. When their father dies, their roles are revealed, and they struggle to make sense of their destiny.

Zindel, Lizabeth, **Girl of the Moment**. Viking Young Adult, 2007. MS/HS. 288 pages.
ISBN-10: 0670062103

Lily's summer internship with the teenage celebrity Sabrina Snow seems like a dream come true. However, the dream turns into a nightmare when Lily finds that Sabrina is a manipulative, demanding prima donna, who is impossible to please.

TOP TEN FOR TEENS - 2007

1) The Nature of Jade (Caletti)

2) Carpe Diem (Cornwall)

3) Ravenhill (Hillmer)

4) Strays (Koertge)

5) Wicked Lovely (Marr)

6) Eclipse (Meyers)

7) My Mother the Cheerleader (Sharenow)

8) Unwind (Shusterman)

9) 7 Days in the Hot Corner (Trueman)

10) Extras (Westerfield)

"G" RATED TOP TEN – 2007

1) The Traitor's Gate (Avi)

2) Igraine the Brave (Funke)

3) Getting Air (Guttman)

4) Harlem Summer (Meyers)

5) Maximum Ride – Saving the World and Other Extreme Sports (Patterson)

6) Paint the Wind (Ryan)

7) The Invention of Hugo Cabret (Selznik)

8) The New Policeman (Thompson)

9) Way Down Deep (White)

10) Reaching for Sun (Zimmer)

BEST BETS FOR 2008

1) The Seer of Shadows (Avi)

2) Peeled (Bauer)

3) Masterpiece (Broach)

4) Graceling (Cashore)

5) The Hunger Games (Collins)*

6) Little Brother (Doctorow)*

7) The Diamond of Darkhold (DuPrau)

8) The Circle of Blood (Ferguson)*

9) The Battle for Skandia (Flanagan)

10) Beastly (Flinn)

11) The Diamond of Drury Lane (Golding)

12) Suite Scarlett (Johnson)

13) The Disreputable History of Frankie Landau-Banks (Lockhart)*

14) Jellico Road (Marchetta)

15) The Missing Girl (Mazer) *

16) The Boxer and the Spy (Parker)

17) Maximum Ride: The Final Warning (Patterson)

18) How to Build a House: a novel (Reinhardt)*

19) The House of Djinn (Staples)

20) Generation Dead (Waters)*

*May be inappropriate for younger readers

TERRIFIC TITLES FOR 2009

1) Wintergirls (Anderson)*

2) Fire (Cashor)

3) City of Glass (Clare)

4) Catching Fire (Collins)

5) Along for the Ride (Dessen)

6) Tropical Secrets: Holocaust Refugees in Cuba (Engle)

7) Jessica's Guide to Dating on the Dark Side (Fantaskey)

8) Operation Redwood (French)

9) If I Stay (Gale)*

10) Den of Thieves (Golding)

11) North of Beautiful (Headley)

12) Scat (Hiassen)

13) My Most Excellent Year: A Novel of Love, Mary Poppins, & Fenway Park (Kluger)

14) Bonechiller (McNamee)

15) Dog on It (Quinn)

16) Punkzilla (Rapp)*

17) When You Reach Me (Stead)

18) Radiant Darkness (Whitman)

19) This Full House (Wolff)*

20) Once Was Lost (Zarr)*

COMPELLING READS FOR 2010

1) Brightly Woven (Bracken)

2) Heist Society (Carter)

3) Clockwork Angel (Clare)

4) Mockingjay (Collins)

5) Matched (Condie)

6) Incarceron (Fisher)

7) Revolution (Donnelly)

8) Hearts at Stake (Harvey)

9) Paper Daughter (Ingold)

10) Girl in Translation (Kwon)

11) Scumble (Law)

12) I Am Number Four (Lore)

13) Finnikin of the Rock (Marchetta)

14) The Sky Is Everywhere (Jandy)*

15) Before I Fall (Oliver)

16) Ship Breaker (Bacigalupi)

17) By the Time You Read This, I'll Be Dead (Peters)*

18) Linger (Stiefvater)

19) Somebody Everybody Listens To (Supplee)

20) Leviathan (Westerfeld and Thompson)

NOVELS IN VERSE

Recently many well-known authors have written novels in free or blank verse. Reluctant teen and middle level readers frequently respond well to the shorter format and are aided by the predictability and definite rhythms in the novel in verse. In addition, many young adult readers, regardless of reading ability, appreciate the fact that poetry portrays an event, a feeling or an idea in brief, descriptive, precise words.[1] Novels in verse provide the opportunity to study not only the content of these novels, but also the poetic techniques and language that make them such a pleasure to read.

Tracy Vaughn Zimmer's *Reaching for Sun* is a novel about a girl with cerebral palsy that tells the story in a seventh-grader's voice in a series of free-verse poems. Josie lives on a farm with her grandmother and mother with whom she shares a passion for plants and gardening. When wealthy, but neglected, Jordan moves into a mansion in the development next door, he and Josie find they share a love of science and nature. For the first time in her life Josie has a friend and she begins to blossom and gain confidence in herself. The author integrates botanical images throughout the story and the poetic structure and imagery enhance this heartwarming story.

Before students begin the book introduce them to many of the poetic techniques and devices that the author uses in *Reaching for Sun*. Have them identify examples of these techniques throughout the novel. Then focus on the content of the story. Present students with guided questions that must be answered by identifying the poetic language that suggests the answer to the question. For example, when asked how Josie feels about herself, students might say she feels like a "dandelion in a purple petunia patch." which means that she feels different from the other students. She feels ugly in comparison to all the beautiful girls around her and like she doesn't fit in.

---

[1] Young, Becky. "Have You Read Any Good Poems Lately? Novels in Verse." http://www.courses.unt.edu/efiga/HistoryAndEthnography/TrendsProjects/young/home_pagebecky_young.htm. October, 20, 2009.

REACHING FOR SUN
by Tracey Vaughn Zimmer

Poetic Devices
Metaphor
Simile
Repetition
Rhythm
Imagery
Stanzas
Alliteration
Personification
Onomatopoeia

Poetic Device Questions

1) In the introduction to Winter the author quotes William Shakespeare. "Then let not winter's ragged hand deface in thee thy summer." What might winter and summer stand for in addition to seasons? What poetic device is this?

2) What are taunts compared to on page 4? What poetic device is this? What does this description mean?

3) How is repetition used on page 8? How does it create rhythm?

4) Describe the imagery of the holiday feast on page 24.

5) What is the logic behind the stanza breaks in the poem "Presents" on page 29?

6) Find three examples of alliteration on page 55.

7) What is being personified on page 113? Discuss how personification enhances the description.

8) What is the onomatopoeia on page 129?

9) Find at least three additional examples of metaphors.

10) Find at least three additional examples of similes.

11) Find at least three additional examples of imagery.

Content Guided Questions

When applicable, answer the following questions by quoting a poetic phrase from the text and then explain how it answers the question.

Example: How does Josie feel about herself?

Answer: She feels like a "dandelion in a purple petunia patch." which means that she feels different from the other students. She feels ugly in comparison to all the beautiful girls around her and like she doesn't fit in.

1) How does the author choose the titles for the poems/chapters? Choose three and explain why you think they are effective.

2) How does Josie feel about Mom's expectations for her? (46)

3) What is Jordan like? (63)

4) Characterize Natalie and her friends. (71)

5) What is cerebral palsy? (74)

6) How does Josie feel about what she is learning from Jordan? (77)

7) Explain why Josie wants summer to be a "wildflower seed mix." (81)
8) What is Gran suggesting Josie can learn from a philodendron? (92)
9) How does Josie feel about Jordan going to science camp? (94)
10) How does Josie feel about swimming? Why? (98)
11) What is Mom's new job? (15) How does Mom feel about it? (105)
12) Explain what is meant by "I'm sure seasons have changed before the man and woman rush into the bedroom." (125)
13) Choose at least 3 poetic phrases that describe how Josie feels at the hospital while waiting to hear about Gran. (128)
14) What does Gran's purse symbolize? (134)
15) Analyze the rhythm of the poem on page 137.
16) How is the silence between Mom and Josie like kudzu? (142)
17) How does Josie feel about Gran coming home from Lazy Acres? (153)
18) Why is it so hard for Josie to be truthful with her mother about therapy?
19) How has Gran changed ?(167-168)
20) Explain

> I'm the wisteria vine
> growing up the arbor of this
> odd family
> reaching for sun.
> (181)

How does it explain the theme of the story?

ADDITIONAL TITLES FOR NOVELS IN VERSE

Author	Titles
Bell, Krista.	No Strings.
Bingham, Kelly.	Shark Girl.
Burg, Ann	All the Broken Pieces.
Chaltas, Thalia.	Because I Am Furniture.
Cormier, Robert.	French Town Summer.
Creech, Sharon.	Love that Dog.
	Hate the Cat.
Engle, Margarita	Tropical Secrets: Holocaust Refugees in Cuba.
	The Firefly Letters: A Suffragette's Journey to Cuba
Frost, Helen.	Keesha's House.
Glenn, Mel.	Jump Ball: a basketball season in poems.
	Split Image – a story in poems.
Grimes, Nikki.	Bronx Masquerade.
Herrera, Juan Felipe.	CRASHBOOMLOVE.
Herrick, Steven.	The Simple Gift: A Novel.
	Love, Ghosts, & Facial Hair.
	A Place Like This.
Hesse, Karen.	Out of the Dust.
	Witness.
Hopkins, Ellen	Glass.
	Fallout.
	Impulse.
	Identical.
	Tricks.
Janesczko, Paul.	Stardust Otel.

Koertge, Ron.	Shakespeare Bats Clean Up.
	Brimstone Journals.
	Shakespeare Makes the Playoffs.
Mack, Tracy.	Birdland.
Mass, Wendy	Heaven Looks a Lot Like the Mall.
Meyers, Walter Dean	Street Love.
Sandell, Lisa Ann	Song of the Sparrow.
Schlitz, Laura Amy	Good Masters! Sweet Ladies!
Schroeder, Lisa	Chasing Brooklyn.
	I Heart You, You Haunt Me.
	Far From You.
Smith, Kirsten	The Geography of Girlhood.
Sones, Sonya.	one of those hideous books where the mother dies.
	What my mother doesn't know.
	Stop Pretending-
	what happened when my big sister went crazy.
	What my girlfriend doesn't know.
Wayland, April Halprin.	Girl Coming in for a Landing.
Wild, Margaret.	Jinx.
Wolf, Allan	Zane's Trace.
Wolff, Virginia Euwer.	Make Lemonade.
	True Believer.
	This Full House.
Yeomans, Ellen	Rubber Houses.
Zimmer	42 Miles.

Guiding Questions for Literature Circles for Novels in Verse

1) How is the novel structured? (ex. Is each chapter a poem? Does it have a title?)

2) If the chapters/poems are titled, how does the author chose titles? How do they enhance the story?

3) Find examples of the following poetic devices in your novel.

Metaphor	Stanzas
Simile	Alliteration
Repetition	Personification
Rhythm	Onomatopoeia
Imagery	

4) Give a brief summary of the plot of the story. What is the problem or conflict in the story?

5) Who is/are the main character(s) in the story? Does the character(s) change in the story? If so, how?

6) How does the poetic language enhance the content of the novel?

7) Is there a particular theme to the imagery? If so, what is it and why do you think the author chose it. (Example: In *Reaching for Sun* the images are usually botanical, because the main characters have a passion for plants and gardening.)

8) What is the theme of the story?

USING EMBEDDED RESEARCH IN CREATIVE WRITING

In his article "Creating Possibilities: Embedding Research into Creative Writing," Jason Wirtz coins the term embedded research. Embedded research is information that is embedded so seamlessly into the story that it enriches the detail and realism in the story without seeming didactic. Students might ask, "What is the difference between historical fiction and fiction with embedded research?" In answer to that question I would say that historical fiction has main characters, who actually existed in situations that actually happened. Stories with embedded research are about fictional characters in situation that might actually have existed or involve accurate details about what takes place. For example, in *The Traitor's Gate* by Avi the main character's father is in a nineteenth century debtor's prison in London. In *Paint the Wind* by Pam Munoz Ryan, the author did a great deal of research about the plight of wild horses so as to include realistic situations in the story.

Initially, have the students read a book from the following list and identify the embedded research in the story. In literature circles have them discuss how the embedded research enhanced the story. You may want to use the following questions for a think sheet to use as a guide for discussion.

BOOKS WITH EMBEDDED RESEARCH
GUIDING DISCUSSION QUESTIONS

1) Search for evidence of embedded research in the story that makes the writing captivating and believable. List at least five examples of details that you found.
2) Think about how the story would have been different without the embedded research. Pick at least one example of the embedded research. Note the page so that you can read the passage aloud with and without the example in your small group discussion.
3) Discuss how the passage would have been different without it. What questions can be answered if the research details are included?
4) Is there evidence of the author's research in the book? If so, explain. For example, is there an author's note about the research he/she did? Is there a bibliography about texts he/she used? Are there acknowledgements to experts whose advice was solicited?
5) What aspects of the story have been researched? If an aspect has been researched, give a detail to support your claim.
Example ideas:
Location
Time Period
Political Issues
Scientific Ideas
Artistic Details
Cultural Details
Literary Details
Other

FICTION WITH EMBEDDED RESEARCH

Ain, Beth Levine. **The Revolution of Sabine**. Candlewick; 1 edition, 2008. MS. 224 pages. ISBN-13: 978-0763633967

In pre-revolution Paris, Sabine Durand, an aristocrat who wants more out of life than a suitable match, contemplates the possibility of determining her own fate. Inspired by *Candide* and Michael, her childhood friend and servant who introduces her to Ben Franklin, Sabine finds the courage to defy her parents' wishes for her to marry and seek her own destiny. The Author's Notes give background information about the time period.

Anderson, Laurie Halse. **Chains**. Simon & Schuster Children's Publishing, 2008. MS. 320 pages. ISBN-13: 978-1416905851

During the Revolutionary War, enslaved Isabel expects to be freed when her master dies, but instead she and her sister are sold to Loyalists who mistreat them. Isabel is enlisted by the rebels to smuggle information to them and suffers disastrous consequences. A detailed author's note provides information about the author's research in a question and answer format.

Avi. **Hard Gold**. Hyperion Book CH, 2008. MS. 240 pages. ISBN-13: 978-1423105190

I Witness: Hard Gold: The Colorado Gold Rush of 1859: A Tale of the Old West is the latest installment in Avi's I Witness series. 14-year-old Early Whitcomb's family is about to lose their Iowa farm, so Early's 19-year-old Uncle Jesse heads to Cherry Creek in Colorado where he hopes to find gold. All he seems to find, however, is trouble. Early sets off with the Bunderly family in their Conestoga wagon to search for Jesse and help him find the gold that will save their family.

Avi. **The Traitor's Gate**. Atheneum/Richard Jackson Books, 2007. MS. 368 pages. ISBN-10: 0689853351

This story takes place in nineteenth century London where the main character's father is thrown in debtor's prison. The realistic historical background enhances the story which involves the main character trying to unravel the mystery of the treachery surrounding his father's problems.

Balliett, Blue. **The Calder Game**. Scholastic Press; 1st edition, 2008. MS. 400 pages. ISBN-13: 978-0439852074

Calder, Petra and Tommy are once again involved in the world of art and intrigue when Calder travels to England with his father and goes missing along with a sculpture by Alexander Calder. Author's notes and illustrations by Helquist introduce readers to Alexander Calder's art, as well as new codes and puzzles for readers to ponder.

Choldenko, Gennifer. **Al Capone Shines My Shoes**. Dial, 2009. MS. 288 pages. ISBN-13: 978-0803734609

In the sequel to *Al Capone Does My Shirts* Moose Flanagan thinks he is indebted to the mobster and worries his family will be kicked off Alcatraz Island if anyone finds out. A foot noted end chapter entitled "Alcatraz Island…What Really Happened?" gives readers background information for the book's setting and characters.

Curtis, Christopher Paul. **Elijah of Buxton**. Scholastic Press, 2007. MS. 288 pages. ISBN-10: 0439023440

Buxton is an actual Canadian settlement established in 1849 by the abolitionist Reverend William King. Reverend King, a white Presbyterian minister, was an abolitionist who bought a plot of land in Canada and offered refuge to escaped slaves. The author's note details the realistic aspects of the setting and historic figures who visited there.

Dean, Claire. **Girlwood**. Houghton Mifflin; 1 edition, 2008. MS. 256 pages. ISBN-13: 978-0618883905

Information about herbs, their uses and warnings for would-be experimenters begin each chapter of this book about a girl whose older sister runs away and is believed to be hiding in the woods that are soon to be cut down to make room for a new subdivision. To complicate matters their parents are separated and their herbalist grandmother, who is trying to help in the search, is ill. The main character is trying to learn all she can about herbal remedies, as well as save the magical forest which has always been her refuge.

Doctorow, Cory. **Little Brother**. Tor Teen, 2008. MS/HS. 384 pages. ISBN-13: 978-0765319852

Techno-geek Marcus and his gaming buddies are ditching school when terrorists blow up the Bay Bridge in San Francisco. Agents from the Department of Homeland Security find the kids suspicious and detain them for six days of intensive interrogation and torture. After his release, Marcus uses his technological skills to fight back against governmental electronic surveillance and restrictions which threaten to take away people's privacy and personal freedom. In an afterword the author includes informative articles from a security expert and an Xbox hacker and provides an extensive bibliography including books, websites, and magazines for further information about how we contribute to our own lack of privacy.

Donnelly, Jennifer. **Revolution**. Delacorte Books for Young Readers, 2010. MS/HS. 496 pages. ISBN-10: 0385737637

After her brother's murder sends Andi into a suicidal tailspin, her father takes her to Paris where he is doing DNA tests on a heart thought to belong to Louis XVII, the doomed son of Marie Antoinette. While there, Andi finds Alexandre Paradis's diary which chronicles the royal family's last days during the French revolution. The author's note at the end includes bibliographical references.

Dowd, Siobhan. **Bog Child**. David Fickling Books. MS. 336 pages. ISBN-13: 978-0385751698

While pilfering peat in the Irish hills, eighteen-year-old Fergus McCann discovers the perfectly preserved body of a dwarf, who was apparently murdered 2000 years ago. Archeologists are called in to study the find, and Fergus falls in love with Cora, the lead archeologist's daughter. As he worries about his brother who is a Long Kesh political prisoner on a hunger strike, smuggles packages for the IRA and pursues Cora, Fergus begins dreaming about the life of the bog child whom he names Mel. An author's note gives background information about events and organizations that were involved in the Northern Ireland conflict in 1981.

Farmer, Nancy. **The Land of the Silver Apples**. Atheneum/Richard Jackson Books, 2007. MS. 496 pages. ISBN-10: 1416907351

The author has done a great deal of research about Norse legends and includes an extensive appendix with information about religion, Pictish symbols, and runes. A detailed bibliography of her research is also available.

Fletcher, Christine. **Ten Cents a Dance**. Bloomsbury USA Children's Books; 1st edition, 2008. MS/HS. 368 pages. ISBN-13: 978-1599901640

In this historical novel set in Chicago in the 1940s, 15-year-old Ruby quits school and secretly takes a job as a dance hall instructor to support her ailing mother and sister. She's drawn to the easy money, the pretty clothes and "bad boy" Paulie, who is a mobster wannabe. Although she seems to be able to avoid the advances of the men at work, she is drawn into the Paulie's gangster lifestyle and wonders how she can avoid being a bad influence on her impressionable younger sister. This well researched story was inspired by the experiences of Fletcher's great aunt.

Gardner, Sally. **The Red Necklace.** Dial, 2008. MS. 384 pages. ISBN-13: 978-0803731004

The French Revolution is the backdrop for this tale of intrigue when Gypsy magician Yann and the young heiress Sido are pitted against the evil Count Kalliovski. Sido's father, who loathes her, has promised her to the count and Yann is determined to save her. However, a series of murder victims begin to surface with a necklace of garnets around their necks, and Yann and Sido find themselves in danger of becoming the next victims. At the book's end, the author provides further historical background on late-18th-century France.

Haddix, Margaret Peterson. **Sent**. Simon & Schuster Children's Publishing, 2009. MS. 320 pages. ISBN-13: 978-1416954224

In the second book of The Missing Series, Jonah and Katherine attempt to save Alex and Chip, the royal princes who were snatched out of time before their deaths in London in 1483. The four kids travel back in time and try to thwart the murder plans of the boys' evil uncle, Richard III, without altering history more than necessary.

Haddix, Margaret Peterson. **Sabotaged**. Simon & Schuster Children's Publishing, 2010. MS. 384 pages. ISBN-13: 978-1416954248

The third book in the Missing series finds Jonah and Katherine traveling back in time with Andrea, who is Virginia Dare, the first child born in the Roanoke Colony. Along the way the lose the Elucidator, which allows them to time travel. Andrea meets her grandfather and the kids find out their trip has actually been sabotaged by an adult known as Second.

Hawking, Lucy and Stephen. **George's Secret Key to the Universe**
Simon & Schuster Children's Publishing, 2007. MS. 304 pages. ISBN-10: 1416954627

Noted physicist Stephen Hawking and his daughter have incorporated many lessons about the universe in this fantasy story. It is illustrated with line drawings, diagrams, charts and full color photos of real images from space.

Hoffman, Mary. **The Falconer's Knot: A Story of Friars, Flirtation and Foul Play.** Bloomsbury USA Children's Books, 2007. MS/HS. 288 pages. ISBN-10: 1599900564

Set in Renaissance Italy, this is a tale of a young nobleman who seeks sanctuary in a friary after being wrongly accused of murder. The realistic depiction of the day to day life of nuns and friars is woven around accurate descriptions of the process they used to create the pigments that they sold to artists for painting frescoes in Italian churches.

Hooper, Mary. **Newes from the Dead**. Roaring Brook Press, 2008. MS/HS. 272 pages. ISBN-13: 978-1596433557

Hanged for the crime of infanticide in England in 1610, Anne, a teenage housemaid, regains consciousness in her coffin. Meanwhile Robert Matthews, a young medical student, is getting ready to assist surgeons who are going to dissect her. When he notices movement of her eyelids he alerts the surgeons who revive her. Based on a true story detailed in a pamphlet published in 1650. The author includes a copy of the pamphlet and an author's note at the end of the book.

House, Silas. **Eli the Good**. Candlewick, 2009. MS. 304 pages. ISBN-13: 978-0763643416

It's the summer of 1976 and ten-year-old Eli Book's usual summer routine is interrupted by the arrival of his Aunt Nell, who has just been diagnosed with breast cancer. An anti-war activist, Nell tangles with Eli's Vietnam vet father, who is struggling with flashbacks, and runs interference between Eli's rebellious sister and their mother. As Eli watches his family combust around him, he wonders how he can help them find peace.

Kadohata, Cynthia, **A Million Shades of Gray**. Atheneum; 1 edition, 2010. MS. 216 pages. ISBN-13: 978-1416918837

Y'Tin, a 13-year-old Vietnamese elephant handler, dutifully attends school, but all he really cares about is taking care of Lady, his elephant. When the Americans leave South Vietnam in 1975 and the North Vietnamese massacre his village, Y'Tin flees, but then finds himself trying to protect Lady and survive in the jungle, while searching for his family in the midst of war. (Author's note included)

Karr, Kathleen. **Born for Adventure**. Marshall Cavendish Children's Books, 2007. MS. 200 pages. ISBN-10: 076145348

Young Tom Ormsby joins Henry Morton Stanley on his 1887 expedition to Africa. This thrilling historical tale illustrates the problems the explorers encountered with jungle diseases and wild animal attacks, as well as the political intrigue surrounding Stanley's motivation for the trip.

Kelly, Jacqueline. **The Evolution of Calpurnia Tate**. Henry Holt and Co. (BYR); 1 edition, 2009. MS. 352 pages. ISBN-13: 978-0805088410

Thwarting societal expectations, 12-year-old Callie pursues her desire to become a scientist in rural Texas in 1899. Although she has six brothers, only one other family member shares her interest, her gruff intimidating grandfather, who happens to own a copy of Charles Darwin's new book, *The Origin of the Species*. Callie and Granddaddy bond over their curiosity about the natural world and discover a new plant species along the way.

Kerr, P. B. **One Small Step**. Margaret K. McElderry, 2008. MS. 320 pages. ISBN-13: 978-1416942139

In 1969 thirteen-year-old Scott is secretly flying military training planes with his father who is an Air Force flight instructor. When Scott gains notoriety by crash-landing a plane, NASA recruits him for a top secret mission to the moon. Accompanied by two chimps, Scott follows his dream and goes where no man has gone before.

Kidd, Ronald. **On Beale Street**. Simon & Schuster Children's Publishing, 2008. MS/HS. 256 pages. ISBN-13: 978-1416933878

In the summer of 1954 in Memphis, Johnny Ross, a 15-year-old white boy, discovers Beale Street, the heart of the Negro blues and music scene. He begins working at Sun Records for Sam Phillips and meets Elvis Presley who is just beginning to record there. Readers will love learning about the Nashville music scene and the beginnings of rock and roll.

Kidd, Ronald. **The Year of the Bomb**. Simon & Schuster Children's Publishing, 2009. MS. 208 pages. ISBN-13: 978-1416958925

In 1955 Paul and his friends, who love horror movies, are ecstatic to find out *The Invasion of the Body Snatchers* is being filmed in their town. Visiting the set, they meet two FBI agents posing as extras, who are investigating people with possible Communist ties. McCarthyism, as well as the intrigue about a Russian spy who worked at Los Alamos on the atomic bomb, are woven into this historical novel.

Konigsburg, E.L. **The Mysterious Edge of the Heroic World**. Ginee Seo Books, 2007. MS. 256 pages. ISBN-10: 1416949720

One of the main characters, Amadeo dreams of someday making an important discovery, and he thinks there are possibilities among the neighbor's belongings, particularly a piece of art by Modigliani. Amadeo's godfather is preparing an exhibit of Degenerate Art for the Sheboygan Art Center. Readers will learn about the Nazis confiscating paintings by many famous artists, supposedly because they were immoral.

Lasky, Kathryn. **The Last Girls of Pompeii**. Viking Juvenile, 2007. MS. 160 pages. ISBN-10: 0670061964

Born with a withered arm, Julia is an embarrassment to her family and is about to be sent to live in a temple. Her beautiful slave Sura is to be sold as a concubine. Every day life of an upper class family in Pompeii is accurately depicted, as Vesuvius looms in the background threatening to erupt.

Liu, Cynthea. **The Great Call of China**. Puffin, 2009. MS. 224 pages ISBN-13: 978-0142411346

In this Students Across the Seven Seas offering, Chinese-born Cece heads off to Xi'an China to learn about anthropology, but she has an ulterior motive. Adopted by an American couple when she was two years old, Cece wants to visit the orphanage where she spent the first two years of her life and find out about her heritage.

Myers, Walter Dean. **Harlem Summer**. Scholastic Press, 2007. MS. 176 pages. ISBN-10: 043936843X

Although the main character and the story are fictional, many of the supporting characters are famous figures from the Harlem Renaissance. There is an appendix that details all the famous characters and places, which also includes pictures.

Myers, Walter Dean. **Sunrise Over Fallujah**. Scholastic Press, 2008. MS. 304 pages. ISBN-13: 978-0439916240

Over his parents' objections, Robin Perry leaves Harlem and joins the army instead of heading off to college. He is assigned to a Civil Affairs unit in Iraq, where he and his comrades are instructed to win over the Iraqi people, not an easy job in the "fog of war." A glossary is included which explains many of the terms and acronyms used when talking about the war in Iraq.

Napoli, Donna Jo. **The Smile**. Dutton Juvenile, 2008. MS. 240 pages. ISBN-13: 978-0525479994

In an artful blending of fact and fiction, the author explores the mystery behind the enigmatic smile of Leonardo da Vinci's Mona Lisa. Monna Elisabetta is looking forward to her thirteenth birthday party when her mother suddenly dies. The event is cancelled and Elizabetta turns to working alongside her father in his silk business to deal with her grief. When her father's friend Leonardo introduces her to Giuliano de Medici, they develop a mutual admiration for each other. However, the Medici family's political problems and Elizabetta's father's plans for her betrothal to another man, thwart the lovers' secret plans to marry.

Newton, Robert. **Runner**. Knopf Books for Young Readers, 2007. MS . 224 pages ISBN-10: 0375837442

Sixteen-year-old Charlie seeks solace in running after is father dies in Melbourne, Australia in 1919. He catches the eye of Squizzy Taylor, a notorious mobster, who actually ruled the mob world at this time. Against his mother's wishes Charlie becomes a courier for him and encounters the many problems this kind of life would actually entail.

Paulsen, Gary. **Woods Runner**. Wendy Lamb Books; 1 edition, 2010. MS. 176 pages. ISBN-13: 978-0385738842

In this depiction of the American Revolution, 13-year-old Samuel, whose parents have moved to a woodland settlement for peace and quiet, returns from hunting to find his home burned to the ground and his parents missing. He sets off to find them and along the way encounters vicious Red Coats and Hessians, as well as helpful rebels. In alternating chapters historical notes provide background information to help the reader understand the atrocities of this war.

Peet, Mal. **Tamar**. Candlewick 2007. MS/HS. 432 pages. ISBN-10: 0763634883

In separate narratives Tamar, a teenage girl, struggles to understand her grandfather's suicide, and the same man works with the local Nazi resistance movement in Holland during WWII. The accurate depiction of life in the underground makes WWII come alive for young readers.

Preble, Joy. **Dreaming Anastasia: A Novel of Love, Magic, and the Power of Dreams**. Sourcebooks Jabberwocky , 2009. MS. 320 pages. ISBN-13: 978-1402218170

In this supernatural romance, 16-year-old Anne Michaelson has recurring dreams involving Anastasia Romanov, who is being held captive by the witch Baba Yaga. Ethan

Kozinsky, who has been searching for years to find the girl who has been predestined to save Anastasia, appears at Anne's high school to enlist her help. Anne, who is fearful of getting involved, cannot deny her attraction to Ethan and get caught up in the intrigue.

Roberts, Judson. **Dragons from the Sea** (The Strongbow Saga –Book Two). HarperTeen, 2007. MS/HS. 352 pages. ISBN-10: 0060813008

The second book in the Strongbow Saga finds Halfdan Hrorikson fighting with the Danes against the Franks. He has joined the crew of Jarl Hastein on *The Gull* and gets involved in the fray when they decide to attack the Franks. The world of the ninth-century Vikings is accurately portrayed in this tale of battle and revenge.

Roberts, Judson. **The Road to Vengeance (The Strongbow Saga: Book 3).** HarperTeen , 2008. MS/HS. 352 pages. ISBN-10: 0060813040

The third book in the Strongbow Saga chronicles the Danish campaign against the Franks. Roberts directs readers to www.strongbowsaga.com where they can find historical military details, as well as a wealth of information about everyday Viking life. Roberts is also available for school visits and workshops.

Ryan, Pam Munoz. **Paint the Wind**. Scholastic Press, 2007. MS. 336 pages. ISBN-10: 0439873622

Alternating stories between Artemisia, the dam who has just given birth to Klee, and Maya, the eleven-year-old girl who moves from her strict grandmother's home to a ranch in Wyoming, *Paint the Wind* is a horse lover's dream. The author has done a lot of research about wild horses. There's a glossary of terms, as well as suggested sites to read more about the plight of wild horses.

Sandell, Lisa Ann. **Song of the Sparrow**. Scholastic Press, 2007. HS. 416 pages ISBN-10: 0439918480

In 490 A.D. 16-year-old Elaine of Ascolat lives with her father in King Arthur's base camp. The accurate portrayal of the conflict between the English and the Saxons creates a realistic background for this story of a young girl who with the aide of Gwynivere helps King Arthur.

Scott, Elaine. **Secrets of the Cirque Medrano**. Charlesbridge Publishing, 2008. 216 pages. ISBN-13: 978-1570917127

This story behind Picasso's Family of Saltambiques, as imagined by the author, involves 14-year-old Brigitte, who works in her aunt's Montmartre café, frequented by Pablo Picasso, circus performers and Russian diplomats. In an author's note Elaine Scott provides more details about Picasso's life, the actual Cirque Medrano and the Russian Imperialist Secret Police.

Selznik, Brian. **The Invention of Hugo Cabret.** Scholastic Press, 2007. MS. 533 pages. ISBN-10: 0439813786

This novel blends narrative, illustrations, photographs and cinematic images. The history of automatons is explored and George Méliés, the father of science fiction movies, is one of the main characters.

Sharenow, Robert. **My Mother the Cheerleader**. Laura Geringer Books, 2007. HS. 297 pages. ISBN-10: 061148972

The history of desegregation of the public schools in New Orleans is seen through the eyes of Louise Collins, who attends the school where six-year-old African-American Ruby Bridges enrolls.

Slayton, Fran Cannon. **When the Whistle Blows**. Philomel, 2009. MS. 160 pages. ISBN-10: 0399251898

In a series of short stories involving seven consecutive Halloweens, the life of Jimmy Cannon plays out in West Virginia during the 1940s. Starting out as a twelve-year-old, Jimmy matures from an adventuresome child into a young man.

Smith, Sherri L. **Flygirl**. Putnam Juvenile, 2009. MS. 256 pages. ISBN-13: 978-0399247095

In 1941 African American Ida Mae Jones, whose father taught her to fly his crop dusting plane, applies for the Women Airforce Service Program(WASP) to help with the war effort at home. However, in order to do so, she has to leave her family and friends and pass as white. She completes a rigorous training program and flies dangerous missions, all the while guarding the secret that would put an end to her military career. An author's note adds information about the WASP program.

Trueman, Terry. **Hurricane**. HarperCollins, 2008. MS. 144 pages. ISBN-13: 978-0060000189

This story is a fictional account of Hurricane Mitch in 1998 which was one of the worst storms to ever hit the Caribbean. It is told from the perspective of Jose, a thirteenyear-old boy living in a small village in Honduras. An addendum links this novel with the events surrounding Hurricane Katrina.

Turnball, Ann. **Forged in the Fire**. Candlewick, 2007. MS/HS. 320 pages. ISBN-10: 0763631442

The prejudice against Quakers in nineteenth century London is explored, as well as the fire which just about destroyed the city. This is the sequel to *No Shame, No Fear*, which is about the romance that blossoms between a Quaker girl and a non-Quaker boy and the problems they face.

Voelkel, J & P. **Middleworld**. Smith & Sons, Imprint of Smith and Kraus Pub. Inc., 2007. MS. 400 pages. ISBN-10: 1575255618

In the first book of The Jaguar Stones Trilogy, Max Murphy, a fourteen-year-old video game loving kid from Boston, finds himself battling the Ancient Maya Lords of Death. His parents are archeologists who accidentally unleash forces of destruction when they travel to Central America on an archeological dig. It is up to Max, the Maya chosen one, to sort out the mess. Detailed appendices about Mayan life are included.

WRITING A SHORT STORY WITH EMBEDDED RESEARCH

Now that the students have studied a book with embedded research, the next step is for the students to do the research for their own story. Initially the teacher could lead a class discussion about research students have done in the past and then move on to topics in which they might be interested. Have the students meet in small groups to brainstorm subjects that might lend themselves to the creative writing project. Each student should come up with two or three ideas that he/she can explore. When they get to the library and begin their research, students may find that one of their ideas is a dead end or doesn't really inspire story ideas. You may assign a formal two to three page paper with a bibliography or you may want to go about it more informally and just require notes and bibliographic information. Remind students that as they go about their research, they should begin thinking about a story in which to weave the information they find. Suggested topic ideas:[2]

Exploring places and Times
       Bermuda Triangle
       Irish Potato Famine
Exploring People and Perspectives
       Lindsay Lohan
       Derek Jeter
Inspirational
       Lance Armstrong
       Oprah Winfrey
Empathetic
       Illegality of Marijuana
       Pro Choice issues
Current Events and Pop Culture
       Cloning
       Reality Television
Historically significant
       Roswell, New Mexico
       Assassination of a president

Once the research piece is completed, give the students an opportunity to brainstorm story ideas with a classmate. Begin the activity by reviewing the following graphic organizer with the class. Give them examples of student ideas that have worked. For example, one of Jason Wirtz's students researched Al Capone and then wove the information into a story called "Memoirs of a Gangster Protégé," in which the main character worked for Al Capone. This is somewhat similar to what Robert Newton did in *Runner*, where Charlie Feehan worked for an Australian mobster. If a student researched a personal issue, such as having a disease like diabetes or cystic fibrosis, he/she could weave personal experiences into the story. Tracy Zimmer's book *Reaching for Sun*, which is about a girl with cerebral palsy, might inspire students to go in this direction.

---

[2] Wirtz, Jason. "Creating Possibilities: Embedding Research into Creative Writing," *English Journal*, Volume 95, Number 4 (March 2006) 23-27.

GRAPHIC ORGANIZER
FOR
SHORT STORY WITH EMBEDDED RESEARCH

Setting

    Location

    Atmosphere

    Time

Characters

    Main Character

        Physical description

        Distinct Personality (Think about Voice)

    Additional Character(s)

        Physical description

        Distinct Personality

        Historical

    Dialogue ideas

Plot Development

    Introduction

    Conflict/Problem

        Depth of information to create clarity

        Researched ideas to incorporate?

    Climax

    Resolution

Point of View

    First person

    Third person

    Omniscient

Now that students have brainstormed and organized their ideas, they are ready to write a rough draft. It is helpful to discuss the grading rubric prior to writing so that they know what to focus on. An example rubric follows:

Short Story with Embedded Research Rubric

5- Outstanding

3- Satisfactory

1- Needs Work

Setting

_____ (5) The location, atmosphere and time are clearly portrayed and enhance the story

_____ (3) The setting is described but may be missing a key element or doesn't permeate the story

_____(1) The setting is insufficiently described or isn't mentioned at all.

Characters

_____ (5) The characters are clearly drawn, including physical descriptions, as well as distinct personalities that are revealed by dialogue

_____(3) The characters are described but distinct personalities are vague and the dialogue lacks authenticity

_____ (1) Little or no character description and dialogue

Plot with Embedded Research

_____(5) The plot has a clear beginning, middle, and end with researched details seamlessly embedded in the story

_____(3) The plot has a clear beginning, middle and end but the researched details are lacking or are not embedded.

_____(1) There is little or no embedded research evident in the plot

Mechanics

_____(5) Few or no errors in punctuation, sentence structure, and spelling

_____(3) Some errors in punctuation, sentence structure and spelling, but they don't interfere with the story.

_____(1) Many errors in punctuation, sentence structure and spelling that are very distracting for the reader

UNITS WHICH FOCUS ON AN ESSENTIAL QUESTION

Example Essential Question: What does it mean to be human?

UNIT OVERVIEW

Loosely based on the scaffolding approach, this unit starts with very structured activities on a book the whole class reads. There is a great deal of teacher direction. Try to choose a book that is accessible to readers at a variety of reading levels. The culminating experience involves a response to the essential question using examples from the book to support one's ideas. An example unit, using *Freak the Mighty* by Rodman Philbrick, follows.

The final section of the unit involves choosing an independent book from a list of choices that lend themselves to answering the essential question. The list includes books at a variety of reading levels. Suggested titles from 2007-9 follow. Students can also choose their own book with approval from the teacher. After reading the book they do an independent project, which they present to the class, which focuses on the essential question.

CLASS BOOK – *Freak the Mighty* by Rodman Philbrick

Day 1 – Anticipatory lesson
Introduce the essential question. Let students know they will be writing an essay answer to the question for the culminating experience.

> What does it mean to be human?
>> Think in terms of:
>> Physical attributes
>> Human connections
>> Ability to reflect on the human experience

Introduce *Freak the Mighty* and discuss what students might predict will happen.
Give students a calendar with each day's assigned reading.
Hand out guiding questions for first assignment.

Guiding Question for Chapters 1-3 (pages 1-14)
1) What does Max mean by "I never had a brain until Freak came along…"
2) When Max was little, what was his method of communicating with others? How do you predict it will change?
3) Why do you think Kevin (Freak) is obsessed with robots?
4) Why does Kevin refer to Max as earthling? How does Max feel about it?
5) What physical limitations does Kevin have? How do these limitations change the way he relates to others?

Day 2
Have a class discussion for Chapters 1-3. Use the guiding questions to structure the discussion.
Assign Chapters 4-6 (pages15-33)

Guiding Questions for Chapters 4-6
1) Why is Kevin obsessed with King Arthur and the Knights of the Round Table?
2) What is unusual about Kevin's vocabulary? How does Max relate to it?
3) Why is Kevin's mother afraid of Max?
4) Max cries because he's happy. (p. 27) Discuss this phenomenon.
5) Why is Tony D a bully?

Day 3
Discuss Chapters 4-6
Assign Chapters 7-9 (pages 34-53)

Guiding Questions for Chapters 7-9
1) Explain "Freak the Mighty." How do Max and Kevin compliment each other?
2) Why does Grim offer Max coffee? How is it symbolic of Grim's new attitude toward Max?
3) When Max and Kevin swear by blood, why do they use saliva?
4) According to Kevin, what is the purpose of the Experimental Bionics Unit at the hospital?
5) Kevin says, "Life is dangerous." Do you agree? Why or why not?

Day 4
Discuss Chapters 7-9.
Assign Chapters 10-11 (pages 54-71)

Guiding Questions for Chapters 10-11
1) What is the quest Max and Kevin go on? Why does Kevin turn it into such an ordeal?
2) What is the foreshadowing on page 62? What do you predict will happen?
3) What are the New Tenements? Why are they called the New Testaments? Discuss puns as a form of humor.
4) Why is Iggy afraid to harass Max?
5) What happened to Kevin's father? How does Kevin feel about him?

Day 5
Discuss Chapters 10-11.
Assign Chapters 12-14 (pages 72-92)

Guiding Questions for Chapters 12-14
1) Why is Max switched from classes for learning disabled students to Kevin's classes? Why do Grim and Gram allow this change?
2) How do the other students relate to Freak the Mighty?
3) Why won't Max speak in class? Write? How does Kevin change this?
4) How does Max feel about the incident in the cafeteria? What does Kevin tell him about it?
5) How does Max's family feel about his father getting out of prison on parole?

Day 6
Discuss Chapters 12-14
Assign Chapters 15-17. (pages 93-114)

Guiding Questions Chapters 15-17
1) Explain what Kevin gives Max for Christmas and how Max feels about it.
2) What came down the chimney? What is this expression an allusion to? Why is it funny?
3) How does Killer Kane say he has changed since being in prison?
4) Do you think Max believes him? Why or why not?
5) How do Loretta and Iggy feel about Killer Kane?

Day 7
Discuss Chapters 15-17
Assign Chapters 18-20 (115-134)

Guiding Questions for Chapters 18-20
1) What are Max's father's plans for them? What do these plans show about his true feelings about religion?
2) Max's father says, 'Never trust a cripple." What does he mean? Do you agree? Why or why not?
3) Why do you think Loretta and Iggy help Max? What does this say about their humanity?
4) How does Kevin outsmart Killer Kane?
5) Max's father assumes Max was too young to remember his mother's death. How did she die? Why do you think he remembers it?

Day 8
Discuss Chapters 18-20.
Assign Chapters 21-23 (pages 135-152)

Guiding Questions for Chapters 21-23.
1) Why does Gwen tell Kevin he has to be extra careful? (p137)
2) What is Kevin's special operation? Why doesn't Gwen know about it?
3) What present does Kevin give Max at the hospital? Why do you think he gives it to him?
4) What is a tracheotomy? How does Kevin feel about having one?
5) What does Kevin mean by "my present manifestation"? (p. 149)

Day 9
Discuss Chapters 21-23
Assign Chapters 24-25 and the dictionary. (pages 152-169)

Guiding Questions for Chapters 24-25
1) Describe Max's reaction to Kevin's death.
2) What advice does Loretta give Max?
3) How does Max use Kevin's present?
4) Begin to think about the essential question for the test. What examples from the book support your ideas about what it means to be human?

Day 10
Discuss Chapters 24-25 and Review for the test.

INDEPENDENT BOOK PROJECTS

Character Locker

Using a shoe box to simulate a locker, create a "locker" which contains items the main character would own. (miniatures or pictures are suggested for large items. i.e. matchbook car corvette if that's what the main character drove) The locker should include a minimum of 8 items. Be prepared to present the locker to the class and explain how the items you included reflect the story and the humanity of the character.

Alphabet Poster

Create a poster that has 26 words related to the book, one that starts with each letter of the alphabet. Try to make the words reflect the humanity of the characters (For example in *Freak the Mighty* Kevin had a large Vocabulary). For Q, X, and Z feel free to choose words that include the letter rather than start with them. Be prepared to present your poster to the class and to explain how each word is related to the story.

Picture Book

Create a picture book which summarizes the book you read. It should summarize the story, but try to focus on the humanity of the characters in the story. (For example, when Kevin and Max become Freak the Mighty, Max felt as if they were super human because Kevin was brilliant and Max was unusually large physically.) No more than one quarter of each page should be text. Include a picture that reflects the text. The picture may be drawn, cut from a magazine, or computer generated from the internet or clip art. Be prepared to read your book to the class.

Powerpoint Presentation

Create a power point presentation reflecting the issues presented in your book as to what it means to be human. For example, in *Freak the Mighty*, Kevin refers to Max as an earthling, which sets Max to pondering the term. (p. 11) The project could identify all the different types of earthlings which appear in the book and include a reflection on their similarities and differences.

BOOK SUGGESTIONS FOR INDEPENDENT PROJECT

Anderson, Laurie Halse. **Twisted**. Viking Juvenile, 2007. HS. 256 pages.
ISBN-10: 0670061018

Bacigalupi, Paolo. **Ship Breaker**. Little, Brown Books for Young Readers; 1 edition, 2010. MS/HS. 336 pages. ISBN-13: 978-0316056212

Bodeen. S. A. **Compound**. Feiwel & Friends, 2008. MS. 256 pages. ISBN-10: 0312370156

Brande, Robin. **Evolution, Me and Other Freaks of Nature**. Knopf Books for Young Readers, 2007. MS/HS. 272 pages. ISBN-10: 0375843493

Brooks, Kevin. **Being**. The Chicken House. 2007. MS/HS. 336 pages. ISBN-10: 0439899737

Caletti, Deb. **The Nature of Jade**. Simon & Schuster Children's Publishing. 2007. MS/HS. 304 pages ISBN-10: 1416910050 Clements, Andrew. **Extra Credit**. Atheneum, 2009. MS. 192 pages. ISBN-13: 978-1416949299

Condie, Ally. **Matched**. Dutton Juvenile, 2010. MS. 369 pages.ISBN-13: 978-0525423645

Crowley, Suzanne **The Very Ordered Existence of Merilee Marvelous**. Greenwillow, 2007. MS. 384 pages. ISBN-10: 0061231975

De Vita, James. **The Silenced**. Eos, 2007. MS/HS. 512 pages. ISBN-10: 0060784628

Dogar, Sharon. **Waves.** Chicken House Ltd, 2007. MS/HS, 352 pages. ISBN-10: 1905294247.

Haddix, Margaret Peterson. **Found**. Simon & Schuster Children's Publishing, 2008. MS. 320 pages. ISBN-10: 1416954171

Koertge, Ron. **Strays**. Candlewick (May 8, 2007) MS/HS. 176 pages. ISBN-10: 0763627054

Malley, Gemma. **The Declaration**. Bloomsbury USA Children's Books, 2007. MS. 320 pages. ISBN-10: 1599901196

Maberry, Jonathan. **Rot and Ruin**. Simon & Schuster Children's Publishing, 2010. MS/HS. 464 pages. ISBN-13: 978-1442402324 McNamee, Graham. **Bonechiller**. Wendy Lamb Books, 2008. MS/HS. 304 pages. ISBN-13: 978-0385746588

Meyer, Stephenie. **Breaking Dawn**. Little, Brown Young Readers, 2008. MS/HS. 768 pages. ISBN-10: 031606792X

Nelson, Blake. **They Came From Below**. Tor Teen (2007) MS/HS. 304 pages. ISBN-10: 0765314231

Patterson, James. **Maximum Ride – Saving the World and Other Extreme Sports**. Little, Brown Young Readers, 2007. MS. 416 pages. ISBN-10: 0316155608

Shusterman, Neal. **Unwind**. Simon & Schuster Children's Publishing, 2007. MS/HS. 352 pages. ISBN-10: 1416912045

Soto, Gary. **Mercy on these Teenage Chimps.** Harcourt Children's Books, 2007. MS. 160 pages. ISBN-10: 0152060227

Testa, Dom. **The Comet's Curse**. Tor Teen, 2009. MS. 240 pages. ISBN-13: 978-0765321077

Thompson, Kate. **The New Policeman**. HarperTeen, 2007. MS. 448 pages. ISBN-10: 0061174270

Waters, Daniel. **Kiss of Life**. Hyperion Book CH, 2009. MS/HS. 416 pages. ISBN-13: 978-1423109235

Yancy, Rick. **Monstrumologist**. Simon & Schuster Children's Publishing; 1St Edition edition, 2009. MS/HS. 448 pages. ISBN-13: 978-1416984481

Zimmer, Tracie Vaughn. **Reaching for Sun**. Bloomsbury USA Children's Books, 2007. MS. 144 pages. ISBN-10: 1599900378

NOVELS WITH ALTERNATING VOICES

Novels with alternating voices are becoming more and more popular. There are two different ways the author employs this device. One includes **multiple narrators**, where the voices are aware that they are telling the story. The other uses **multiple reflector characters**, where there are alternating characters whose consciousnesses are revealed by an external narrator, but they are not narrating the story.

When discussing novels with alternating voices, it is important to understand the basic components of point of view. According to John Lye, a professor at Brock University, "One of the main factors that determines the meaning of the story is who is telling the story, and how. There are many 'points of view' from which a story can be told. By 'point of view' we generally mean two things: 1) the relation of the narrator to the action of the story — whether the narrator is, for instance, a character in the story, or a voice outside of the story; 2) the relation of the narrator to the issues and the characters that the story involves."[3]

There are various ways to tell the story. Each way of telling it may bring a different emphasis, different knowledge, and different ways in which readers process the story. According to Professor Lye, there are five questions to consider when discussing the point of view from which a story is told, the final question being, how many narrators are there? The following information is an abbreviation of information he provides for his English students at Brock University.

I. From where is the story being told?

An **external narrator** is not in the story. He/she is aware the he is telling a story and may comment on the story being told. When the readers know the thoughts, experiences and feelings of a character in the story through the external narrator, the character is known as a **reflector character**. The reflector character is not aware of being the subject of the narration and is not telling the story, but is only having his/her experiences reported. The story may be told by the external narrator so that the readers know more about the fate or motivations of other characters than the main characters (**position of irony**) or so that the readers know no more than the characters know (**position of suspense**.)

An **internal narrator** is a character in the story and is aware that he or she is telling a story. The internal narrator may be a **protagonist** (main characters around whom the action centers) or just an observer of the protagonists' lives. The internal narrator may tell the story as it is happening or after he or she has lived through it (retrospectively). The **retrospective narrator** knows more than the reader and is in a position of irony in relation to the events of the story.

---

[3] Lye, John. Narrative Point of View: Some Considerations. www.brocku.ca/english/courses. June 8, 2008.

II. **How much does the narrator know?**

This question may arise with both external and internal narrators. Limited knowledge is expected with internal narrators, because the reader is seeing the story from only one point of view. With external narrators the reader may think that narrator knows everything and read the story with trust. However, it is also possible that the external narrator does not understand what is happening and misrepresents the truth. The question of what the narrator knows is different from what the narrator chooses to tell the reader.

III. **How reliable is the narrator?**

The reliability of narrators varies. It is dependent on what the narrators know, what their intentions are, and what their biases are. With the internal narrator, who is a character in the story, reliability can also involve the character's age or intellectual capability. For instance, a particularly young character, or a retarded or senile character may not really understand what is happening in the story and misrepresent the truth.

IV. **What is the narrator's orientation?**

How does the narrator view the various issues raised in the story? This question involves several different issues. **Distance:** Is the narrator emotionally close or distant to the story he/she is narrating? **Interest:** Does the narrator share in the "stakes of the story? Or is the narrator apparently uninterested or disinterested? **Sympathy:** Does the narrator empathize with the characters, judge them or approach them as an impartial observer? **Voice:** What is the narrator like? What is his/her attitude about the subject of the story? What are his/her ideological positions?

V. **How many narrators are there**?

Multiple narrators can take several forms. First, there may be more than one internal narrator who is telling the story. They may show different perspectives about the same events. If so, "what happened" maybe told several times. (*Harmless*) Or the story may be told in a linear fashion with different characters telling successive chapters of the story that may overlap somewhat. (*How to Be Bad*). Finally, the multiple narrators may be telling the different stories that are taking place in different locals, but are ultimately related. (*I Wanna Be Your Joey Ramone*).

Again, multiple narrators are different from **multiple reflector characters**. Multiple narrators are voices aware that they are telling the story. Multiple reflector characters are characters whose consciousnesses are revealed by an external narrator, but they are not narrating the story. (*Forever in Blue: The Fourth Summer of the Sisterhood*)

ALTERNATING VOICES UNIT OF STUDY

In ***The Missing Girl***, Norma Fox Mazer has taken the alternating voice style of writing to the next level by including four different narrators, using three different points of view. This psychological thriller's narrators reveal the details of the abduction of a young girl by a psychopathic pedophile. The story is told by an external narrator from the points of view of the abductor and Beauty, the victim's oldest sister. Fancy, the victim's developmentally delayed sister, gives her view of the story in first person and Autumn, the youngest sister, who is the one abducted, tells the story in second person singular. Suspense builds throughout the story, as readers witness the pedophile stalking the sisters and wait for the abduction, as he decides which one to abduct. Then after the abduction, they root for Autumn as she tries to outwit the man who has imprisoned her. Autumn's confinement in the kidnapper's home is terrifying. The abuse is not overly graphic, but there are some chilling sequences. This book provides a unique opportunity to study alternating voices that include an external narrator and two internal narrators, as well as first, second and third person points of view.

THE MISSING GIRL
By Norma Fox Mazer
A Novel with Alternating Voices

1) There are four different voices in *The Missing Girl*. Identify each voice and from what point of view the story is told.
   a. The Stalker – external narrator
   b. Beauty – external narrator
   c. Fancy – first person
   d. Autumn – second person
2) How reliable is each narration?
   a. The Stalker narration by an external narrator reliably represents his demented thought processes.
   b. Beauty is the oldest sister and her narration by an external narrator is reliable.
   c. Fancy is the developmentally delayed sister and her narration is not reliable.
   d. Autumn is 11 years old and the sister who is abducted. Although she is young, the story is happening to her and her narration is fairly reliable.
3) Why does the author choose these four characters?
   a. The Stalker – His narration increases the suspense and provides a chilling look into his thought process.
   b. Beauty – Her narration gives a credible outsider's view.
   c. Fancy – Aptly named, Fancy gives a fanciful view of what's happening from a young child's point of view.
   d. Autumn – Her narration provides a first hand look at what it feels like to be abducted and held prisoner, as well as allows the reader to know her plans for escape.

4) How does this writing style increase the suspense of the story?

> The reader knows what the pedophile is thinking and wonders which sister he will abduct and how he will go about it. The reader also sees the story from the oldest sister's credible point of view, as well as a subplot about her involvement with a boy, which readers wonder about. Fancy's first person narration reveals that she views the abduction as a fantasy story where her sister is a princess and the abductor is a monster. Finally, Autumn's narration allows the reader to witness her imprisonment from both her and the pedophile's point of view, which heightens the suspense about whether she will escape.

5) Is the reader in a position of irony (knows more than the main characters) or a position of suspense (knows no more than the main characters)?
    a. The reader is in a position of irony in that he/she knows that the pedophile is contemplating abducting one of the sisters, whereas they do not. However, there is still a lot of suspense as to which one he will abduct.
6) Describe the orientation of each voice. How close to the story is each voice and does this person share in the stakes?
    a. The pedophile is very close to the story and is very involved in the stakes.
    b. Beauty is close to the story but is not closely involved in the imprisonment. She is on the outside trying to find her sister.
    c. Fancy is close to the story in that her sister is the one abducted, but her mental issues color the way she views the situation.
    d. Autumn's stakes are the highest because she is the one abducted.
7) How do you feel about each of the narrators and reflector characters?
   (Answers will vary)
8) How does the story end? Discuss the last three chapters and why the author chose to end the story this way.
    a. The third to the last chapter is an article from the Bremen Herald (the community newspaper) reporting that a badly decomposed body had been discovered in a marshy cove of the Niskcogee River. The reader presumes it is the body of the pedophile who abducted Autumn.
    b. The second to the last chapter is from Autumn's point of view. It details how protective Beauty has now become and how Autumn, who never used to feel special, now believes that she is a combination of all of her sisters' best qualities. This chapter gives the reader insight about Autumn's recovery from her ordeal.
    c. The last chapter is from Fancy's point of view. She is telling a fairy tale to her class about a monster who kidnapped a princess and locked her in a tower and how the princess escaped. The reader presumes this is Fancy's view of what happened to her sister.
9) In your opinion, why did the author choose the alternating voice format to tell the story? (answers will vary)
10) How would the story have been different if the story had been told by one character? By only an omniscient narrator? (answers will vary)

NOVELS WITH ALTERNATING VOICES

GUIDING QUESTIONS FOR LITERATURE CIRCLES

1) Are the alternating voices in the story narrators or reflector characters?

2) If there are multiple narrators, list them. From what point of view does each narrator tell the story?

3) If there is an external narrator telling the story of several reflector characters, list the reflector characters.

4) If there are multiple narrators, why did the author choose these particular characters to narrate the story?

5) What is the narrator's orientation? Answer the following questions for each of the narrators.

> a. Distance: Is the narrator emotionally close or distant to the story he/she is narrating?

> b. Interest: Does the narrator share in the "stakes of the story? Or is the narrator apparently uninterested or disinterested?

> c. Sympathy: Does the narrator empathize with the characters, judge them or approach them as an impartial observer?

> d. Voice: What is the narrator like? What is his/her attitude about the subject of the story? What are his/her ideological positions?

6) How reliable is the narrator(s)? Explain your answer.

7) How does the multiple narrator or reflector character format of the story enhance the story? Why do you think the author chose this particular format?

8) How does the story change depending on which character tells the story?

9) Is the reader in a position of irony (knows more than the characters) or a position of suspense (knows no more than the characters)?

10) How does the story end? Who is the narrator or which reflector character's point of view is used? Why?

11) How would the story be different, if it did not have multiple narrators or reflector characters?

NOVELS WITH ALTERNATING VOICES

Adlington, L.J. **Cherry Heaven**. HarperTeen , 2008. MS. 464 pages. ISBN-10: 006143180X

Anderson, Jody Lynn. **The Secrets of Peaches**. HarperTeen, 2007. MS/HS. 304 pages. ISBN-10: 0060733087

Asher, Jay. **13 Reasons Why**. Razorbill, 2007. HS. 304 pages. ISBN-10: 1595141715

Baker. E.D. **Wings: A Fairy Tale**. Bloomsbury USA Children's Books, 2008. MS. 320 pages. ISBN-13: 978-1599901930

Barkley, Brad and Hepler, Heather. **Jars of Glass**. Dutton Juvenile, 2008. MS/HS. 208 pages. ISBN-13: 978-0525479116

Brashares, Ann. **Forever in Blue**. Delacorte Books for Young Readers, 2007. MS/HS.400 pages. ISBN-10: 0385729367

Galante, Cecilia. **The Patron Saint of Butterflies**. Bloomsbury USA Children's Books; 1st edition, 2008. MS/HS. 304 pages.**ISBN-13: 978-1599902494**

Giles, Gail. **What Happened to Cass McBride?** Little, Brown Young Readers, 2007. MS/HS. 240 pages. ISBN-10: 0316166391

Hartinger, Brent. **Split Screen: Attack of the Soul-Sucking Brain Zombies/Bride of the Soul Sucking Brain Zombies**. HarperTeen, 2007. HS. 304 pages. ISBN-10: 0060824085

Henkes, Kevin. **Bird Lake Moon**. Greenwillow, 2008. MS. 192 pages. ISBN-13: 978-0061470769

Hernandez, David. **No More Us for You**. HarperTeen, 2009. MS/HS. 288 pages. ISBN-13: 978-0061173332

Hooper, Mary. **Newes from the Dead**. Roaring Brook Press, 2008. MS/HS. 272 pages ISBN-13: 978-1596433557

Hopkins, Ellen. **Identical**. Margaret K. McElderry, 2008). HS. 576 pages. ISBN-10: 1416950052

Hopkins, Ellen. **Fallout**. Margaret K. McElderry, 2010. HS. 672 pages. ISBN-13: 978-1416950097

Hopkins, Ellen. **Tricks**. Margaret K. McElderry; 1 edition, 2009. HS. 640 page. ISBN-13: 978-1416950073

Hughes, Mark Peter. **Lemonade Mouth**. Delacorte Books for Young Readers, 2007. MS/HS. 352 pages. ISBN-10: 0385733925

Kluger, Steve. **My Most Excellent Year: A Novel of Love, Mary Poppins, & Fenway Park**. Puffin; Reprint edition, 2009. MS/HS. 416 pages. ISBN-13: 978-0142413432

Kuehnert, Stephanie. **I Wanna Be Your Joey Ramone**. MTV, 2008. HS. 352 pages. ISBN-10: 1416562699

Levine, Gail Carson. **Ever**. HarperCollins, 2008. 256 pages. ISBN-10: 0061229628

Levithan, David. **Love is the Higher Law**. Knopf Books for Young Readers, 2009. HS. 176 pages. ISBN-13: 978-0375834684

Lockhart, Mlynowski and Myracle. **How to Be Bad**. HarperTeen, 2008. MS/HS. 336 pages. ISBN-10: 006128422X

Mackler, Caroline. **Tangled**. HarperTeen; 1 edition, 2009. MS/HS. 320 pages. ISBN-13: 978-0061731044

Mazer, Norma Fox. **The Missing Girl**. HarperTeen, 2008. MS/HS. 288 pages. ISBN-10: 0066237769.

Mlynowski, Sarah. **Gimme a Call**. Delacorte Books for Young Readers, 2010. MS. 320 pages. ISBN-13: 978-0385735889

Reinhardt, Dana. **Harmless**. Wendy Lamb Books, 2007. MS/HS. 240 pages. ISBN-10: 0385746997

Shusterman, Neal. **Unwind**. Simon & Schuster Children's Publishing , 2007. 352 pages. ISBN-10: 1416912045

Weaver, Will. **Saturday Night Dirt**. Puffin, 2008. MS. 272 pages. ISBN-10: 014240392X

Wiess, Laura. **Leftovers.** MTV, 2008. HS. 256 pages .ISBN-13: 978-1416546627

CLASSIC CONNECTIONS

Literature and film are filled with retellings of classic stories with a modern twist. In fact Phillip Pullman (His Dark Materials Trilogy) theorizes that there are only a few plots in the literature and identifies them as follows.

1) **Cinderella**- an under-regarded boy or girl overcomes all odds and comes out a winner.
2) **Little Red Riding Hood** – seduction of innocence
3) **Beauty and the Beast** – ugly monster is transformed by the love of an innocent
4) **Romeo and Juliet** – boys meets girl, boy loses girl, boy finds girl
5) **Tristan and Isolde**- the eternal love triangle
6) **Shane** – the incorruptible avenger
7) **Psycho** – the horrible thing coming out of the dark
8) **Orpheus and Eurydice** – the lost beautiful thing which is always sought after and never quite found
9) **Achilles** – the fatal flaw
10) **Faust** – the debt that must be paid
11) **The Flying Dutchman** – the hero is cursed for some wrong doing and has to wander forever, searching for the thing that will redeem him
12) **The Quest for the Holy Grail** – something (happiness, freedom, vengeance, victory, self-knowledge or love) is sought above all other things and everything is subordinated to finding it.

He goes on to suggest that there are several superficial ways to change the story.

1) by changing the narrating voice
2) by changing the point of view
3) by changing the protagonist (e.g. making the Prince the central character in Cinderella)
4) by changing the setting (Cinderella in New York City)
5) by changing the medium (e.g. word to pictures, prose to verse)
6) by adding a new character (e.g. Cinderella's first boyfriend)
7) by taking away one of the fundamental elements (e.g. no step sisters in Cinderella)
8) by contradiction (e.g. fairy godmother hinders Cinderella)
9) by changing the order of events (e.g.Cinderella and Prince meet before the ball)

Many modern YA authors are following this time honored tradition of retelling a classic story in a modern setting (*Beastly* by Alex Flinn) or incorporating elements of a classic in a modern tale (*Saving Juliet* by Suzanne Selfors). By having students read and compare the classic and the related modern novel, teachers can expose kids to plots that form the backbone of literature and help them appreciate the clever variations that the modern authors imagine.

RETELLING OF A CLASSIC TALE

BEASTLY by Alex Flinn

Beastly by Alex Flinn is an updated version of *Beauty and the Beast* which is set in New York City. In her author's note at the end of the book Alex Flinn details the history of the classic tale and the many versions available. Have students read one of the versions of *Beauty and the Beast* and then read *Beastly*. The following questions can be used as a guide for a comparative study of the two versions.

1) Read the author's note at the end of *Beastly*. Choose one of the classic versions of *Beauty and the Beast* she suggests and read it.
2) Why did Alex Flinn choose to write an updated version of the classic tale? As you read *Beastly*, begin to think about the differences between it and the classic version.
3) In the introduction to *Beastly* Mr. Anderson is moderating the Unexpected Changes chat group online. Who are the members of the chat group and which fairy tale does each represent?
4) From what point of view is each version of the story told?
5) In each version the Prince is changed into a beast. Why was each guy changed into a beast and who performed the transformation?
6) What part do the parents of Beauty and the Beast play in each of the versions?
7) Describe the young maiden who can save the Beast in each version. How does she get lured into his lair?
8) In each version what does the Prince do during the endless days of imprisonment? How does this help with his transformation?
9) Where and why does Alex Flinn employ the chat room scripts?
10) Into what segments does Alex Flinn divide the story? Why do you think she separates the story into these different parts?
11) What is the theme(s) of *Beastly*? Is it in any way changed from the theme of the classic version?
12) What are some of the messages about teenage behavior that the author of *Beastly* wishes to convey?
13) Review Philip Pullman's list of ways the author goes about changing a classic tale. What are the techniques that Alex Flinn uses in *Beastly* to retell *Beauty and the Beast* with a modern twist?
14) Which version did you prefer?
15) Why do you think people enjoy reading updated versions of stories they already know?

Titles with Classic Connections

New Title	Classic Connection
Also Known as Harper (Leal)	To Kill a Mockingbird
Another Faust (Nayeri)	Faust
Ash (Lo)	Cinderella
Avalon (Cabot)	King Arthur
At Face Value (Franklin)	Cyrano de Bergerac
The Battle of the Labyrinth (Riordan)	Greek Myths
Book of the Thousand Days (Hale)	Grimm's Maid Maleen
Cindy Ella (Palmer)	Cinderella
Confessions of a Triple Shot Betty (Gehrman)	Much Ado About Nothing
Crazy Beautiful (Baratz-Logstead)	Beauty and the Beast
Cupid (Lester)	Eros and Psyche
A Curse As Dark as Gold (Bunce)	Rumpelstiltskin
Dark Dude (Hijuelos)	Huck Finn
Ella Enchanted (Levine)	Cinderella
Enter Three Witches (Cooney)	Macbeth
Enthusiasm (Shulman)	Pride and Prejudice
Eye of the Crow (Peacock)	Sherlock Holmes
Fairest (Levine)	Sleeping Beauty
The Extraordinary Adventures of Alfred Kropp series (Yancy)	King Arthur
The Fat Girl (Sachs)	Pygmalion
Girlfriend Material (Kantor)	The Sun Also Rises
Goddess Bootcamp (Childs)	Greek Mythology
Going Bovine (Bray)	Don Quixote
The Gospel According to Larry (Tashjian)	Walden
Guinevere's Gift (McKenzie)	King Arthur
Here Lies Arthur (Reeve)	King Arthur
If I Have a Wicked Stepmother, Where's My Prince? (Kantor)	Cinderella
Jekyll Loves Hyde (Fantaskey)	Dr. Jekyll and Mr. Hyde
The Juliet Club (Harper)	Romeo and Juliet
	Much Ado About Nothing
Just Ella (Haddix)	Cinderella
Kiss in Time (Flinn)	Sleeping Beauty

The Last Knight (Bell)	Don Quixote
Little Brother (Doctorow)	*1984*
The Night Tourist (Marsh)	Orpheus and Erydice
Nobody's Princess (Friesner)	Helen of Troy
Nobody's Prize (Sequel)	
Oh My Gods (Childs)	Greek Mythology
Pandora Gets Jealous (Hennesy)	Pandora's Box (Greek Myth)
Pandora Gets Vain (Hennesy)	
Pandora Gets Lazy (Hennesy)	
Pride and Prejudice and Zombies	Pride and Prejudice
Radiant Darkness (Whitman)	Greek Mythology
Runemarks (Harris)	Norse Legends
Saving Juliet (Selfors)	Romeo and Juliet
The Song of the Sparrow (Sandell)	King Arthur
Snakehead (Halam)	Greek Mythology
Suite Scarlett (Johnson)	Hamlet
Sun and Moon, Ice and Snow (George)	East o' the Sun and West o' the Moon
	Beauty and the Beast
The Case of the Left-Handed Lady (Springer)	Sherlock Holmes
The Case of the Bizarre Bouquets (Springer)	Sherlock Holmes
The Grimm Legacy (Shulman)	Grimm Fairy Tales
The Hunger Games (Collins)	Theseus and the Minotaur
The Last Olympian (Riordan)	Greek Mythology
The Revolution of Sabine (Ain)	Candide
The Story of Edgar Sawtelle (Wroblewski)	Hamlet
The Witches' Guide to Cooking with Children (McGowan)	Hansel and Gretel
Troy High (Norris)	Illiad
*Undercove*r (Kephart)	Cyrano de Bergerac
The Willoughbys (Lowry)	*Little Women* and many other classics "stuffed with orphans, nannies and long-lost heirs."
Wings: A Fairy Tale (Baker)	Midsummer Night's Dream
Wondrous Strange	Midsummer Night's Dream

Blogging about Social Awareness

According to Robert Selman, the chair of Harvard Graduate School of Education's Human Development and Psychology department, "Good children's literature not only raises moral dilemmas, but also generates the feelings that are associated with situations where moral conflict and confusion exists." He suggests that through reading about social conflict students can vicariously experience the resolution of problem situations. "The more one practices ethical awareness in conjunction with other students, the better s/he will get at it. If our inevitable ethical mistakes can be contained or corrected, if they can be truly felt, if they are the kinds of ethical errors that do not cause irreversible damage to self or to others, then as we go through school, we will have built up immunity, resilience, and capacity for resistance to becoming ethically lost. Better yet, we may take a road that leads to making things better in this world."[4]

Literature circles that focus on social awareness can be grouped according to topic. For example, a variety of books focus on the issue of prejudice in its many different forms. Questions that relate to prejudice in general can be applied to many different situations presented in young adult books. If your class has a blog site, the discussion might be held through blogging rather than the traditional setting.

Modeling the discussions you would like students to have can be done by first reading and discussing one book with the entire class. A fun way to start this unit would be to have students read *Generation Dead* by Daniel Waters. Many students, who are members of a particular minority group that is being discussed, are uncomfortable during class discussions. In *Generation Dead* the prejudice is against zombies, so the issue can be discussed without any student thinking he/she is being targeted.

Waters, Daniel. **Generation Dead**. Hyperion Book CH, 2008. MS/HS. 400 pages. ISBN-13: 978-1423109211

When dead teenagers start coming back to life, prejudice against these "living impaired" kids is rampant at Oakvale High. Phoebe, who is a Goth girl, finds herself attracted to Tommy, the leader of the undead. She and her best friends Adam and Margi join the Undead Studies group to see if they can begin to understand the phenomenon and bridge the rift in the student body that prejudice has created.

The book has a great deal of internet support, including a Generation Dead wiki where students can post comments: http://flumeaward.wikispaces.com/Generation+Dead. Tommy has a blog entitled "My So Called Undeath – My Life as a Zombie" at http://mysocalledundeath.blogspot.com where readers can subscribe to posts and comments. The author, Daniel Waters, has a personal website at http://danielwaters.com/ where he blogs and readers can post comments to which he responds. The website for the book, http://www.gendead.com, includes a "Zombie Quiz" for girls which encourages readers to take a stance on issues related to dating. Although the majority of readers posting comments are girls, this is definitely a boy friendly book.

Generation Dead is the first book in a series. Students who particularly enjoy *Generation Dead* might want to read the sequel *Kiss of Life*. The *Horn Book* review of the novel suggests, "This nuanced take on an old horror staple proves a surprisingly effective platform for explorations of grief, loyalty, justice, and social change."

Waters, Daniel. **Kiss of Life**. Hyperion Book CH, 2009. MS/HS. 416 pages.ISBN-13: 978-1423109235

In the sequel to *Generation Dead*, Adam, who has sacrificed himself to save Phoebe's life, has now returned as one of the undead. Zombies are being blamed for various crimes that are taking place and there is a mystery surrounding the Hunter Foundation's experiments. Phoebe now finds herself with not one, but two undead boyfriends.

After the class completes *the Generation Dead* unit, have them choose individual books which involve issues of prejudice and answer the literature circles discussion questions. Then hold traditional literature circle discussions or have students blog about the book they read on a class blog site. Additional social awareness topics might include substance abuse, self images issues such as eating disorders, gender issues, religious extremism, global conflict issues, and environmental awareness.

---

[4] Bucuvalas, Abigail. *Teaching Social Awareness – An Interview with Larsen Professor Robert Selman.* http://www.gse.harvard.edu/news/features/selman02012003.html, July 8, 2009.

Social Awareness Literature Circle Questions
Prejudice

1) What is prejudice?

2) Which character(s) in the novel is struggling with issues of prejudice? Explain

3) How are these issues impacting his/her life?

4) What does the main character do to cope with the oppressions he/she is feeling?

5) What is the setting of the story? What impact do the issues of prejudice have on the setting?

6) Which characters in the story add to the problems? How?

7) Which characters are supportive and how do they show their support?

8) What stereotypes are associated with the prejudicial issues?

9) Are cliques formed among the kids in the story, according to prejudices and stereotypes of others who are different from themselves? Explain

10) What is the nature of the discrimination? How has it developed over time?

Additional Titles which Focus on Prejudice

Alexie, Sherman. **The Absolutely True Diary of a Part-Time Indian**. Little, Brown Young Readers, MS/HS. 2007. 240 pages. ISBN-10: 0316013684

    With illustrations by cartoonist Ellen Forney, this semi-autobiographical novel tells the story of a bright hydrocephalic Native American boy, who is the target of bullies and loves to draw. Transferring to a white high school, he attempts to rise above life on the reservation where alcoholism is rampant.

Issue: Native Americans

Alvarez, Julia. **Return to Sender**. Knopf Books for Young Readers, 2009. MS. 336 pages. ISBN-13: 978-0375858383

    Tyler's family is forced to hire illegal Mexican workers to save their Vermont farm when his father is injured in a tractor accident. Although he has conflicting feelings about their right to be in the United States, he befriends Mari, the oldest of the three daughters who is worried about her missing mother and incarcerated uncle. Her family lives in constant fear of discovery and Tyler struggles to do the right thing.

Issue: Illegal immigrants

Blundell, Judy. **What I Saw and How I Lied**. Scholastic Press. MS/HS. 288 pages. ISBN-13: 978-0439903462

    In this National Book Award winning novel, fifteen-year-old Evie and her mother Beverly accompany her stepfather Joe, who has recently returned from WWII, to Palm Beach, Florida where Evie falls for Peter, an army buddy of Joe's that he's been avoiding. After a boating accident and a suspicious death, her parents become murder suspects and Evie has to examine her loyalties and consider that her perceptions about her mother may have been wrong all along.

Issue: Anti-Semitism

Burd, Nick. **The Vast Fields of Ordinary**. Dial, 2009. HS. 320 pages. ISBN-13: 978-0803733404

    During an eventful summer before college, Dade Hamilton watches his parents marriage implode, his relationship with sort of boyfriend Pablo fizzle, and the media's obsessive coverage of an autistic girl's disappearance unfold. He toils away at a boring job at Food World and feels lost and invisible, until he meets Alex Kincaid, an openly gay drug dealer, with whom he falls in love.

Issue: Homosexuality

Burg, Ann. **All the Broken Pieces**. Scholastic Press, 2009. MS. 224 pages. ISBN-13: 978-0545080927

    In this novel-in-verse Matt Pin, a twelve-year-old Vietnamese boy who has been adopted by an American family, is haunted by his past in which his father abandons him, his little brother is maimed by a land mine and his mother sends him off to America. He is adored by his new little brother and is a star pitcher on the school baseball team, but he struggles with the prejudice of his teammates and his memories of the atrocities of war.

Issue: Vietnamese immigrants

Choldenko, Gennifer. **Al Capone Shines My Shoes**. Dial 8, 2009. MS. 288 pages. ISBN-13: 978-0803734609

    In the sequel to *Al Capone Does My Shirts* Moose Flanagan thinks he is indebted to the mobster and worries his family will be kicked off Alcatraz Island if anyone finds out. With his mentally impaired sister off at the Esther P. Marinoff school, he thought his problems were

solved, but he receives a gangster's note in his laundry that may mean they've just begun.
Issue: Mentally impaired

de la Pena, Matt. **Mexican WhiteBoy**. Delacorte Books for Young Readers, 2008. MS. 256 pages. ISBN-13: 978-0385733106

Biracial baseball player, Danny Lopez, doesn't feel like he fits in with his dad's Mexican culture, nor the white culture at school. The baseball field is the only place he is comfortable. If he could only get control of his blazing fast ball, it might be his ticket to acceptance. When he meets Uno, an African American street thug with issues of his own, they team up on and off the field to navigate their problems.
Issue: Biracial kids

Ehrenberg, Pamela. **Ethan Suspended.** Eerdmans Books for Young Readers, 2007. MS. 336 pages. ISBN-10: 0802853242
Ethan Oppenheimer is sent to live with his old fashioned grandparents in Washington, D.C., after he is suspended from his suburban school in Pennsylvania. The only white student at his new junior high school, he finds it impossible to fit in.

Issue: Reverse Discrimination

Elkeles, Simone. **Perfect Chemistry**. Walker Books for Young Readers, 2008. MS/HS. 368 pages. ISBN-13: 978-0802798220
When Brittany Ellis, the school's golden girl, and Alex Fuentes, a Latino Bloods gang member, are assigned as chemistry lab partners, they clash immediately. However, as they get to know each other, they are surprised to find they have a lot in common and an undeniable attraction begins to smolder. Complications in both their lives find them turning to each other for support and ultimately romance.

Issue: Inter-racial dating

Engle, Margarita. **The Firefly Letters: A Suffragette's Journey to Cuba.** Henry Holt and Co. (BYR), 2010. MS. 160 pages. ISBN-13: 978-0805090826

This novel-in-verse chronicles the three months suffragette Fredrika Bremer spent in Cuba in 1851. The story focuses on three oppressed women: Fredrika, an upper class girl from Sweden, Cecilia, a teenage slave who is her translator, and Elena, a teenager whose family owns Cecilia. Elena, who is kept a virtual prisoner on her family's estate, finds herself envying the other two women's relative freedom.

Issue: Woman Suffrage

Hijuelos, Oscar. **Dark Dude**. Atheneum, 2008. HS. 448 pages ISBN-13: 978-1416948049
Rico Fuentes is a "dark dude" in 60's Harlem. Although he is Cuban-American, his light skin makes him the target of bullies of all races. He takes refuge in comic books and science fiction; but when harassment at school becomes unbearable, his best buddy turns to drugs, and his parents threaten to send him to military school, he heads off to a hippie commune in Wisconsin where he discovers, "Where you are, doesn't change who you are."

Issue: African Americans

Ingold, Jeanette. **Paper Daughter**. Harcourt Children's Books, 2010. MS. 224 pages. ISBN-13: 978-0152055073

Maggie Chen, an aspiring journalist who is still reeling from her father's death, takes an internship at a Seattle newspaper, where she uncovers a story that links her father's death to political corruption. At the same time she is investigating her father's lies about his family origins, which are related to a story about Fai-yi Li, a Chinese immigrant, whose narrative alternates with Maggie's.

Issue: Chinese Immigration

Jones, Traci L. **Finding My Place**. Farrar, Straus and Giroux (BYR), 2010. MS. 192 pages. ISBN-13: 978-0374335731

In 1975 Tiphanie, a talented African American girl, finds herself transferring to a predominately white school, when her parents, veterans of the civil rights movement, insist she must "uphold the race." Although she struggles at first, she is befriended by Jackie Sue, a hippie from the trailer park, who hides her problems behind a brash personality and a large vocabulary. Their complicated friendship enables Tiphanie, who is struggling with parental pressure, as well as racism at school, to cope; but ultimately it is she who has to be the strong one, as Jackie Sue's problems spiral out of control.

Issue: African Americans

Kerr. M.E. **Someone Like Summer**. HarperTeen, 2007. MS/HS. 272 pages. ISBN-10: 0061140996

In this story of star crossed lovers, blond blue-eyed Annabel is in love with Esteban, an illegal immigrant from Columbia. Prejudice is rampant in the town. Although Annabel's father, who is a contractor, hires the illegals, he doesn't want his daughter dating one of them, and Esteban's older sister calls Annabel "flour face" and thinks all white girls are loose. Will they be able to defy the odds and remain together?

Issue: Illegal immigrants

Levithan, David and John Green. **Will Grayson, Will Grayson**. Dutton Juvenile, 2010. HS. 304 pages. ISBN-13: 978-0525421580

In alternating chapters two characters named Will Grayson tell the story of Tiny Cooper, "The world's largest person who is really, really gay." Heterosexual Will Grayson is Tiny's best friend and homosexual will grayson, who writes in lower case letters because he's clinically depressed, becomes Tiny's boyfriend. Together they tell a story of friendship, infatuation and changing to become the person you really want to be.

Issue: Homosexuality

Myers, Walter Dean. **Riot**. EgmontUSA, 2009. MS. 192 pages. ISBN-13: 978-1606840009

The New York Draft Riots of 1863 are the subject of this novel which is written in screenplay format. 15-year-old Claire, the biracial daughter of a black man and an Irish woman, witnesses the tensions explode between the blacks in New York City and the Irish youth who are angry about the being drafted to fight for the freedom of people they see as job competition.

Issue: African-Americans and Irish Immigrants in the 19th Century

Na, An. **The Fold**. Putnam Juvenile, 2008. MS. 192 pages. ISBN-13: 978-0399242762

Joyce Park longs to be as beautiful as her older sister so that she can capture the attention of John Ford Kang, a popular, gorgeous classmate. When Joyce's wealthy aunt offers her cosmetic surgery to add a fold to her eyelids, she is at first appalled, then tempted. She wonders if she conforms more closely to conventional standards of beauty, will she gain the self-confidence she is lacking and win JFK's heart?

Issue: Asian Americans

Powers, J.L. **The Confessional.** Knopf Books for Young Readers, 2007. HS. 304 pages. ISBN-10: 0375838724

When a Mexican terrorist blows up himself and a bridge in El Paso, Texas, tension between the Mexican students and white students at a Catholic boys school heats up. Then white Mac Malone beats up Bernie Martinez and ends up dead the next day. Mac's best friend Greg Gonzalez attempts to find Mac's murderer and in the process stirs up a lot of questions about loyalties, faith and personal responsibility.

Issue: Mexican Immigrants

Smith, Sherri L. **Flygirl**. Putnam Juvenile, 2009. MS. 256 pages.
ISBN-13: 978-0399247095
In 1941 African American Ida Mae Jones, whose father taught her to fly his crop dusting plane, applies for the Women Airforce Service Program to help with the war effort at home. However, in order to do so, she has to leave her family and friends and pass as white. She completes a rigorous training program and flies dangerous missions, all the while guarding the secret that would put an end to her military career.

Issue: African American Females

Woodson, Jacqueline. **Peace, Locomotion**. Putnam Juvenile, 2009. MS. 144 pages.
ISBN-13: 978-0399246555

This sequel Woodson's novel-in-verse, *Locomotion*, find Lonnie Collins Motion writing letters to his sister Lili who is living with a separate foster family after their parents die in a fire. Lonnie is coming to turns with his living situation with Ms. Edna and worries with her about Jenkins, her grown son who is "over there fighting in the war." When Jenkins returns with physical and emotional problems, Lonnie begins longing for peace for his new family, his community and the world.

Issue: African Americans

Yoo, David. **Stop Me If You've Heard This One Before**. Hyperion Book CH, 2008. MS/HS. 384 pages. ISBN-13: 978-1423109075

Korean-American Albert Kim has decided to be an "intentional loser" at his new high school, until he gets involved with Mia Stone when they are both working at the local inn for the summer. Mia has recently broken up with her super jock boyfriend Ryan and is using the job as a distraction. Just as Albert and Mia's relationship is heating up, Ryan is diagnosed with cancer and Mia spends most of her time trying to help him. Albert is frustrated and confused as he tries to navigate the stormy seas of first love.

Issue: Korean Americans

Zenatti, Valerie. **A Bottle in the Gaza Sea**. Bloomsbury USA Children's Books; 1st edition, 2008. MS/HS. 160 pages. ISBN-13: 978-1599902005

When Naim, a Palestinian boy, finds a note in bottle on the beach, he begins communicating with Tal, the Israeli girl who wrote the note and had her brother throw it into the sea in Gaza. Through their email correspondence they develop a relationship that bridges the political chasm between their two countries.

Issue: Israeli/Palestinian conflict

Stories with a Soundtrack

Just as many movies have soundtracks that help define characters and move the plot forward, more and more books are including musical references that create a mood and provide background information. Frequently, the main characters bond over a shared love of music or friendships are initiated by one character introducing another to his or her favorite tunes. If readers have a working knowledge of the music incorporated in a novel, it helps them understand the personality of the characters and the stage upon which the story is played out. A variety of projects can be assigned to help students explore the story soundtrack and analyze how it impacts the story.

First, students can create a **playlist of songs** that are mentioned in the book and websites that can be accessed for sampling the music. If students have iTunes accounts, which are free, they can listen to thirty seconds of the song. Many groups have their own websites, which also provide samplings of the group's music. Googling the artist and song title frequently brings up a You Tube video of the song. Have students keep a running list of the songs mentioned in the book. Encourage them to listen to each song on the internet as they come across it in the book, so that they can reflect on how the song enhances the story. *Audrey, Wait!* by Robin Benway is a perfect book for this project because each chapter starts with a line from a popular song that acts as a chapter title and reflects the mood and what's happening in the chapter. (See example playlist project on the next page.) The reflection can be done song by song or a general reflection as to how the musical references enhanced the story as a whole.

Second, students who **play an instrument** can find the music to some of the songs mentioned in the book and record themselves playing them or perform them for the class. Tablatures for songs are frequently available for free on the internet. A book that particularly lends itself to this project is *The New Policeman* by Kate Thomson. Sheet music for a traditional Irish fiddle tune is provided at the end of each chapter.

Third, students can create a **wiki** which summarizes the story, mentioning songs that are referenced by the characters or author. They can provide links to the songs or information about the musicians within the wiki summary. There are a variety of wiki creation sites that are free, but many school districts have particular wiki software that they sanction. Wikispot and Wikispaces provide free wiki creation software on the internet, but may contain advertising.

Fourth, if the novel references one particular artist, for example *Debby Harry Sings in French* or *I Wanna Be Your Joey Ramone*, students may want to do a project which focuses on that particular musician and his/her music. Students could do research and create a **biographical project** about the artist which includes a discography. The project could be very open ended. A power point presentation which includes pictures and music downloads of the artist and his/her music, as well as information on how the music relates to the book would be very effective.

Of course, another option would be to allow students to design their own project that explores the novel's "soundtrack" and how it enhances character development and impacts the story.

Example Project

Audrey, Wait! Playlist

Group	Song	Website
My Chemical Romance	"Here Comes the Sound"	www.mychemicalromance.com
Mew	"156"	www.myspace.com/mew
Cowboy Junkies	"Bea's Song"	www.cowboyjunkies.com
The Velvet Underground	"Rock & Roll"	www.thevelvetunderground.co.uk/
Deathcab for Cutie	"Transatlanticism"	www.deathcabforcutie.com
Red Hot Chili Peppers	"Minor Thing"	www.redhotchilipeppers.com
The Cure	"Doing the Unstuck"	www.thecure.com
Radiohead	"Fake Plastic Trees"	www.radiohead.com
Fallout Boy	"Get Busy Living or Get Busy Dying"	www.falloutboyrock.com
Patti Smith	"Beneath the Southern Cross"	www.pattismith.net
Jimmy Eat World	"A Praise Chorus"	www.jimmyeatworld.com
Oasis	"Don't Look Back in Anger"	www.oasisinet.com
Belle & Sebastian	"Sukie in the Graveyard"	www.belleandsebastian.com
The Libertines	"Up the Bracket"	www.myspace.com/thelibertines
Pete Yorn	"Just Another"	www.peteyorn.com
The Strokes	"Barely Legal"	www.thestrokes.com
Jack's Mannequin	"Dark Blue"	www.jacksmannequin.com
Franz Ferdinand	"Take Me Out"	www.franzferdinand.co.uk
Voxtrot	"Biggest Fan"	www.voxtrot.net
Cartel	"A"	www.myspace.com/cartel
The Sounds	"Much too Long"	www.myspace.com/thesounds
Taking Back Sunday	"MakeDamnSure"	www.takingbacksunday.com
New Found Glory	"All Downhill From Here"	www.myspace.com/newfoundglory
Hellogoodbye	"All Your Love"	www.hellogoodbye.net
Joanna Newsom	"Peach, Plum, Pear"	www.myspace.com/joannanewsom
Regina Spektor	"Fidelity"	www.myspace.com/ reginaspektor
The Knife	"Heartbeats"	www.myspace.com/theknife
REM	"E-bow the Letter"	www.myspace.com/rem
The Academy Is…	"Slow Down"	www.theacademyis.com
Green Day	"Jesus of Suburbia"	www.greenday.com
The White Stripes	"I Think I Smell a Rat"	www.whitestripes.com
The Decemberists	"Of Angels and Angles"	www.thedecemberists.com
Yeah, Yeah, Yeahs	"Cheated Hearts"	www.yeahyeahyeahs.com
The Doves	"The Last Broadcast"	www.myspace.com/thedovesmyspace
Valencia	"Away We Go"	www.myspace.com/valencia
Guided by Voices	"Fair Touching"	www.gbv.com
AFI	"Summer Shudder"	www.myspace.com/afi
Stars	"Your Ex-lover Is Dead"	www.myspace.com/stars
Arcade Fire	"Windowsill"	www.arcadefire.com
Bloc Party	"Positive Tension"	www.blocparty.com
Anberlin	"Audrey, Start the Revolution"	www.anberlin.com

Reflection:

As I read *Audrey, Wait!*, I used iTunes to play 30 seconds of the song that was referenced at the beginning each chapter. I noted the artist and song, as well as a website for further information on my playlist. In her biographical information the author states: "Like Audrey, Robin Benway listens to her music way too loud, has an awesome best friend, and has attended more concerts than any human being should." Robin Benway's knowledge of alternative rock music is extensive. Many of the songs were relatively obscure and I listened to the group's most popular song, as well as the one that was referenced.

Many of the bands had a similar musical sound. Jack's Mannequin, Voxtrot, and TakingBackSunday are all fairly mainstream bands with great hooks sung by male lead singers. I thought about this particular sound when I was thinking about what Evan, Audrey's rock star ex-boyfriend, and his band would sound like. Joanna Newsom, Regina Spektor and the YeahYeahYeahs have female lead singers that have a similar tone quality. I thought these bands reflected when Audrey was trying to cope with her emotions and was feeling the most defiant. There were many British groups such as Franz Ferdinand and The Velvet Underground, which gave me some background for Simon Lolita's group.

In *Audrey, Wait!* particular lyrics from the songs were very important because they functioned as chapter titles and gave the reader a hint as to what would happen in the chapter and how Audrey was feeling. For example, the first chapter was entitled "Don't You Just Love Goodbyes?" from Mew's "156." This signaled Audrey's breakup with Evan and let the reader know that Audrey is very sarcastic. Chapter 4 was entitled "Making islands where no islands should go…" from Deathcab for Cutie's "Transatlanticism." In this chapter Audrey was talking about her relationship with Evan and how sometimes she felt very alone when she was with him because he was so obsessed with his music. "Lying awake in the garden, trying to get over your stardom..." from Pete Yorn's "Just Another" reflects how Audrey felt when the video for Evan's song "Audrey, Wait!" came out and it mirrored their breakup exactly. "So if you're lonely, you know I'm here waiting for you…" from Franz Ferdinand's "Take Me Out," is the title of the chapter where James, Audrey's co-worker at the ice cream store, defends her and then asks her out and they share their first kiss in the freezer. "You're everything I want, because you're everything I'm not…" from TakingBackSunday's "MakeDamnSure," is the chapter title for the chapter about James and Audrey's first date. She is so depressed about her notoriety and lack of privacy, that she finds his normalness attractive. "I'm sorry won't cut it for the rest of your life..." in Valencia's "Away We Go," refers to Evan finally calling Audrey and apologizing and then asking her to appear with him on MTV. "Live through this and you won't look back" from the Stars' "Your Ex-lover is Dead" introduces the beginning of Audrey's brutally candid performance on the show. She did not follow the cue cards and poured out all her feelings that had been bottled up. "As streetlights sing on Audrey's song.." from Anberlin's "Audrey Start the Revolution" wraps up the book and her "happily ever after."

The music references in *Audrey, Wait!* not only were informative, they also created a tone for the story. Audrey was definitely an alternative rock kind of girl. I was introduced to many new bands, as well as obscure songs from bands with which I am familiar. Listening to the songs on iTunes, I got a sense of the music which was being referenced in the story, whether it was the fictional music of rock groups in the novel, or actual bands which Audrey or other characters were listening to. This was truly a unique read which will appeal to a variety of readers, especially those who are music buffs. The book and music references were so popular that there is actually an IMix soundtrack for the book that you can buy on iTunes. The songs included on the soundtrack are as follows:

Audrey Waits! Soundtrack

Song	Artist
Cheating Hearts	Yeah Yeah Yeahs
Rock and Roll	The Velvet Underground
A Praise Chorus	Jimmy Eat World
Whatever happened to my rock	Black Motor Underground
Lying is the most fun a girl can have	Panic at the Disco
Just a Girl	No Doubt
405	Deathcab for Cutie
Just Another	Pete Yorn
Heartbeats	Jose Gonzalez
Your Ex-Lover is Dead	Stars

In addition, a contest was held for readers to record their own version of the song *Audrey, Wait!* Two guys from the band The XYZ Affair won the contest and their song can be heard on You Tube. You Tube also has a site organized with videos of many of the songs from bands and songs mentioned in the book.

SUGGESTED FORMAT FOR THE REFLECTION

Introduction

Students should identify how they accessed the music and created the play list. Additional information about the author or background about the bands could also be included.

General Overview

Students should identify the genre of music included in the book, or the different varieties of music if there are more than one. What the music choices reflect in terms of characters' personalities and plot points could also be included.

Story Summary

Students should summarize the story through musical references.

Conclusion

Students should reflect on whether or not the use of music references was effective and how it impacted their enjoyment of the book.

Additional Information

Of course, any additional information that is unique to the story can be included, such as the actual IMix Soundtrack that is available for *Audrey, Wait*, as well as the contest winner information for the Audrey, *Wait!* contest and the You Tube video site.

Novels with Soundtracks

Benway, Robin. **Audrey, Wait!** Razorbill, 2008. MS/HS. 313 pages. ISBN-13: 978-1595141910
Music: Alternative Rock and Roll

Blank, Jessica. **Karma for Beginners**. Hyperion Book CH, 2009. MS/HS. 320 pages. ISBN-13: 978-1423117513
Music: Classic rock and '80s New Wave

Brothers, Meagan. **Debbie Harry Sings in French**. Henry Holt and Co. (BYR); 1st edition, 2008. MS/HS. 240 pages. ISBN-13: 978-0805080803
Music: Debbie Harry/Blondie

Castelluci, Cecil. **Beige**. Candlewick, 2007. MS/HS. 320 pages. ISBN-10: 0763630667
Music: Punk rock

Cohn, Rachel. **Very LeFreak**. Knopf Books for Young Readers; 1 edition, 2010. HS. 320 pages. ISBN-13: 978-0375857584
Music: Rock and Roll

Dessen, Sarah. **Just Listen**. Speak, 2008. MS. 400 pages. ISBN-13: 978-0142410974.
Music: Rock and roll

Donnelly, Jennifer. **Revolution**. Delacorte Books for Young Readers, 2010. MS/HS. 496 pages. ISBN-10: 0385737637
Music: Classical, Rock and Roll, Hip Hop

Eulberg, Elizabeth. **The Lonely Hearts Club**. Point; 1 edition, 2009. MS.320 pages. ISBN-13: 978-0545140317
Music: Beatles

Forman, Gayle. **If I Stay**. Dutton Juvenile (April 2, 2009) 208 pages. ISBN-13: 978-0525421030
Music: Cello, rock and roll

Going, K.L. **King of the Screwups**. Harcourt Children's Books; 1 edition, 2009. MS/HS. 320 pages. ISBN-13: 978-0152062583
Music: Glam rock

Hughes, Mark Peter. **Lemonade Mouth**. Delacorte Books for Young Readers, 2007. MS/HS. 352 pages. ISBN-10: 0385733925
Music: Jingles, garage bands

Kidd, Ronald. **On Beale Street**. Simon & Schuster Children's Publishing, 2008. MS/HS. 256 pages. ISBN-13: 978-1416933878
Music: Rock and Roll, Elvis Presley, Blues

Kluger, Steve. **My Most Excellent Year: A Novel of Love, Mary Poppins, & Fenway Park**. Puffin; Reprint edition, 2009. MS/HS. 416 pages. ISBN-13: 978-0142413432
Music: Musicals

Levithan, David and John Green. **Will Grayson, Will Grayson**. Dutton Juvenile, 2010. HS. 304 pages. ISBN-13: 978-0525421580
Music: Musicals

Kuehnert, Stephanie. **I Wanna Be Your Joey Ramone**. MTV, 2008. HS. 352 pages. ISBN-10: 1416562699
Music: The Ramones

Madigan, L.K. **Flash Burnout**. Houghton Mifflin Books for Children, 2009. MS/HS. 336 pages. ISBN-13: 978-0547194899
Music: Rock and Roll

Myers, Walter Dean. **Harlem Summer**. Scholastic Press, 2007. MS. 176 pages. ISBN-10: 043936843X
Music: Jazz

Printz, Yvonne. **The Vinyl Princess**. HarperTeen, 2009. MS/HS. 320 pages. ISBN-13: 978-0061715839
Music: Rock and Roll

Rapp, Adam. **Punkzilla**. Candlewick, 2009. HS. 256 pages. ISBN-13: 978-0763630317
Music: Punk and rock and roll

Skovron, Jon. **Struts and Frets**. Amulet Books, 2009. MS/HS. 304 ISBN-13: 978-0810941748
Music: Rock and Roll and Jazz

Supplee, Suzanne. **Somebody Everybody Listens To**. Dutton Juvenile; 1 edition, 2010. MS. 304 pages. ISBN-13: 978-0525422426
Music: Country Western

Thompson, Kate. **The New Policeman**. HarperTeen, 2007. MS. 448 pages. ISBN-10: 0061174270
Music: Irish ballads

van de Ruit, John. **Spud.** Razorbill, 2007. MS/HS. 352 pages. ISBN-10: 1595141707
Music: Musicals

Woodson, Jacqueline. **After Tupac & D Foster**. Putnam Young Adult, 2008. MS. 160 pages. ISBN-13: 978-0399246548
 Music: Tupac Shakir

ART WORLD CONNECTIONS IN YOUNG ADULT NOVELS

Young adult novels, which explore the characters' connections with the arts, as well as their ability to express themselves through artistic renderings, are becoming more and more prevalent in new YA titles. Many characters in these books escape the conflict in their lives by disappearing into artistic endeavors. Their art work helps them work through problems in a constructive manner.

Ultimately, we as teachers hope to connect with our students by introducing them to books that speak to their passions and dreams. Many of our students are artists who have little opportunity to express themselves artistically in a language arts classroom. The following list of books involves art in one way or another. Invite students to read an art related YA book and then create an artistic project that reflects what they learned from the book. The projects can take many forms, depending on the art form explored in the novel.

Project Ideas

Explore the classic artists whose works inspire the story
> Example: Explore the work of the artist Matisse who inspires Lucy or Chuck Close who inspires Sam in *If I Have a Wicked Step Mother, Where's My Prince?* by Melissa Kantor. Create a power point presentation to detail what you discovered.

Create a piece of art work using the art form explored in the book
> Example: Create a collage similar to the ones Terra creates in *North of Beautiful* by Justina Chen Headley. (Suggestion: have the collage reflect who you are and display the elements on a silhouette of your profile.)

Make a video of a scene inspired by the story or recreate a scene from the book.
> Example: Chronicle events in your recent history such as Viola does for her year at Prefect Academy in *Viola in Reel Life* by Adriana Trigiani.

Make a digital picture album which includes pictures related in some way to the story. Include captions explaining the connection.
> Example: In *Flash Burnout* by L.K. Madigan, Blake Hewson does a collection of "lonely shots" that include Marissa's drug addict mother, whereas Marissa focuses on flowers for her photo essay. Choose a topic and create a photo essay of your own and explain how you were inspired by the book.

Create a book cover with an artistic rendering that you feel captures the essence of the book.
> Example: Pick an idea from the book *Same Difference* by Siobhan Vivian and create a sidewalk chalk drawing reflecting it. Photograph the sidewalk art and use it to design a book cover for *Same Difference*.

Alexie, Sherman. **The Absolutely True Diary of a Part-Time Indian**. Little, Brown Young Readers, MS/HS. 2007. 240 pages. ISBN-10: 0316013684

Art form: Cartoons

Amato, Mary. **Invisible Lines**. EgmontUSA, 2009. MS. 336 pages. ISBN-13: 978-1606840108

Art form: Drawing and cartoons

Avi. **The Seer of Shadows**. HarperCollins, 2008. MS. 208 pages. ISBN-10: 0060000155

Art form: photography

Balliett, Blue. **The Calder Game**. Scholastic Press; 1st edition, 2008. MS. 400 pages. ISBN-13: 978-0439852074

Art form: Alexander Calder sculptures

Brasheres, Ann. **Forever in Blue**. Delacorte Books for Young Readers, 2007. MS/HS. 400 pages. ISBN-10: 0385729367

Art form: Painting, film
Broach, Elise. **Masterpiece**. Henry Holt and Co. (BYR), 2008. MS. 304 pages. ISBN-13: 978-0805082708
Art Form: Pen and Ink drawings and Albrecht Durer

Carter, Ally. **Heist Society**. Hyperion Book CH, 2010. MS. 304 pages. ISBN-13: 978-1423116394

Art form: Classical artists' painting

Crane, E.M. **Skin Deep**. Delacorte Books for Young Readers, 2008. MS. 288 pages. ISBN-10: 0385734794

Art form: Raku pottery

Doyle, Roddy and others. **Click.** Arthur A. Levine Books, 2007. MS/HS. 256 pages. ISBN-10: 0439411386

Art form: photography

Gallagher, Liz. **The Opposite of Invisible**. Wendy Lamb Books, 2008. MS/HS. 160 pages. ISBN-10: 0375841520

Art form:Animation

Headley, Justina Chen. **Girl Overboard**. Little, Brown Young Readers, 2008. MS/HS. 352 pages. ISBN-13: 978-0316011303

Art form: Manga

Headley, Justina Chen. **North of Beautiful**. Little, Brown Young Readers; 1 edition, 2009. 384 pages. ISBN-13: 978-0316025058

Art form: Collage

Hoffman, Mary. **The Falconer's Knot: A Story of Friars, Flirtation and Foul Play.** Bloomsbury USA Children's Books, 2007. MS/HS. 288 pages. ISBN-10: 1599900564

Art form: Frescos in Renaissance Italy

Howell, Simmone. **Notes from the Teenage Underground.** Bloomsbury, 2007. HS. 335 pages. ISBN-10: 1582348359
 Art form: film (Andy Warhol)

Konigsburg, E.L. **The Mysterious Edge of the Heroic World.** Ginee Seo Books, 2007. MS. 256 pages. ISBN-10: 1416949720
Art form: Degenerate Art and Modigliani

Madigan, L.K. **Flash Burnout**. Houghton Mifflin Books for Children, 2009. MS/HS. 336 pages. ISBN-13: 978-0547194899

Art form: Photography

Magnum, Lisa. **The Hourglass Door**. Shadow Mountain, 2009. MS. 432 pages.
ISBN-13: 978-1606410936

Art form: Leonardo Da Vinci

Napoli, Donna Jo. **The Smile**. Dutton Juvenile, 2008. MS. 240 pages. ISBN-13: 978-0525479994

Art form: Leonardo Da Vinci

Scott, Elaine. **Secrets of the Cirque Medrano**. Charlesbridge Publishing, 2008. 216 pages. ISBN-13: 978-1570917127

Art form: Picasso

Selznik, Brian. **The Invention of Hugo Cabret.** Scholastic Press, 2007. MS.
533 pages. ISBN-10: 0439813786

Art: Graphic drawings and Film –George Melies

Trigiani, Adrianna. **Viola in Reel Life**. HarperTeen, 2009. MS. 288 pages. ISBN-13: 978-0061451027

Art form: film making

Vivian, Siobhan. **Same Difference**. Push, 2009. MS. 304 pages. ISBN-13: 978-0545004077

Art form: Sidewalk chalk drawing and others

Watson, Sasha. **Vidalia in Paris**. Viking Juvenile, 2008. MS/HS. 288 pages. ISBN-13: 978-0670010943

Art form: copying the classics

Additional Titles involving classic artists
From the Mixed Up Files of Mrs. Basil E. Frankweiler - Konigsburg – Michaelangelo
Chasing Vermeer – Balliett – Vermeer
The Wright 3 – Balliett – Frank Lloyd Wright
If I Have a Wicked Stepmother, Where's My Prince? – Kantor – Matisse, Close, & others
The Truth About Forever – Dessen – sculpture
The Girl with the Pearl Earring – Chevalier – Vermeer
Girl in Hyacinth Blue-Vreeland – Vermeer
The Da Vinci Code – Brown – Leonardo da Vinci

CULTURAL COMPARISONS

Young adult novels about kids from different cultures lend themselves to teaching the writing of comparison contrast essays. The unit's introduction should include a preview of the writing project. Depending on the students' level of sophistication, the essay can range from a simple four paragraph essay to a fully developed paper, where each topic is explored in great detail. As students are reading their novel, they should be noting similarities and differences between their own culture and the culture represented in the book. Brainstorming issues that vary from culture to culture, such as governments, food, religion, climate, holidays and living conditions, will help students organize their search.

Jean Kwok's *Girl in Translation* lends itself to this assignment. Drawing on Kwok's personal experience, this debut novel tells the story of a Chinese immigrant who must make the transition between cultures. After her father's death, Ah Kim, 11, leaves Hong Kong in the 1980s and moves with her mother to the US. Her mother's older sister, who owns a garment factory in Brooklyn, gives Ma a job bagging skirts and an unheated, roach infested apartment in the slums. Ma winds up working 12-hour-plus days in the factory. Ah Kim, now known as Kimberly, joins her after school hours and together they perform the exhausting job well into the night, when Kim's classmates are studying. When Kimberley starts public school, she speaks little English, but she excels in math and science. Her teacher at first thinks she's cheating, but after further examination reveals Kimberley's brilliance, the teacher recommends her for a scholarship to a prestigious private school. Eventually, she ends up at Yale and then Harvard Medical School. More intriguing are her relationships with her best friend Annette, a Chinese-American boy who works at the factory, an Anglo boyfriend and of course, her struggle to rectify her new American life with the old world expectations of her mother.

Comparison/Contrast Worksheet

You may want to give students a worksheet to use in tracking similarities and differences as they read the book. The following notes for *Girl in Translation* can be used as an example for students.

Similarities between the main character and the reader

Topic	Similarity
Friendship	Kimberley has a best friend who is more privileged that she is
Education	Kimberley excels at math and science and gets a scholarship to college
Employment	Kimberley works in a library during high school

Differences

Topic	Main Character	Reader
Family	Mother & daughter Father died	Mother, father, sister, and brother
Government	Communist China	Democratic America
Religion	Buddhist	Christian
Food	Rice w/ toppings	Meat and potatoes
Home	Tenement apartment	Suburban home
Behavior	Shy and reclusive	Outgoing

Once the readers have finished their books and their worksheet, they should choose their topics and fill in the following graphic organizer for their essay. A sample four paragraph essay for *Girl in Translation* follows.

GRAPHIC ORGANIZER FOR COMPARISON/CONTRAST ESSAY

I. Introduction
    A. Main Character Introduction
        1) Cultural background_____
        2) Defining Characteristics
            a._____
            b._____
    B. Reader Introduction
        1) Cultural background_____
        2) Defining Characteristics
            a. _____
            b._____
    C. Similar yet different thesis

II. Similarities
    A)Topic_____
        1) Detail_____
        2) Detail_____
    B)Topic_____
        1) Detail_____
        2) Detail_____
    C) Topic_____
        1) Detail_____
        2) Detail_____

III. Differences
    A. Topic_____
        1) Main Character
            a. Detail_____
            B. Detail_____
        2) Reader
            a. Detail_____
            b. Detail_____
    B. Topic_____
        1) Main Character
            a. Detail_____
            b. Detail_____
        3) Reader
            a. Detail_____
            b. Detail_____
    C. Topic_____
        1) Main Character
            a. Detail_____
            b. Detail_____
        2) Reader
            a. Detail_____
            b. Detail_____
IV. Conclusion
    A. Restate similar yet different thesis
    B. Summarize similarities
    C. Summarize differences
    D. Wrap-up sentence

Girl in Translation by Jean Kwok tells the story of an eleven-year-old Chinese girl who immigrates with her mother to New York from Hong Kong in the 1980s. It follows her efforts to make the transition between cultures from her arrival in the United States in elementary school through adulthood. Ah Kim is a brilliant student who knows that her academic prowess is the key to her successful assimilation into American culture. I am an American college graduate with a master's degree in educating gifted children. I grew up in the Midwest in a family which includes my mother, father, sister and brother. Although Ah Kim is worlds apart from me culturally, we still have some significant similarities.

Our similarities include valuing education, having a wealthy childhood best friend and working in a library during our formative years. Ah Kim, whose American name is Kimberley, says of school, "It was as if school were a vast machine and I a cog perfectly formed to fit in it." I, too, was well suited to school. Like Kimberley, I am a very good test taker with a natural talent for math. Our families both value education and place a heavy emphasis on achievement. Academia is a world where we both flourished. During our childhoods, Kimberley and I also each had a devoted best friend who was from a much wealthier family. While we spent our summers working, our best friends were off on exotic vacations and international educational trips. Sleepovers were always at the best friend's house, and she introduced us to things we were not exposed to in our less privileged upbringings. Finally, Kimberley and I both worked in a library during high school. Our library duties were fairly undemanding, thus we had a lot of time to read books while we were working, as well as socialize with our friends who came to the library to see us. We were both free to take home books that were deemed too worn out for the library collection. Spending so much time surrounded by books, we both developed a lifelong passion for reading.

Although Kimberley and I have a few similarities, our differences are much more obvious. Kimberley never strayed too far from her Chinese roots. Our childhood homes, religions, and diets are vastly different. Kimberley spent six years living in a rat and roach infested, unheated tenement apartment with her mother. I grew up in a suburban home in Indianapolis, Indiana with an intact nuclear family. I had my own room, whereas Kim slept with her mother on a mattress, which they placed near the stove which was their only source of heat. Their home was filled with religious symbols. They "set up five altars in the kitchen: to the earth god, the ancestors, the heavens, the kitchen god and Kuan Yin. Kuan Yin is the goddess of compassion who cares for all…" My Baptist monotheistic religious background included going to church every Sunday and church camp during the summer. Kim and her mother went to the Buddhist temple and prayed to all the altars in their home on a daily basis. They "lit incense and poured tea and rice wine before the many altars." Whereas Baptists worship one god, Kim prayed to different gods for different things. She said, "We prayed to the local earth god of the building and apartment to grant permission to live there in peace, to the ancestors and heavens to keep away troubles and evil people, to the kitchen god to keep us from starving and to Kuan Yin to bring us our hearts' desires." Her diet consisted mainly of rice with a variety of toppings. Where my family's meals consisted mainly of meat and potatoes, Kim and her mother occasionally had fish, tofu, or lichee nuts to compliment the rice. When Kim got sick, her mother plied her with pulverized deer antlers, crushed crickets and octopus tentacles. My mother's remedies included chicken soup, aspirin and Robutusin. Although Kimberley ultimately became a doctor and was able to afford a much higher standard of living, she and mother never completely left behind their Chinese culture and beliefs.

As I read *Girl in Translation*, I was constantly struck by the cultural differences that separated Kimberley from her American classmates. Her impoverished childhood, Buddhist beliefs, and Chinese cultural traditions made it difficult for her to relate to the students who attended the private school she attended. Yet like me, she valued education and academic success, sought the companionship of a best friend and loved reading. Her ultimate success in matriculating to Yale and Harvard medical school are testimony to her successful transition between cultures.

Recommended Novels for Cultural Comparisons

Alvarez, Julia. **Return to Sender**. Knopf Books for Young Readers, 2009. MS. 336 pages. ISBN-13: 978-0375858383

Culture: Mexican immigrants

Apelqvist, Eva. **Swede Dreams**. Puffin. 2007. MS/HS. 224 pages. ISBN-10: 0142407461

Culture: Swedish

Beah, Ishmael. **A Long Way Gone – Memoirs of a Boy Soldier**. Sarah Crichton Books, 2007. HS. 240 pages. ISBN-10: 0007247087

Culture: Africa – Sierra Leone in the 1990s

Cornwell, Autumn. **Carpe Diem**. Feiwel & Friends, 2007. MS/HS. 368 pages. ISBN-10: 0312367929

Culture: Maylaysia, Cambodia, and Laos

de la Pena, Matt. **Mexican WhiteBoy**. Delacorte Books for Young Readers, 2008. MS. 256 pages. ISBN-13: 978-0385733106

Culture: Hispanic

Engle, Margarita. **The Firefly Letters: A Suffragette's Journey to Cuba.** Henry Holt and Co. (BYR), 2010. MS. 160 pages. ISBN-13: 978-0805090826

Culture: Cuba in 1851

Engle, Margarita. **Tropical Secrets: Holocaust Refugees in Cuba**. Henry Holt and Co. (BYR); 1 edition, 2009. MS.208 pages. ISBN-13: 978-0805089363

Culture: Jewish refugee in Cuba during WWII

Fukuda, Andrew Kia. **Crossing**. AmazonEncore, 2010. MS/HS. 217 pages. ISBN-13: 978-1935597032

Culture: Chinese American

Headley, Justina Chen. **North of Beautiful**. Little, Brown Young Readers; 1 edition, 2009. 384 pages. ISBN-13: 978-0316025058

Culture: Chinese

Jones, Traci L. **Finding My Place**. Farrar, Straus and Giroux (BYR), 2010. MS. 192 pages. ISBN-13: 978-0374335731

Culture: African American in 1975

Kadohata, Cynthia, **A Million Shades of Gray**. Atheneum; 1 edition, 2010. MS. 216 pages. ISBN-13: 978-1416918837

Culture: South Viet Namese in 1975

Kephart, Beth. **The Heart is Not a Size**. HarperTeen; 1 edition, 2010. MS. 256 pages. ISBN-13: 978-0061470486

Culture: Mexican

Kwok, Jean. **Girl in Translation**. Riverhead Hardcover, 2010. MS/HS. 304 pages. ISBN-13: 978-1594487569

Culture: Chinese immigrant in the 1980s

Liu, Cynthea. **The Great Call of China**. Puffin, 2009. MS. 224 pages.ISBN-13: 978-0142411346

Culture: Chinese

Medina, Meg. **Milagros: Girl from Away**. Henry Holt and Co. (BYR), 2008. MS. 288 pages ISBN-13: 978-08050823

Culture: Carribbean

Na, An. **The Fold**. Putnam Juvenile, 2008. MS. 192 pages. ISBN-13: 978-0399242762
Culture: Asian American

Park, Linda Sue. **A Long Walk to Water**. Clarion Books, 2010. MS. 128 pages. ISBN-13: 978-0547251271

Culture: Lost Boys of the Sudan

Sheth, Kashmira. **Boys without Names**. Balzer + Bray, 2010. MS. 316 pages. ISBN-13: 978-0061857607

Culture: Mumbai, India

Staples, Suzanne Fisher. **The House of Djinn**. Farrar, Straus and Giroux, 2008. MS. 224 pages. ISBN-10: 0374399360

Culture: Islamic culture in Pakistan

Supplee, Suzanne. **When Irish Guys Are Smiling**. Puffin, 2008. MS. 224 pages. ISBN-10: 0142410160.

Culture: Irish

Venkatraman, Padma. **Climbing the Stairs**. Speak, 2010. MS.272 pages. ISBN-13: 978-0142414903

Cuture: Bombay, India in 1941

Watson, Sasha. **Vidalia in Paris**. Viking Juvenile, 2008. MS/HS. 288 pages. ISBN-13: 978-0670010943

Culture: French

Zenatti, Valerie. **A Bottle in the Gaza Sea**. Bloomsbury USA Children's Books; 1st edition, 2008. MS/HS. 160 pages. ISBN-13: 978-1599902005

Cultures: Palestinian and Israeli

AUTHOR STUDY

When students find a book they like, they frequently want to read more by that author. The selection of new young adult books in *What's New in Young Adult Novels?* has many offerings from authors who have proven track records. Invite students to read the latest title from a particular author, and then do a biographical study of the author. Investigating the author's background may shed light on elements of his/her life that have influenced or have been woven into their stories. The internet is a great source for biographical information and many of the authors have blogs in which they share personal information. Finally, have students select another of the author's books to read.

After they have completed these three steps have them present the information to the class. Ideas for this project might include an author poster or brochure which has short reviews of the two books read, as well as biographical information and additional titles by the author. If they want to do a performance, have them do an "Author's Visit."[5] The student comes to class as the author, talks to the class and has one of his/her friends interview him/her. Creative costuming might include Pam Munoz Ryan wearing cowgirl clothes or Julius Lester wearing a Roman toga.

Students might want to choose current titles from the following authors. Additional titles by the same author are also suggested.

Anderson, Laurie Halse. <u>**Twisted**</u>.
> *Speak*
> *Fever 1793*
> *Catalyst*
> *Wintergirls*

Avi. <u>**The Traitor's Gate.**</u>
> *The True Confessions of Charlotte Doyle*
> *The Seer of Shadows*
> *Crispin-The End of Time*
> *Hard Gold*

Bauer, Joan. <u>**Peeled**</u>.
> *Hope Was Here*
> *Backwater*
> *Rules of the Road*
> *Sticks*

Blume, Judy. <u>**BFF**. **Two novels by Judy Blume--Just As Long As We're Together/Here's to You, Rachel Robinson.**</u>
> *Are You There God? It's Me Margaret*
> *Fudge*
> *Superfudge*
> *Then Again Maybe I Won't*
> *Tiger Eyes*

Brooks, Kevin. <u>**Being**</u>.
> *The Road of the Dead*
> *Kissing the Rain*
> *Martyn Pig*
> *Black Rabbit Summer*
> *Lucas*

Cabot, Meg. <u>**Airhead**</u>.
> *The Princess Diaries (series)*
> *An American Girl*
> *Avalon High*
> *How to Be Popular*
> *Being Nikki*

---

[5] Blasingame, James. *Books That Don't Bore 'Em*. Scholastic Teaching Resources. 2007. 106.

Cooney, Caroline. Enter Three Witches.
The Face on the Milk Carton
Diamonds in the Shadows
Driver's Ed
If the Witness Lied

Creech, Sharon. The Castle Corona.
Walk Two Moons
Absolutely Normal Chaos
Chasing Redbird
Bloomability

Crutcher, Chris. Deadline.
Whale Talk
Crazy Horse Electric Game
Chinese Handcuffs
Ironman

Curtis, Christopher Paul. Elijah from Buxton.
Bud, Not Buddy
The Watsons Go to Birmingham, 1963
Bucking the Sarge

Dessen, Sarah. Along for the Ride.
The Truth About Forever
Just Listen
Lock and Key
Dreamland
This Lullaby

Draper, Sharon. November Blues.
Fire in the Rock
Copper Sun
The Battle of Jericho
Tears of a Tiger
Forged by Fire

Farmer, Nancy. The Land of the Silver Apples.
The Ear, the Eye and the Arm
The Sea of Trolls
The House of the Scorpion
A Girl Named Disaster

Haddix, Margaret Peterson. Found. (Series)
Double Identity
Turnabout
Shadow Children Series
Just Ella

Funke, Cornelia. Igraine the Brave.
The Thief Lord
Dragon Rider
Inkheart
Ink Spell

Hobbs, Will. Go Big or Go Home.
Jackie's Wild Seattle
Changes in Latitude
Downriver
Jason's Gold
Ghost Canoe

Kerr. M. E. Someone Like Summer.
  Fell
  Gentlehands
  Dinky Hocker Shoots Smack
  Deliver Us from Evie
Konigsburg, E.L. The Mysterious Edge of the Heroic World.
  From the Mixed Up Files of Mrs. Basil E. Frankwiler
  The View from Saturday
  The Second Mrs. Gioconda
  A Proud Taste of Scarlet and Miniver
Lasky, Kathryn. Ashes.
  Night Journey
  Beyond the Divide
  Beyond the Burning Time
  The Last Days of Pompeii
Le Guin, Ursula. Powers.
  Voices
  Gifts
  The Wizard of Earthsea
  The Tombs of Atuan
  The Farthest Shore
Lester, Julius. Cupid-A Tale of Love and Desire.
  Day of Tears
  Pharaoh's Daughter: A Novel
  Othello: A Novel
  All Our Wounds Forgiven
Lupica, Mike. The Big Field.
  Travel Team
  Summer Ball
  Heat
  Two-Minute Drill
Mazer, Norma Fox. The Missing Girl.
  A Figure of Speech
  Silver
  Girlhearts
  Taking Terri Mueller
McKinley, Robin. Dragonhaven.
  The Blue Sword
  The Hero and the Crown
  Beauty
  Spindle's End
Myers, Walter Dean. Sunrise Over Fallujah.
  Game
  Harlem Summer
  Monster
  Somewhere in the Darkness
  Hoops
  Scorpions
Peck, Richard. On the Wings of Heroes.
  A Long Way from Chicago
  A Year Down Yonder
  Here Lies the Librarian
  The River Between Us

Pullman, Phillip. Once Upon a Time in the North.
                Ruby in the Smoke (Sally Lockhart Series)
                   The Shadow in the North
                   The Tiger in the Well
                   The Tin Princess
          The Golden Compass (Dark Materials Series)
                   The Subtle Knife
                   The Amber Spyglass

Rinaldi, Ann. Juliet's Moon.
      Or Give Me Death
      The Coffin Quilt
      Come Juneteenth
      An Unlikely Friendship

Ryan, Pam Munoz. Paint the Wind.
      Esperanza Rising
      Becoming Naomi Leon
      Riding Freedom
      The Dreamer

Sleator, William. Test.
      The House of Stairs
      Interstellar Pig
      Into the Dream
      Duplicate
      Strange Attractors

Soto, Gary. Mercy on these Teenage Chimps.
      Baseball in April
      Living Up the Street
      A Simple Plan
      Accidental Love

Spinelli, Jerry. Smiles to Go
      Maniac Magee
      Stargirl
      Love, Stargirl
      Eggs
      Milkweed

Strasser, Todd. Boot Camp.
      The Wave
      Can't Get There From Here
      Give a Boy a Gun
      How I Created My Perfect Prom Date

White. Ruth. Way Down Deep.
      Belle Prater's Boy
      The Search for Belle Prater
      Memories of Summer
      Sweet Holler Creek
      Weeping Willow

Woodson, Jacqueline. Peace, Locomotion.
      Miracle's Boys
      Feathers
      The Other Side
      Locomotion
      After Tupac and D Foster

AMAZON WEB PAGE PROJECT

When I attended the Colorado Teen Literature Conference a couple years ago, one of the most intriguing sessions I attended, "Integrating Technology in a Best Practices Language Arts Classroom,"[6] was led by Betsey and Charles Coleman from Colorado Academy in Denver, Colorado. One of their suggested activities for the classroom, the "Camazon" project, instructs students in creating a mock Amazon web page for an assigned book. The project not only has students using the latest technology, but also requires them to use higher level thinking skills in reflecting on their reading. For an Amazon web page, students include product details and a list of the author's other books, write spotlight reviews, create a "customers who bought this book also bought/viewed these books," section, and write an email to a friend about the book. Students make connections between the books they have read and the book they are reviewing; they use their own voice to respond, and they provide evidence in their spotlight reviews.

For the Colorado Academy "Camazon" web page project, students were grouped and given a limited number of texts to choose from that were coming-of-age novels. Last year the technological aspect of the project was done using Dreamweaver. The final projects were quite sophisticated, including hyperlinks, music, moving graphics, and interactive elements. Handouts included detailed guidelines about how to use various computer programs, how to write in each genre, and how the projects would be assessed. Kimberly Jans, Colorado Academy's upper school technology coordinator, helped create a project template for the students to use and Sophie Swanson created the evaluation rubric. To view several creative examples of this project online, readers can go to http://mustangs.coloacad.org/homeimages/camazon/ca_amazon.htm . One of my favorite examples for the book *Hard Love* by Ellen Whittlinger includes an inventive use of graphics, as well as music, to enhance to content.

In 2010 students used Glogster EDU to create their projects. According to their website, "Glogster EDU is the leading global education platform for the creative expression of knowledge and skills in the classroom and beyond. They empower educators and students with the technology to create GLOGS - online multimedia posters - with text, photos, videos, graphics, sounds, drawings, data attachments and more." If you are feeling adventuresome, you might want to explore the world of GLOGS. More information can be found at http://www.glogster.com/.

However, the project could also be simplified. Using the following basic ideas for the project, teachers could adapt it in many different ways, including making it an individual assignment, allowing students to choose their own titles, or abbreviating some of the project requirements. If access to or knowledge of technology is limited, teachers could also assign a print project, rather than a web based product.

---

[6] Coleman, Betsey and Charles. *Integrating Technology in a *Best Practices* Language Arts Classroom*, Colorado Teen Literature Conference, April 5, 2008.

AMAZON CHECKLIST

Banner
Camazon heading
This page was created by…your names (just first ones if posted on the web)
Include a short quote from the book that captures its essence. (Example for *Hard Love*
by Ellen Wittlinger: " I am immune to Emotion. I have been ever since I can remember."

Title and Author
Create a button so that viewer can click on author to see his/her other books.
On the other books page you need icons/ images as well as titles of 4 or more books.

Product Details
Cost
Available in Paperback?
Length
Publisher
ISBN
Language

Spotlight Reviews
2 fake reader review of approximately 350 words (3 reviews for extra credit)
Rate the item using the 4 stars system (Put this before each spotlight review)
Include at least one good Spotlight Reviews and one mixed one.
Title and fake author (may be entertaining but not over-the-top silly)

Editorial Reviews
Taken from somewhere else
Cited
Link created if editorial is too long

Better Together
Project book title and another related to it (use cover images from the internet)
Not another novel by the same author
Write a short paragraph about why you put these two titles together

Customers who bought this book also bought or viewed
At least 4 books and a paragraph (short) of explanation explaining the relationship
between the two

Email a friend
E-mail format
Interesting visuals
Email language (very different from formal review

AMAZON WEB PAGE RUBRIC

CONTENT

Banner
- o First Names
- o Title and Author
- o Link to other books written by author and images of those books

Product Details
- o Cost
- o Available in Paperback?
- o Length
- o Publisher
- o ISBN
- o language

Spotlight Reviews
- o 2 reviews each approximately 350 words (or 3 for extra credit)
- o positive review
- o mixed review (not negative)
- o number of people who found them helpful
- o star system
- o title and fake author (entertaining but not silly or over-the-top)

Editorial Review
- o taken from somewhere else
- o cited
- o link created if your editorial is too long

Better Together
- o Another related book
- o Picture of both of the books
- o Paragraph explaining why the books work together

Customers Who Bought This Book Also Bought or Viewed
- o Four books with cover picture
- o Title/author
- o Comparison for each with main book.
  Use specific details. It is not a summary

Email a Friend
- o Email format
- o Interesting visuals
- o Email language
- o VERY DIFFERENT from other reviews

CREATIVITY
- o Interesting backgrounds
- o Music that is appropriate for your book
- o Flash and movement

MECHANICS
- o Readability
- o Titles italicized unless they are links
- o Is language appropriate in each section to purpose and tone (spotlight reviews, email)
- o Have you checked EVERY WORD and sentence for grammatical and spelling errors?

PREPARING FOR AN AUTHOR VISIT

If you want a successful author visit, it is always wise to prepare your students before the author arrives. Of course, having the students read one or more of the author's books is preferable, but very rarely does one have access to enough copies to do this. Therefore, the following steps are helpful in giving the students enough background so that they are actively engaged with the author and his/her presentation. Prepare a packet of information for language arts teachers to present in their classrooms. Then have the teachers send students who are sincerely interested in hearing the author talk.

1) Visit the author's website, if he/she has one.
2) Introduce biographical information about the author. The web is an easy place to find out about his/her life.
3) Discuss other books the author has written, especially if his/her newest title is a sequel.
4) Generally, the author is on tour to promote his/her latest book. Most kids will not have read it. Read it yourself, if possible.
5) Give the students background information about the current book, such as a synopsis and current reviews of the book that praise it.
6) Finally, pick excerpts to read to the kids that will get them excited about it.
7) Limit the audience. An intimate setting with 50-100 well-prepared kids creates a much better climate than an auditorium filled with all the students in the school whether they want to be there or not.

Example Author Visit Preparation Packet for Teachers

David Clement-Davies
New Book: *FELL*
Sequel to *THE SIGHT*
1) Biographical information about Author
Clement-Davies was born in 1964 and went to Westminster School and Edinburgh University. There, Clement-Davies read History and English literature, specializing in the Italian Renaissance, and Russian literature and society. For many years, he dreamed of one day becoming an actor, taking a drama course and working in theater. However, he was also interested in writing and soon became a freelance travel journalist.

His first novel, *Fire Bringer*, was a tremendous success. According to his website, he had many inspirations for the book: "…Nature and the wild have always played a big part in his writing. Perhaps it was the rich memories of part of his childhood growing up in Wales, or just the wonderful animal books he has read."

Clement-Davies lives in a little mountain home in the Andalusia region of Spain for much of the year, but he also lives in London. He has written a musical, two adult novels, and is currently working on a play, set in the present and the 17th century, called *Startled Anatomies*, alongside his children's books. [7]

2) Author's Website
His website www.davidclementdavies.com is spectacular, but not at all printable. Kids can go to the computer lab and access the website, or if the teacher has a Smart Board, he/she can project the website for the class.

3) Bibliography of Young Adult Novels by Clement-Davies
Fire Bringer
Fire Bringer is a story about Rannoch, a red deer who is born in ancient Scotland on the night his father is murdered. He is born with a white mark on his head. A prophecy foretells that a deer with this mark will bring freedom to the herd of red deer known as the Herla, who have been under the control of Sgorr, the evil Lord of the Herds.

---

[7] David Clement-Davies. http://en.wikipedia.org/wiki/David_Clement-Davies. October 21, 2009

The Sight

The Sight, Clement-Davies's second novel, is set in Transylvania and is about a pack of wolves. The alpha female of the pack, is about to give birth to a litter. The pack is hiding from Morgra and her raven Kraar. Morgra is a wolf who possesses the Sight, which is the ability to look through the eyes of the bird. Morgra reveals that one of the cubs, Larka, will also have the Sight, and she hopes to use the cub's powers to take control of the world.

The Alchemists of Barbal

Armed with a simple stone talisman, Silas Root sets off for Barbal, a walled city where Mardak the Dark reigns. Silas hopes to confront and defeat Mardak and secure the release of the Lord Alchemist, whom Marduk has imprisoned. Although his journey is difficult, the future of magic depends on Silas's success.

The Telling Pool

Rhodri Falcon and his crusader father become entangled in the war of a king and the nefarious schemes of an manipulative sorceress – one who literally steals men's hearts. From the magic Telling Pool, Rhodri must discover the hero within him, which is linked to ancient heroes, and ultimately, save the day.

4) Background information about the author's latest book - *Fell*

In this sequel to *The Sight* David Clement-Davies tells the story of Fell, the black wolf whose betrayal of his family in *The Sight* almost led to the enslavement of all wolves by the evil Morgra. Wandering alone in the forests of Transylvania, lost in the pain of his sister Larka's death, Fell rejects their shared gift of seeing into the minds of others. It is only when a message comes from his old friend Skart, the eagle, that Fell begins to accept his destiny: to enter the world of humans and restore a lost girl to her family, thus healing the wounds of a divided kingdom.

5) Read aloud excerpts:

Pages 9—13
This selection is a recap of *The Sight* and reintroduces Fell, the black wolf who is a main character.
Pages 18-20
This selection introduces Alin (Alina), a girl who is posing as a boy. She is said to be a changeling and is in hiding. Actually, she is the sister of the boy who was stolen by wolves in *The Sight*, and of course, is of noble birth.
Page 118
If you have time, read the chapter, "The Girl and The Wolf," where Fell and Alina first meet. It is very exciting and whets the reader's appetite for more.

Creative Writing Focus

Although it is still preferable to invite students who have read the author's work, successful book talks can also be organized around creative writing issues. Invite creative writing classes to the talk and encourage students to ask questions about the writing process, such as the following:

1) Where do you get your ideas?
2) How did you decide you wanted to be a writer?
3) What motivated you to write your latest book?
4) Describe the timeline between spark and publication. What happened along the way?
5) Describe your writing routine.
6) Do you outline your stories before you start writing? Why or why not?
7) Describe your revision process.
8) How did you go about getting published?
9) Have your books been optioned for film? Would you want to work on the screenplay?
10) What authors/books have inspired you?
11) Do you have a website? If so, who maintains it?
12) Do you blog? Twitter?
13) What are you working on now?
14) What are you reading right now?

WHAT ARE LITERATURE CIRCLES?

If you have a variety of new young adult novels that fit a certain theme, you can suggest what Deborah Hipes calls Book Bundles. A great way to use them in the classroom is to have students read different books that have a common theme and then discuss them in literature circles.

Defining Literature Circles

1. Students **choose** their own reading materials.

2. **Small temporary groups (4- 6 kids)** are formed, based upon book choice.

3. Different groups can read **different books.**

4. Groups meet to discuss their reading.

5. Kids use written or drawn **notes** to guide both their reading and discussion.

6. Discussion **topics** can come from the students or fit a particular theme.

7. Group meetings aim to be **open, natural conversations about books**, so personal connections, digressions, and open-ended questions are welcome.

8. In newly-forming groups, students may play a rotating assortment of task **roles.**

9. The teacher serves as a **facilitator**, not a group member or instructor.

10. Evaluation is by **teacher observation** and **student self evaluation.**[8]

---

[8] "What are literature circles?" http://www.literaturecircles.com/article1.htm. August 6, 2007.

BOOK BUNDLES

The book bundles section includes books that have similar themes. The fantasy book bundles activities include Quest of the Young Fantasy Hero, as well as Vampires, Werewolves and Faeries. I also have a list of "Candy Bar" books which refers to books that may be fun reads for students, but are basically light hearted stories about fairly superficial issues such as boyfriend/girlfriend problems, strict parents, or cliques/popularity. Ideas for books and activities to use with boys follows the Candy Bar books which primarily appeal to girls. The Mystery bundle, The Damaged Kids bundle, the Teens Dealing with Death bundle, the Young Athletes bundle, the Sexual Identity bundle, and the Dystopian Societies bundle include guiding questions that could be used for literature circles. The Science Connection bundle also has suggestions for areas of scientific study that could be paired with each book.

Quest of the Young Fantasy Hero

With the success of J.K. Rowling's Harry Potter series many authors are attempting to capitalize on the popularity of this genre. Young readers of this genre may be interested in the structure of the quest novel and how authors employ it. The following titles have a similar tone to the Harry Potter books, yet attempt to create a world of their own. After students read the title, have them analyze it using the "Quest of the Fantasy Hero" worksheet.

Bracken, Alexandra. **Brightly Woven**. EgmontUSA, 2010. MS. 368 pages. ISBN-13: 978-1606840382

Breathed, Berkeley. **Flawed Dogs: The Novel: The Shocking Raid on Westminster**. Philomel, 2009. MS. 208 pages. ISBN-13: 978-0399252181

Carey, Janet Lee. **Stealing Death**. EgmontUSA, 2009. MS. 368 pages. ISBN-13: 978-1606840092

Cashore, Kristin. **Graceling**. Juvenile. MS. 480 pages. ISBN-13: 978-0152063962

Colfer, Eoin. **Airman**. Hyperion Book CH, 2008. MS. 416 pages ISBN-13: 978-1423107507

DuPrau, Jeanne. **The Diamond of Darkhold**. Random House Books for Young Readers, 2008. MS. 304 pages. ISBN-13: 978-0375855719

Farmer, Nancy. **The Land of the Silver Apples**. Atheneum/Richard Jackson Books, 2007. MS. 496 pages. ISBN-10: 1416907351

Flanagan, John. **The Battle for Skandia.**. (The Ranger's Apprentice: Book 4). Philomel, 2008. MS. 272 pages ISBN-10: 0399244573

Flanagan, John. **The Icebound Land.** (The Ranger's Apprentice: Book 3). Philomel, 2007. MS. 260 pages. ISBN-10: 0399244565

Funke, Cornelia. **Igraine the Brave**. Chicken House Ltd, 2007. MS. 224 pages. ISBN-10: 0439903793

Gaiman, Neil. **The Graveyard Book**. HarperCollins, 2008. 320 pages. ISBN-13: 978-0060530921

George, Jessica Day. **Sun and Moon, Ice and Snow**. Bloomsbury USA Children's Books, 2008. MS. 336 pages. ISBN-13: 978-1599901091

Hanley, Victoria. **Violet Wings**. EgmontUSA, 2009. MS.368 pages. ISBN-13: 978-1606840115

Kingsley, Kaza. **Erec Rex –The Dragon's Eye**. Firelight Press, Inc., 2007. MS. 400 pages. ISBN-10: 0978655532

Kirkbride, Tom. **Gamadin**. Emerald Book Company. MS. 446 pages. ISBN-13: 978-1934572061

Klass, David. **Whirlwind**. Farrar, Straus and Giroux (BYR), 2008. MS/HS. 304 pages. ISBN-10: 0374323089

Kress, Adrienne. **Alex and the Ironic Gentleman**. Weinstein Books, 2007. MS. 320 pages. ISBN-10: 160286005X

Landy, Derek. **Skulduggery Pleasant**. HarperCollins, 2007. MS. 400 pages. ISBN-10: 0061231150

Law, Ingrid. **Scumble**. Dial, 2010. MS. 416 pages. ISBN-13: 978-0803733077

Marchetta, Melina. **Finnikin of the Rock**. Candlewick; 1 edition, 2010. MS/HS. 416 pages.
ISBN-13: 978-0763643614

McMann, Lisa. **Gone**. Simon Pulse; 1 edition, 2010. 214 pages. ISBN-13: 978-1416979180

Patterson, James. **Maximum Ride: The Final Warning**. Little, Brown and Company, 2008. MS. 272
pages. ISBN-10: 0316002860

Patterson, James. **Maximum Ride – Saving the World and Other Extreme Sports**. Little, Brown Young
Readers, 2007. MS. 416 pages. ISBN-10: 0316155608

Patterson, James. **Max**. Little, Brown and Company, 2009. MS. 320 pages. ISBN-13: 978-0316002899

Peterfreund, Diana. **Rampant**. HarperTeen, 2009. HS. 416 pages.ISBN-10: 0061490008

Riordan, Rick. **The Battle of the Labyrinth**. Hyperion, 2008. MS. 368 pages. ISBN-10: 1423101464

Riordan, Rick. **The Last Olympian**. Disney Hyperion Books for Children, 2009. MS. 400 pages. ISBN-
13: 978- 1423101475

Rothfuss, Patrick. **The Name of the Wind**. DAW, 2008. MS/HS. 736 pages.
ISBN-13: 978-0756404741

Rowling, J.K. **Harry Potter and the Deathly Hallows**. Arthur A. Levine Books, 2007. MS. 759 pages.
ISBN-10: 0545010225

Ryan, Carrie. **The Forest of Hands and Teeth**. Delacorte Books for Young Readers,   2009. MS/HS.
320 pages. ISBN-13: 978-0385736817

Sage, Angie. **Physik**. Katherine Tegen Books, 2007. MS. 560 pages. ISBN-10: 0060577371

Sage, Angie. **Queste**. Katherine Tegen Books, 2008. MS. 608 pages. ISBN-10: 0060882077
Sensel, Joni. **The Humming of Numbers**. Henry Holt and Co. (BYR), 2008. MS/HS. 256 pages.
ISBN-13: 978-0805083279

Soesbee, Ree. **Pillar of Flame**. Mirrorstone, 2007. MS. 256 pages. ISBN-10: 0786942487

Yancy, Rick. **Alfred Kropp – The Seal of Solomon**. Bloomsbury USA Children's Books, 2007. MS. 336
pages. ISBN-10: 1599900459

Westerfeld, Scott and Keith Thompson. **Leviathan**. Simon Pulse; Reprint edition, 2010. MS. 464 pages.
ISBN-13: 978-1416971740

Whitcomb, Laura. **The Fetch**. Houghton Mifflin Books for Children; 1 edition, 2009. MS/HS. 384 pages.
ISBN-13: 978-0618891313

Yancy, Rick. **Alfred Kropp – The Seal of Solomon**. Bloomsbury USA Children's Books, 2007. MS. 336
pages ISBN-10: 1599900459

Young, E.L. **Storm: The Infinity Code**. Dial, 2008. MS. 336 pages. ISBN-10: 0803732651.

Young, E.L. **Storm: The Ghost Machine**. Dial, 2008. MS. 320 pages. ISBN-13: 978-0803732674

Quest of the Young Fantasy Hero

Common traits of heroes found frequently in young adult literature
Hero or Heroine:

       1) has family MIA (either dead or away from home)
       2) longs for adventure
       3) must travel on quest
       4) has 3 to 7 tasks to perform
       5) meets people with enchanted powers for good
       6) has companions that are not always humans
       7) confronts the dark world of evil forces
       8) battles strange creatures
       9) wins out against evil
       10) proves that pain and sorrow must come before joy
       11) receives honor of some kind

Analyze your book by filling in the following Story Outline on another sheet of paper. Number of tasks, obstacles, companions, evil forces, steps in achieving task and honors may vary.[9]

I. Hero or heroine's origin
II. Setting
      A. Time
      B. Place
III. Deed or Tasks to be Performed
IV. Wise older person(s) who help
V. Obstacles to overcome
      A.
      B.
VI. Companions – name and describe
      A.
      B.
VII. Evil Forces – name and describe
VIII. Steps in achieving the task
      A.
      B.
IX Honors received
      A.
      B.

---

[9] Polette, Nancy, and Hamlin, Marjorie. *Exploring Books with Gifted Children*. Libraries Unlimited. ©1980.

VAMPIRES, WEREWOLVES, FAIRIES, AND ANGELS

Although this element of the fantasy genre may seem like fluff, there is a lot of information about these fictional characters around which the authors have spun their tale. For example, Melissa Marr starts each chapter of *Wicked Lovely* with a quote from various books that explain fairy lore. Steven Krensky has a series entitled *Monster Chronicles* which includes historical information about vampires and werewolves, as well as other monsters. Each book includes a selected bibliography, further reading and website suggestions, movies and TV treatments and an index.[10] In her *Encyclopedia of Angels* Rosemary Guiley has compiled information including the evolution of the angel in Western thought, the origins of angels, their manifestation in other cultures, and present angel philosophy.[11] Have students read one of the following titles and then do research on whichever fantastic being is incorporated in the novel. Then they can compare the author's portrayal to the researched information they have found. Additional titles are suggested if the students want to read more books involving vampires, werewolves, fairies or angels.

New Titles

Baker. E.D. **Wings: A Fairy Tale**. Bloomsbury USA Children's Books, 2008. MS. 320   pages. ISBN-13: 978-1599901930

Block, Francesca Lia. **The Frenzy**. HarperTeen, 2010. HS. 272 pages.ISBN-13: 978-0061926662

Bray, Libba. **The Sweet Far Thing.** Delacorte Books for Young Readers, 2007. MS/HS. 832 pages. ISBN-10: 0385730306

Cast, P.C. and Kristin. **Chosen: House of Night Novel – Book 3**. St. Martin's Griffin, 2008. HS. 320 pages. ISBN-13: 978-0312360306

Clare, Cassandra. **City of Bones**. Simon Pulse, 2008. MS/HS. 512 pages. ISBN-10: 1416955070

Clare, Cassandra. **City of Ashes**. Margaret K. McElderry, 2008. MS/HS. 464 pages. ISBN-10: 1416914293

Clare, Cassandra. **City of Glass**. Margaret K. McElderry, 2009. 560 pages. ISBN-13: 978-1416914303

Clare, Cassandra. **Clockwork Angel**. Margaret K. McElderry, 2010. MS/HS. 496 pages. ISBN-13: 978-1416975861

Clement-Moore, Rosemary. **Prom Dates from Hell**. Delacorte Books for Young Readers, 2007. MS/HS. 320 pages. ISBN-10: 0385734123

De Lint, Charles. **Dingo**. Puffin, 2008. MS. 224 pages. ISBN-10: 0142408166

De La Cruz, Melissa. **Masquerade: A Blue Bloods Novel.** Hyperion, 2007. MS/HS. 320 pages. ISBN-10: 0786838930

De la Cruz, Melissa. **Revelations**. Hyperion Book. MS. 272 pages. ISBN-13: 978-1423102281

Despain, Brea. **The Dark Divine**. EgmontUSA, 2009. MS/HS. 384 pages. ISBN-13: 978-1606840573

Fantaskey, Beth. **Jessica's Guide to Dating on the Dark Side**. Harcourt Children's Books; 1 edition, 2009. MS/HS. 368 pages.ISBN-13: 978-0152063849

---

[10] Krensky, Steven *Monster Chronicles*. Lerner Publications Company. Minneapolis. 2007.
[11] Guiley, Rosemary. *The Encyclopedia of Angels*. Checkmark Books. New York. 2004.

Fitzpatrick, Becca. **Hush, Hush**. Simon & Schuster Children's Publishing, 2009. MS/HS. 400 pages. ISBN-13: 978-1416989417

Fitzpatrick, Becca. **Crescendo**. Simon & Schuster Children's Publishing, 2010. MS/HS 432 pages. ISBN-13: 978-1416989431

Gray, Claudia. **Evernight**. HarperTeen, 2008. MS. 336 Pages. ISBN-13: 978-0061284397

Gray, Claudia. **Stargazer**. HarperTeen; 1 edition, 2009. MS/HS. 336 pages. ISBN-13: 978-0061284403

Gray, Claudia. **Hourglass**. HarperTeen; 1 edition, 2010. MS/HS. 352 pages. ISBN-13: 978-0061284410

Harvey, Alyxandra. **Hearts at Stake**. Walker Books for Young Readers; 1 edition, 2010. MS. 256 pages. ISBN-13: 978-0802720740

Harvey, Alyxandra. **Blood Feud**. Walker Books for Young Readers, 2010. MS. 272 pages. ISBN-13: 978-0802720962

Jones, Carrie. **Need**. Bloomsbury USA Children's Books, 2008. MS. 320 pages. ISBN-13: 978-1599903385

Kagawa, Julie. **The Iron King**. Harlequin; Original edition, 2010. MS. 368 pages. ISBN-13: 978-0373210084

Livingston, Lesley. **Wondrous Strange**. HarperTeen, 2008. MS. 336 pages. ISBN-13: 978-0061575372

Livingston, Lesley. **Darklight**. HarperTeen; 1 edition, 2009. MS. 320 page. ISBN-13: 978-0061575402

Marr, Melissa. **Fragile Eternity**. HarperCollins, 2009. MS. 400 pages. ISBN-13: 978-0061214714

Marr, Melissa. **Wicked Lovely**. HarperTeen, 2007. MS/HS. 336 pages. ISBN-10: 0061214655

Marr, Melissa. **Ink Exchange**. HarperTeen, 2008. MS/HS. 336 pages. ISBN-10: 006121468X

Mead, Richelle. **The Vampire Academy**. Razorbill, 2007. HS. 332 pages. ISBN-10: 159514174X.

Meyer, Stephenie. **Breaking Dawn**. Little, Brown Young Readers, 2008. MS/HS. 768 pages. ISBN-10: 031606792X

Meyer, Stephenie. **Eclipse**. Little, Brown Young Readers, 2007. MS/HS. 640 pages. ISBN-10: 0316160202

Pierce, Meredith. **The Dark Angel.** Little, Brown Young Readers, 2007. MS/HS 256 pages. ISBN-10: 0316067237

Pike, Aprilynne. **Wings**. HarperTeen, 2009. MS. 304 pages. ISBN-13: 978-0061668036

Pike, Aprilynne. **Spells**. HarperTeen; 1 edition, 2010. MS.368 pages. ISBN-13: 978-0061668067

Selfors, Suzanne. **Coffeehouse Angel**. Walker Books for Young Readers, 2009. MS/HS. 288 pages. ISBN-13: 978-0802798121

Smith, Cynthia Leitich. **Eternal**. Candlewick, 2009. MS/HS. 320 pages. ISBN-13: 978-0763635732

Smith, Cynthia Leitich. **Tantalize**. Candlewick, 2007. MS/HS. 336 pages. ISBN-10: 0763627917

Smith, Tara Bray. **Betwixt**. Little, Brown Young Readers, 2007. MS/HS. 496 pages. ISBN-10: 031606033X

Stiefvater, Maggie. **Shiver**. Scholastic Press; 1 edition, 2009. MS/HS. 400 pages. ISBN-13: 978-0545123266

Stiefvater, Maggie. **Linger**. Scholastic Press, 2010. MS/HS. 368 pages. ISBN-13: 978-0545123280

Taylor, Laini. **The Faeries of Dreamdark: Blackbringer**. Putnam Juvenile, 2007. MS/HS. 437 pages. ISBN-10: 0399246304

Thompson, Kate. **The New Policeman**. HarperTeen, 2007. MS. 448 pages. ISBN-10: 0061174270

Turner, Max. **Night Runner**. St. Martin's Griffin; 1 Original edition, 2009. MS. 272 pages. ISBN-13: 978-0312592288

Zink, Michelle. **The Prophecy of the Sisters**. Little, Brown Books for Young Readers; 1 edition, 2010. MS. 368 pages. ISBN-13: 978-0316027410

Additional Series

PC. Cast's *House of Night* series
Darren Shan's *Cirque du Freak* series
Rachelle Mead's *Vampire Academy* series
Holly Black's *Modern Tale of Faerie* series
L J Smith's *Vampire Diaries* series
Rosemary Laurey's *The Vampire Series*
Justin Somper's *Vampirates* Series
Lauren Kate's *Fallen* Series
Alexandra Aldornetto *Halo* Series
Meredith Pierce *The Dark Angel Trilogy*

CANDY BAR BOOKS

This term, coined by Sheila Kaehny, refers to books that are fun reads for students, but are basically light hearted stories about fairly superficial issues such as boyfriend/girlfriend problems, strict parents, or cliques/popularity. Frequently, they are told in first person and the voice is very clever and characteristic of the way teenagers speak. I would suggest using them as independent reads where students examine the voice or using excerpts for teaching voice and point of view.

Anderson, Jodi Lynn. **Love and Peaches**. HarperTeen, 2008. MS. 256 pages. ISBN-13: 978-0060733117

Anderson, Jody Lynn. **The Secrets of Peaches**. HarperTeen, 2007. MS/HS. 304 pages. ISBN-10: 0060733087

Apelqvist, Eva. **Swede Dreams**. Puffin. 2007. MS/HS. 224. ISBN-10: 0142407461

Benway, Robin. **Audrey Wait!** Razorbill, 2008. MS/HS. 313 pages. ISBN-13: 978-1595141910

Brashares, Ann. **Forever in Blue.** Delacorte Books for Young Readers. 2007. MS/HS. 400 pages. ISBN-10: 0385729367.

Bushnell, Candace. **The Carrie Diaries**. Balzer + Bray, 2010. MS/HS. 400 pages. ISBN-13: 978-0061728914

Brashares, Ann. **Three Willows: The Sisterhood Grows**. Delacorte Books for Young Readers, 2009. MS. 336 pages. ISBN-13: 978-0385736763

Cabot, Meg. **Airhead**. Point, 2008. MS. 352 pages. ISBN-10: 0545040523

Cabot, Meg. **Being Nikki**. Point, 2009. MS. 352 pages. ISBN-13: 978-0545040563

Cabot, Meg. **Runaway**. Scholastic Inc.; 1 edition, 2010. MS. 320 pages. ISBN-13: 978-0545040600

Caletti, Deb. **The Fortunes of Indigo Skye**. Simon & Schuster Children's Publishing, 2008. MS/HS. 304 pages. ISBN-10: 1416910077

Caletti, Deb. **The Secret Life of Prince Charming**. Simon Pulse, 2009. MS. 336 pages. ISBN-13: 978-1416959403

Carter, Ally. **I'd Tell You I Love You, But Then I'd Have to Kill You.** Hyperion, 2007. MS. 288 pages.ISBN-10: 1423100042

Carter, Ally. **Cross My Heart and Hope to Spy**. Hyperion, 2007. MS. 240 pages.. ISBN-10: 1423100050

Carter, Ally. **Don't Judge a Girl by Her Cover**. Hyperion Book CH, 2009. MS. 272 pages. ISBN-13: 978-1423116387

Cassidy, Kay. **The Cinderella Society**. EgmontUSA , 2010. MS/HS. 336 pages. ISBN-13: 978-1606840177

Clement-Moore, Rosemary. **Prom Dates from Hell**. Delacorte Books for Young Readers, 2007. HS. 320 pages. ISBN-10: 0385734123

Cohn, Rachel. **Cupcake.** Simon & Schuster Children's Publishing, 2007. MS/HS. 256 pages. ISBN-10: 1416912177

Colasanti, Susane. **Something Like Fate**. Viking Juvenile, 2010. MS/HS. 288 pages. ISBN-13: 978-0670011469

Dessen, Sarah. **Along for the Ride**. Viking Juvenile, 2009). MS. 384 pages.ISBN-13: 978-0670011940

Dessen, Sarah. **Lock and Key**. Viking Juvenile, 2008 MS/HS. 432 pages. ISBN-10: 067001088X.

Dionne, Erin. **Models Don't Eat Chocolate Cookies**. Dial, 2009. MS. 256 pages. ISBN-13: 978-0803732964

Duff, Hilary. **Elixir**. Simon & Schuster Children's Publishing, 2010. MS/HS. 336 pages. ISBN-13: 978-1442408531

Elkeles, Simone. **Rules of Attraction**. Walker Books for Young Readers, 2010. MS/HS. 336 pages. ISBN-13: 978-0802720856

Ferris, Aimee. **Girl Overboard**. Puffin, 2007. MS/HS. 224 pages. ISBN-10: 0142407992

Frankel, Valerie. **American Fringe**. NAL Trade, 2008. HS. 272 pages.
ISBN-10: 045122292X

Fredericks, Mariah**. In the Cards: Love.** Aladdin, 2007. MS. 288 pages
ISBN-10: 0689876556

Fredericks, Mariah**. In the Cards: Fame.** Atheneum/Richard Jackson Books, 2008. MS. 288 pages. ISBN-10: 0689876564

Freitas, Donna. **The Possibilities of Sainthood**. Farrar, Straus and Giroux (BYR); 1st edition, 2008. MA. 280 pages. ISBN-13: 978-03743608

Gallagher, Liz. **The Opposite of Invisible**. Wendy Lamb Books, 2008. MS/HS. 160 pages. ISBN-10: 0375841520

Gehrman, Jody. **Confessions of a Triple Shot Betty**. Dial, 2008. HS. 256 pages.
ISBN-10: 0803732473

Godbersen, Anna. **The Luxe**. HarperCollins, 2007. HS. 448 pages. ISBN-10: 0061345660

Godbersen, Anna. **Rumors: A Luxe Novel**. HarperCollins, 2008. HS. 432 pages.
ISBN-10: 0061345695

Godbersen, Anna. **Envy**. HarperCollins, 2009. MS/HS. 416 pages. ISBN-13: 978-0061345722

Gonzalez, Julie. **Imaginary Enemy**. Delacorte Books for Young Readers, 2008. MS. 256 pages.
ISBN-13: 978-0385735520

Greenwald, Lisa. **My Life in Pink and Green**. Amulet Books, 2009. MS. 272 pages. ISBN-13: 978-0810983526

Han, Jenny. **The Summer I Turned Pretty**. Simon & Schuster Children's Publishing, 2009. MS. 288 pages. ISBN-10: 1416968237

Headley, Justina Chen. **North of Beautiful**. Little, Brown Young Readers; 1 edition, 2009. 384 pages. ISBN-13: 978-0316025058

Helpler, Heather. **The Cupcake Queen**. Dutton Juvenile, 2009. MS. 240 pages.
ISBN-13: 978-0525421573

Hepler, Heather and Brad Barkley. **Dream Factory.** Dutton Juvenile, 2007. MS/HS. 256 pages. ISBN-10: 0525478027

Kantor, Melissa. **The Breakup Bible**. Hyperion Book CH; Reprint edition, 2008. MS. 288 pages. ISBN-13: 978-0786809639

Kuehnert, Stephanie. **I Wanna Be Your Joey Ramone**. MTV, 2008. HS. 352 pages.
ISBN-10: 1416562699

Johnson, Maureen. **Scarlett Fever**. Point; 1 edition, 2010. MS. 352 pages. ISBN-13: 978-043989928

Kantor, Melissa. **Girlfriend Material**. Hyperion Book CH; 1 edition, 2009. MS. 256 pages.
ISBN-13: 978-1423108498

Leavitt, Lindsey. **Princess for Hire**. Hyperion Book CH, 2010. MS. 256 pages.
ISBN-13: 978-1423121923

Lockhart, E. **The Disreputable History of Frankie Landau-Banks**. Hyperion Book CH, 2008. MS. 352 pages.
ISBN-13: 978-0786838189

Lockhart, Mlynowski and Myracle. **How to Be Bad**. HarperTeen, 2008. MS/HS.
336 pages. ISBN-10: 006128422X

Lockhart, e. **The treasure map of boys**. Delacorte Books for Young Readers, 2009. MS. 256 pages.
ISBN-13: 978-0385734264

Mackall, Dandie Daley. **Crazy in Love**. Dutton Juvenile, 2007. MS/HS. 192 pages ISBN-10: 0525477802

Mass, Wendy. **Finally**. Scholastic Press; 1 edition, 2010. MS. 304 pages ISBN-13: 978-0545052429

Mlynowski, Sarah. **Gimme a Call**. Delacorte Books for Young Readers, 2010. MS. 320 pages. ISBN-13: 978-0385735889

Myracle, Lauren. **l8r, g8r**. Amulet. 2007. MS. 240 pages. ISBN-10: 081091266X

Myracle, Lauren. **Peace Love and Baby Ducks**. Dutton Juvenile, 2009. MS. 192 pages. ISBN-13: 978-0525477433

O'Connell, Jenny. **The Book of Luke**. MTV, 2007. HS. 304 pages. ISBN-10:1416520406

Palmer, Robin. **Cindy Ella.** Puffin, 2008. MS. 304 pages. ISBN-10: 014240392X

Palmer, Robin. **Geek Charming**. Puffin, 2009. MS. 288 pages. ISBN-13: 978-0142411223

Rennison, Louise. **Love is a Many Trousered Thing (Confessions of Georgia Nicolson)**. HarperTeen, 2007. MS. 271 pages. ISBN-10: 0060853875

Reynolds, Phyllis Naylor. **Almost Alice**. Atheneum , 2008. MS/HS. 288 pages. ISBN-13: 978-0689870965

Schneider, Robyn. **Better Than Yesterday**. Delacorte Books for Young Readers, 2007. HS. 240 pages. ISBN-10: 0385733453

Schreiber, Mark. **Star Crossed.** Flux, 2007. MS/HS. 305 pages. ISBN-10: 0738710016

Scott, Elizabeth. **Perfect You**. Simon Pulse, 2008. MS. 304 pages. ISBN-10: 1416953558

Scott, Elizabeth. **Something Maybe**. Simon Pulse, 2009. MS. 217 pages. ISBN-13: 978-1608477531

Selfors, Suzanne. **Saving Juliet**. Walker Books for Young Reader, 2008. MS/HS. 256 pages. ISBN-10: 0802797407

Sonnenblick, Jordan. **Zen and the art of faking it**. Scholastic Press, 2007. MS. 272 pages. ISBN-13: 978-0439837071

Spinelli, Jerry. **Love, Stargirl**. Knopf Books for Young Readers, 2007. MS/HS 288 pages. ISBN-10: 0375813756

Spinelli, Jerry. **Smiles to Go**. Joanna Cotler, 2008. MS. 256 pages. ISBN-10: 0060281332

Supplee, Suzanne. **When Irish Guys Are Smiling**. Puffin, 2008. MS. 224 pages. ISBN-10: 0142410160.

Tashjian, Janet. **Larry and the Meaning of Life**. Henry Holt and Co. (BYR), 2008. MS. 224 pages. ISBN-13: 978-0805077353

Tracy, Kristen. **Lost it**. Simon Pulse, 2007. HS. 288 pages. ISBN-10: 1416934758

Trigiani, Adrianna. **Viola in Reel Life**. HarperTeen, 2009. MS. 288 pages. ISBN-13: 978-0061451027

van de Ruit, John. **Spud.** Razorbill, 2007. MS/HS. 352 pages. ISBN-10: 1595141707

van de Ruit, John. **Spud – The Madness Continues…** Razorbill, 2008. MS/HS. 304 pages. ISBN-13: 978-1595141903

Van Draanen, Wendelin. **Confessions of a Serial Kisser**. Knopf Books for Young Readers, 2008. MS. 304 pages. ISBN-13: 978-0375842481

Vega, Denise. **Fact of Life #31**. Knopf Books for Young Readers, 2008. HS. 384 pages. ISBN-13: 978-0375848193

Wiseman, Rosalind. **Boys, Girls, and Other Hazardous Materials**. Putnam; 1 edition, 2010. 288 pages. ISBN-13: 978-0399247965

Yoo, David. **Stop Me If You've Heard This One Before**. Hyperion Book CH, 2008. MS/HS. 384 pages. ISBN-13: 978-1423109075

Ziegler, Jennifer. **How to Not Be Popular**. Delacorte Books for Young Readers, 2008. MS. 352 pages. ISBN-13: 978-0385734653

Zindel, Lizabeth, **Girl of the Moment**. Viking Young Adult, 2007. MS/HS. 288 pages ISBN-10: 0670062103

DEFINITION FOR VOICE

VOICE shows the writer's personality. The writing has a sound different from everyone else's. It contains feelings and emotions so that it does not sound like an encyclopedia article. The reader should be able to sense the sincerity and honesty of the writer.[12]

Guiding Question for Literature Circles

1) From whose point of view is the story told?

2) Describe the tone of the narration.

3) What can you tell about the character's personality from the voice?

4) What is revealed about the character's values?

5) Pick several words or expressions that are representative of the way the character talks. What do they reveal about the character?

6) How is emotion conveyed through the voice?

7) Is figurative language incorporated into the voice?

8) Are standard writing conventions followed or disregarded to create the voice? Explain.

9) How would the story be different if told by a different character?

10) If the story were made into a film, what actor(s) do you think would best portray the main character(s)?

---

[12] Steele, Kim "Definiton for Voice"
http://www.kimskorner4teachertalk.com/writing/sixtrait/voice/definition.html . October 21, 2009

BOOKS FOR BOYS

According to the U.S. Department of Education, school-age boys read a grade and a half lower than girls. Boys read more comic books, baseball cards, magazines and non-fiction than novels. This is not surprising when one considers boys identify with men, who, in general, don't read as many books as women. Boys' tastes in books reflect how their brains are wired. Michael Gurian, author of *Boys and Girls Learn Differently! A Guide for Teachers and Parents,*[13] writes that boys' brains engage in less cross-hemisphere activity than girls'. In other words, boys use only half of their brain at any given time. That means that when boys read, they need an extra jolt of sound, color, motion or some physical stimulation to get their brains up to speed. Thus boys prefer reading sports, adventure stories and fantasies. Give boys the type books they prefer at a level of difficulty that they are comfortable with and they won't be as reluctant to read. Michael Sullivan, author of *Connecting Boys with Books: What Libraries Can Do,*[14] suggests allowing boys to respond to books through drawing, writing, acting and storytelling for better assessment of what they comprehend.

Suggested Activities to Encourage Boys to Engage in Reading Activities[15]

After a reading experience, assign

1) craft activities that reinforce the story

2) drawing a scene from the story

3) acting out the story

4) creating their own version of the tale

5) creating a game board that follows the plot of the story

6) information scavenger hunts

7) competitions

8) storytelling

---

[13] Gurian, Michael. *Boys and Girls Learn Differently! A Guide for Teachers and Parents.* Jossey-Bass. 2002

[14] Sullivan, Michael. *Connecting Boys with Books: What Libraries Can Do.* ALA Editions, 2003.

[15] Sullivan Michel. "Why Johnny Won't Read." *School Library Journal.* August 1, 2004.

Books for Middle Level Boys

Avi, **Hard Gold**. Hyperion Book CH, 2008. MS. 240 pages. ISBN-13: 978-1423105190

Bodeen. S. A. **Compound**. Feiwel & Friends, 2008. MS. 256 pages. ISBN-10: 0312370156

Bosch, Pseudonymous. **The Name of this Book is Secret**. Little, Brown Young Readers, 2007. MS. 384 pages. ISBN-10: 0316113662

Bradbury, Jennifer. **Shift**. Atheneum, 2008. MS. 256 pages. ISBN-13: 978-1416947325

Broach, Elise. **Masterpiece**. Henry Holt and Co. (BYR), 2008. MS. 304 pages. ISBN-13: 978-0805082708

Carman, Patrick. **Into the Mist**. Scholastic Press, 2007. MS. 304 pages. ISBN-10: 0439899524

Choldenko, Gennifer. **Al Capone Shines My Shoes**. Dial (September 8, 2009). MS. 288 pages. ISBN-13: 978-0803734609

Collins, Suzanne. **The Hunger Games**. Scholastic Press, 2008. MS/HS. 384 pages. ISBN-13: 978-0439023481 (Series sequels: *Catching Fire* and *Mockingjay*)

DuPrau, Jeanne. **The Diamond of Darkhold**. Random House Books for Young Readers, 2008. MS. 304 pages. ISBN-13: 978-0375855719

Flanagan, John. **The Icebound Land.** (The Ranger's Apprentice: Book 3). Philomel, 2007. MS. 260 pages. ISBN-10: 0399244565 (Series: The Ranger's Apprentice – 10 books)

French, S. Terrell. **Operation Redwood**. Amulet Books, 2009. MS. 368 pages. ISBN-13: 978-0810983540

Gaiman, Neil. **The Graveyard Book**. HarperCollins, 2008. 320 pages. ISBN-13: 978-0060530921

Gordon, Roderick and Williams, Brian. **Tunnels**. The Chicken House, 2007. MS. 480 pages. ISBN-10: 0439871778

Grisham, John. **Theodore Boone: Kid Lawyer.** Dutton Children's Books; 1 edition, 2010. MS. 263 pages. ISBN-13: 978-0525423843

Guttman, Dan. **Getting Air**. Simon & Schuster Children's Publishing, 2007. MS. 240 pages. ISBN-10: 0689876807

Hawking, Lucy and Stephen. **George's Secret Key to the Universe**.Simon & Schuster Children's Publishing, 2007. MS. 304 pages. ISBN-10: 1416954627

Haddix, Margaret Peterson. **Found**. Simon & Schuster Children's Publishing, 2008. MS. 320 pages. ISBN-10: 1416954171 (Series sequels: *Sent* and *Sabotaged*)

Halam, Ann. **Snakehead**. Wendy Lamb Books, 2008. MS. 304 pages. ISBN-13: 978-0375841088

Herlong, M.H. **The Great Wide Sea**. Viking Juvenile, 2008. MS. 288 pages. ISBN-13: 978-0670063307

Hiaasen, Carl. **Scat**. Knopf Books for Young Readers, 2009. 384 pages. ISBN-13: 978-0375834868

Higgins, F. E. **The Black Book of Secrets**. Feiwel & Friends, 2007. MS. 288 pages. ISBN-10: 0312368445

Higson, Charlie. **Double or Die**. Puffin Books, 2007. MS. 391 pages. ISBN: 0141322032 (Series: The Young James Bond – 5 books)

Hobbs, Will**. Go Big or Go Home**. HarperCollins, 2008. MS. 192 pages. ISBN-10: 0060741414

Horowitz, Anthony. **Snakehead.** Philomel, 2007. MS. 400 pages. ISBN-10: 0399241612 (Series: Alex Rider – 9 books)

Jinks, Catherine. **Genius Squad**. Harcourt Children's Books, 2008. MS. 448 pages. ISBN-13: 978-0152059859

Kingsley, Kaza. **Erec Rex –The Dragon's Eye.** Firelight Press, Inc., 2007. MS. 400 pages. ISBN-10: 0978655532

Kinney, Jeff. **Diary of a Wimpy Kid: Roderick Rules.** Amulet, 2008. MS. 224 pages. ISBN-10: 0810994739 (Series: The Diary of a Wimpy Kid – 5 books)

Landy, Derek. **Skulduggery Pleasant**. HarperCollins, 2007. MS. 400 pages. ISBN-10: 0061231150 (Series: Skulduggery Pleasant – 5 books)

Lupica, Mike**. The Big Field**. Philomel, 2008. MS. 288 pages. ISBN-10: 0399246258

Lupica, Mike. **Summer Ball**. Philomel, 2007. MS. 256 pages ISBN-10: 0399244875

Lupica, Mike. **Million Dollar Throw**. Philomel, 2009. MS. 244 pages. ISBN-13: 978-0399246265

Lupica,, Mike. **Two-Minute-Drill: Mike Lupica's Comeback Kids**. Philomel, 2007. MS. 176 pages. ISBN-10: 0399247157

Myers, Walter Dean. **Game**. Harper Teen, 2008. MS. 224 pages ISBN-10: 0060582944

Paolini, Christopher. **Brisingr**. Knopf Books for Young Readers, 2008. MS. 784 pages. ISBN-13: 978-0375826726 (Series: The Inheritance Cycle)

Parker, Robert B. **Chasing the Bear: A Young Spenser Novel**. Speak, 2010. MS. 176 pages. ISBN-13: 978-0142415733

Patterson, James. **Maximum Ride – Saving the World and Other Extreme Sports**. Little, Brown Young Readers, 2007. MS. 416 pages. ISBN-10: 0316155608 (Series: Maximum Ride – 7 books)

Paulsen, Gary. **Notes from the Dog**. Wendy Lamb Books, 2009. MS. 144 pages. ISBN-13: 978-0385738453

Paulsen, Gary. **Lawn Boy Returns**. Wendy Lamb Books, 2010. MS. 112 pages. ISBN-13: 978-0385746625

Paulsen, Gary. **Woods Runner**. Wendy Lamb Books; 1 edition, 2010. MS. 176 pages. ISBN-13: 978-0385738842

Pratchett, Terry. **Nation**. HarperCollins, 2008. MS. 384 pages. ISBN-13: 978-0061433016

Pullman, Phillip. **Once Upon A Time in the North**. Knopf Books for Young Readers, 2008. MS. 112 pages. ISBN-10: 0375845100.

Riordan, Rick. **The Last Olympian**. Disney Hyperion Books for Children, 2009. MS. 400 pages. ISBN-13: 978-1423101475 (Series: Percy Jackson and the Olympians – 5 books)

Rowling, J.K. **Harry Potter and the Deathly Hallows**. Arthur A. Levine Books, 2007. MS. 759 pages. ISBN-10: 0545010225 (Series: Harry Potter – 7 books)

Sachar, Louis. **The Cardturner**. Delacorte Books for Young Readers, 2010. MS. 352 pages. ISBN-13: 978-0385736626

Sage, Angie. **Queste**. Katherine Tegen Books, 2008. MS. 608 pages.ISBN-10: 0060882077 (Series: Septimus Heap – 5 books)

Somper, Justin. **Vampirates 3: Blood Captain**. Little, Brown Young Readers, 2008. MS. 576 pages. ISBN-13: 978-0316020855 (Series: The Vampirates -5 books)

Soto, Gary. **Mercy on these Teenage Chimps.** Harcourt Children's Books, 2007. MS. 160 pages. ISBN-10: 0152060227

Sleator, William. **Test**. Amulet, 2008. MS/HS. 240pages. ISBN-10: 0810993562

Taylor, Greg. **Killer Pizza**. Feiwel & Friends, 2009. MS. 352 pages. ISBN-13: 978-0312373795

Trueman, Terry. **Hurricane**. HarperCollins, 2008. MS. 144 pages. ISBN-13: 978-0060000189

Voelkel, J & P. **Middleworld**. Smith & Sons, Imprint of Smith and Kraus Pub. Inc., 2007. MS. 400 pages. ISBN-10: 1575255618

Westerfeld, Scott and Keith Thompson. **Leviathan**. Simon Pulse; Reprint edition, 2010. MS. 464 pages. ISBN-13: 978-1416971740 (Sequel: Behemoth)

Yancy, Rick. **Alfred Kropp – The Seal of Solomon**. Bloomsbury USA Children's Books, 2007. MS. 336 pages ISBN-10: 1599900459 (Series: Alfred Kropp – 3 books)

Young, E.L. **Storm: The Infinity Code**. Dial, 2008. MS. 336 pages. ISBN-10: 0803732651. (Series: S.T.O.R.M – 5 Books)

Books for High School Boys

Beah, Ishmael. **A Long Way Gone** – **Memoirs of a Boy Soldier**. Sarah Crichton Books, 2007. HS. 240 pages. ISBN-10: 0007247087

Brooks, Kevin. **Being.** The Chicken House, 2007. MS/HS. 336 pages. ISBN-10: 0439899737

Brooks, Kevin. **Black Rabbit Summer**. Push, 2009. HS. 512 pages. ISBN-13: 978-0545060899

Card, Orson Scott. **Ender in Exile**. Tor Books, 2008. MS/HS. 384 pages. ISBN-13: 978-0765304964

Choyce, Lesley. **Wave Warrior**. Orca Book Publishers, 2007. MS/HS. 105 pages. ISBN-10: 1551436477

Crutcher, Chris. **Deadline.** HarperTeen, 2007. HS. 320 pages. ISBN-10: 0060850892

de la Pena, Matt. **Mexican WhiteBoy**. Delacorte Books for Young Readers, 2008. MS. 256 pages. ISBN-13: 978-0385733106

Doctorow, Cory. **Little Brother**. Tor Teen, 2008. MS/HS. 384 pages. ISBN-13: 978-0765319852

Doctorow, Cory. **For the Win**. Tor Teen; 1 edition, 2010. MS/HS. 480 pages. ISBN-13: 978-0765322166

Fukui, Isamu. **Truancy**. Tor Teen, 2008. MS/HS. 432 pages. ISBN-10: 0765317672

Gill, David Macinnis. **Black Hole Sun**. Greenwillow Books, 2010. MS/HS. 352 pages. ISBN-13: 978-0061673047

Going, K.L. **King of the Screwups**. Harcourt Children's Books; 1 edition, 2009. MS/HS. 320 pages. ISBN-13: 978-0152062583

Green, John. **Paper Towns**. Dutton Juvenile, 2008. MS/HS. 320 pages. ISBN-13: 978-0525478188

Hautman, Pete. **All-in.** Simon & Schuster Children's Publishing, 2007. MS/HS. 192 pages. ISBN-10: 1416913254

Hijuelos, Oscar. **Dark Dude**. Atheneum, 2008. HS. 448 pages ISBN-13: 978-1416948049

Hillmer, Timothy. **Ravenhill.** University of New Mexico Press, 2007. HS. 239 pages. ISBN-10: 0826339859

Hornby, Nick. **Slam.** Putnam Juvenile, 2007. HS. 304 pages. ISBN-10: 0399250484

Joyce, Graham. **TWOC (Taken Without Owner's Consent).** Viking Juvenile, 2007. HS. 224 pages. ISBN-10: 0670060909

Klass, David. **Whirlwind**. Farrar, Straus and Giroux (BYR), 2008. MS/HS. 304 pages. ISBN-10: 0374323089

Koertge, Ron. **Strays.** Candlewick, 2007. MS/HS. 176 pages. ISBN-10: 0763627054

Laser, Michael. **Cheater**. Dutton Juvenile; 1 editior, 2008. MS. 240 pages ISBN-13: 978-0525478263

Lore, Pittacus. **I Am Number Four**. Harper; 1 edition, 2010. MS. 448 pages. ISBN-13: 978-0061969553

Maberry, Jonathan. **Rot and Ruin**. Simon & Schuster Children's Publishing, 2010. MS/HS. 464 pages. ISBN-13: 978-1442402324

McNamee, Graham. **Bonechiller**. Wendy Lamb Books, 2008. MS/HS. 304 pages.
ISBN-13: 978-0385746588

Ness, Patrick. **The Knife of Never Letting Go**. Candlewick, 2009. MS/HS. 496 pages.
ISBN-13: 978-0763645762

Rapp, Adam. **Punkzilla**. Candlewick, 2009. HS. 256 pages. ISBN-13: 978-0763630317

Reeve, Philip. **Here Lies Arthur**. Scholastic Press, 2008. MS. 352 pages.
 ISBN-13: 978-0545093347

Roberts, Judson. **Dragons from the Sea** (The Strongbow Saga –Book Two). HarperTeen, 2007. MS/HS.
352 pages. ISBN-10: 0060813008

Roberts, Judson. **The Road to Vengeance (The Strongbow Saga: Book 3)**. HarperTeen , 2008. MS/HS.
352 pages. ISBN-10: 0060813040
Rothfuss, Patrick. **The Name of the Wind**. DAW, 2008. MS/HS. 736 pages.
ISBN-13: 978-0756404741

Shusterman, Neal. **Unwind**. Simon & Schuster Children's Publishing , 2007. MS/HS.
352 pages. ISBN-10: 1416912045
Smith, Charles R. **Chameleon**. Candlewick; 1 edition, 2008. MS/HS. 384 pages.
ISBN-13: 978-0763630850

Strasser, Todd. **Boot Camp.** Simon & Schuster Children's Publishing, 2007. HS. 256 pages. ISBN-10:
141690848X

Tashjian, Janet. **Larry and the Meaning of Life**. Henry Holt and Co. (BYR), 2008. MS. 224 pages.
ISBN-13: 978-0805077353

Tharp, Tim. **The Spectacular Now**. Knopf Books for Young Readers, 2008. HS. 304 pages.
ISBN-13: 978-0375851797

Trueman, Terry. **7 Days at the Hot Corner**. HarperTeen, 2007. MS/HS. 160 pages. ISBN-10:
0060574941

van de Ruit, John. **Spud**. Razorbill, 2007. MS/HS. 352 pages. ISBN-10: 1595141707

van de Ruit, John. **Spud – The Madness Continues…** Razorbill, 2008. MS/HS. 304 pages.
ISBN-13: 978-1595141903

Weaver, Will. **Saturday Night Dirt**. Puffin, 2008. MS. 272 pages.
ISBN-10: 014240392X

Weaver, Will. **Super Stock Rookie**. Farrar, Straus and Giroux (BYR); 1 edition, 2009. MS. 208 pages.
ISBN-13: 978-0374350611

Weaver, Will. **Checkered Flag Cheater**. Farrar, Straus and Giroux (BYR); 1 edition, 2010. MS/HS. 208
pages. ISBN-13: 978-0374350628

Westerfeld, Scott. **Extras**. Simon Pulse, 2007. MS/HS. 432 pages. ISBN-10: 1416951172

Wooding, Chris. **Malice**. Scholastic Press, 2009. MS. 384 pages. ISBN-13: 978-0545160438

Yancy, Rick. **Monstrumologist**. Simon & Schuster Children's Publishing; 1St Edition edition, 2009.
MS/HS. 448 pages. ISBN-13: 978-1416984481

Yoo, David. **Stop Me If You've Heard This One Before**. Hyperion Book CH, 2008. MS/HS. 384 pages.
ISBN-13: 978-1423109075

BOOK BUNDLE: MYSTERIES

Mysteries are arguably the most popular genre in fiction. Nancy Drew and the Hardy Boys have captivated readers for generations. In teaching the mystery genre, analyzing the author's use of classic mystery techniques can help students understand why mysteries are such "page turners." Foreshadowing, cliff hangers, and red herrings are just a few of the techniques the authors use to keep their readers coming back for more.

New Young Adult Mysteries

Abrahams, Peter. **Reality Check**. HarperTeen; 1 edition, 2009. MS/HS. 336 pages. ISBN-13: 978-0061227660

Adlington, L.J. **Cherry Heaven**. HarperTeen , 2008. MS. 464 pages. ISBN-10: 006143180X

Arnold, Tedd. **Rat Life**. Dial, 2007. MS/HS. 208 pages. ISBN-10: 0803730209

Avi. **Murder at Midnight**. Scholastic Press; 1 edition, 2009. MS. 272 pages. ISBN-13: 978-0545080903

Avi. **The Traitor's Gate**. Atheneum/Richard Jackson Books, 2007. MS. 368 pages. ISBN-10: 0689853351

Bauer, Joan. **Peeled**. Putnam Juvenile, 2008. MS. 256 pages. ISBN-10: 0399234756

Beil, Michael. **The Red Blazer Girls: The Ring of Rocamadour**. Knopf Books for Young Readers, 2009, MS, 304 pages. ISBN-13: 978-0375848148 (Sereis: The Red Blazer Girls)

Berk, Josh. **The Dark Days of Hamburger Halpin**. Random House Children's Books, 2010. MS/HS. 250 pages. ISBN-13: 9780375856990

Blundell, Judy. **What I Saw and How I Lied**. Scholastic Press, 2008. MS/HS. 288 pages. ISBN-13: 978-0439903462

Bradbury, Jennifer. **Shift**. Atheneum, 2008. MS. 256 pages. ISBN-13: 978-1416947325

Brooks, Kevin. **Black Rabbit Summer**. Push, 2009. HS. 512 pages. ISBN-13: 978-0545060899

Carter, Ally. **Don't Judge a Girl by Her Cover**. Hyperion Book CH, 2009. MS. 272 pages. ISBN-13: 978-1423116387

Carter, Ally. **Heist Society**. Hyperion Book CH, 2010. MS. 304 pages. ISBN-13: 978-1423116394

Carter, Ally. **Only the Good Spy Young**. Hyperion Book CH; 1 edition, 2010. MS. 272 pages. ISBN-13: 978-1423128205

Cooney, Caroline. **If the Witness Lied**. Delacorte Books for Young Readers, 2009. MS. 224 pages. ISBN-13: 978-0385734486

Dowd, Siobhan. **Bog Child**. David Fickling Books, 2008. MS. 336 pages. ISBN-13: 978-0385751698

Feinstein, John. **Change-Up: Mystery at the World Series**. Knopf Books for Young Readers, 2009. MS. 320 pages. ISBN-13: 978-0375856365 (Sports Mystery Series – 4 books)

Ferguson, Alane. **The Dying Breath: Forensic Mystery**. Viking Juvenile, 2009. MS/HS. 234 pages. ISBN-13: 978-0670063147 (Series: Forensic Mysteries – 4 books)

Fukuda, Andrew Kia. **Crossing**. AmazonEncore, 2010. MS/HS. 217 pages. ISBN-13: 978-1935597032

Golding, Julia. **The Diamond of Drury Lane**. Roaring Brook Press, 2008. MS.432 pages.ISBN-10: 1596433515

Green, John. **Paper Towns**. Dutton Juvenile, 2008. MS/HS. 320 pages. ISBN-13: 978-0525478188

Haddix, Margaret Peterson. **Found**. Simon & Schuster Children's Publishing, 2008. MS. 320 pages. ISBN-10: 1416954171

Henry, April. **Torched**. Putnam Juvenile, 2009. MS/Hs. 224 pages. ISBN-13: 978-0399246456

Hiaasen, Carl. **Scat**. Knopf Books for Young Readers, 2009. 384 pages. ISBN-13: 978-0375834868

Higson, Charlie. **Double or Die**. Puffin Books, 2007. MS. 391 pages. ISBN: 0141322032

Hoffman, Mary. **The Falconer's Knot: A Story of Friars, Flirtation and Foul Play.** Bloomsbury USA Children's Books, 2007. MS/HS. 288 pages. ISBN-10: 1599900564

Konigsburg, E.L. **The Mysterious Edge of the Heroic World**. Ginee Seo Books, 2007. MS. 256 pages. ISBN-10: 1416949720

Lennon, Stella. **The Amanda Project: Invisible I**. HarperTeen, 2009. MS. 304 pages. ISBN-13: 978-0061742125

Marchetta, Melina. **Jellico Road**. HarperTeen, 2008. MS/HS. 432 pages. ISBN-13: 978-0061431838

Meldrum, Christina. **Madapple**. Knopf Books for Young Readers. MS/HS. 416 pages. ISBN-13: 978-0375851766

Parker, Robert B. **The Boxer and the Spy**. Philomel, 2008. MS/HS. 224 pages. ISBN-13: 978-0399247750

Parker, Robert B. **Edenville Owls**. Puffin, 2008. MS/HS. 208 pages. ISBN-13: 978-01424111612

Peacock, Shane. **Eye of the Crow: The Boy Sherlock Holmes – His First Case.** Tundra Books, 2007. MS. 264 pages. ISBN-10: 0887768504

Quinn, Spencer. **Dog On It: A Chet and Bernie Mystery**. Atria, 2009. MS/HS. 336 pages. ISBN-13: 978-1416585848

Schrefer, Eliot. **The School for Dangerous Girls**. Scholastic Press, 2009. MS/HS. 256 pages. ISBN-13: 978-0545035286

Sherry, Maureen. **Walls Within Walls**. Katherine Tegen Books; 1 edition, 2010. MS. 368 pages. ISBN-13: 978-0061767005

Shulman, Polly. **The Grimm Legacy**. Putnam Juvenile, 2010. MS. 336 pages. ISBN-13: 978-0399250965

Springer, Nancy. **The Case of the Left-Handed Lady: An Enola Holmes Mystery.** Philomel , 2007. MS. 192 pages. ISBN-10: 0399245170 (Series: Enola Holmes Mysteries – 8 books)

Staub, Wendy Corsi. **Lily Dale: Connecting**. Walker Books for Young Readers, 2008. MS. 304 pages. ISBN-13: 978-0802797858 (Series: Lily Dale – 4 books)

Stead, Rebecca. **When You Reach Me**. Wendy Lamb Books; 9th Printing of First Edition edition, 2009. MS.208 pages. ISBN-13: 978-0385737425

Wright, Rachel. **You've Got Blackmail**. Putnam Juvenile, 2009. MS. 208 pages. ISBN-13: 978-0399250941

Young, E.L**. Storm: The Ghost Machine**. Dial, 2008. MS. 320 pages. ISBN-13: 978-0803732674 (Series – 5 books)

Guiding Questions for Literature Circles

1) Define the following mystery story characteristics
    Clues
    Foreshadowing
    Cliff hangers
    Suspects
    Red herrings
    Alibis
    Motives
2) What is the crime?
3) Who is the criminal?
4) What is the criminal's motive?
5) Who are the suspects?
6) Do the suspects have alibis? If so, what are they?
7) Is there a detective? If so, describe him/her. What characteristics make him/her a good detective?
8) What are the classic mystery techniques the author uses to create suspense? Give examples of each from the book.
9) Does the author do anything unusual to make the story unique? (Example: *Dog On It* tells the mystery from a dog's point of view.)
10) Is the mystery part of a series? If so, what is the common thread in all of the stories?

Book Bundle: Damaged Kids

Trauma and abuse during childhood and how abused children deal with the problems that ensue are topics that are explored in many new young adult novels. Frequently, these topics lend themselves to engrossing, yet disturbing, reads that prompt lively discussion. However, many of these books may be inappropriate for the younger reader. The following list includes many new titles involving damaged kids and the issues explored.

Anderson, Laurie Halse. **Twisted**. Viking Juvenile, 2007. HS. 256 pages. ISBN-10: 0670061018
Issues: Social isolation and an abusive parent

Anderson, Laura Halse. **Wintergirls**. Viking Juvenile, 2009. MS/HS. 288 pages. ISBN-13: 978-0670011100
Issues: Eating disorders and cutting

Arnold, Tedd. **Rat Life**. Dial, 2007. MS/HS. 208 pages. ISBN-10: 0803730209
Issue: Mental illness of abused Viet Nam veteran

Avasthi, Swati. **Split**. Knopf Books for Young Readers, 2010. MS/HS. 288 pages. ISBN-13: 978-0375863400
Issue: Parental Abuse

Baratz-Logstead, Lauren. **Crazy Beautiful**. Houghton Mifflin Books for Children, 2009. MS/HS. 208 pages. ISBN-13: 978-0547223070
Issue: Disfigurement
Barkley, Brad and Hepler, Heather. **Jars of Glass**. Dutton Juvenile, 2008. MS/HS. 208 pages.
ISBN-13: 978-0525479116
Issue: Parental mental illness

Barnes, John. **Tales from the Madmen Underground**. Viking Juvenile; 1 edition, 2009. HS. 544 pages.
ISBN-13: 978-0670060818
Issue: Alcoholism

Bloss, Josie. **Albatross**. Flux; 1 edition, 2010. MS/HS. 240 pages .ISBN-13: 978-0738714769
Issue: Abusive boyfriend

Charlton-Trujillo, E.E. **Feels Like Home.** Delacorte Books for Young Readers, 2007. MS/HS. 224 pages.
ISBN-10: 0385733321
Issues: Guilt and abandonment

Cohn, Rachel. **You Know Where to Find Me**. Simon & Schuster Children's Publishing, 2008. MS/HS. 208 pages.
ISBN-10: 0689878591
Issues: Suicide and substance abuse

de Guzman, Michael. **Finding Stinko.** Farrar, Straus and Giroux , 2007. MS. 144 pages. ISBN-10: 0374323054
Issue: Abandonment

De la Pena, Matt. **We Were Here**. Delacorte Books for Young Readers, 2009. MS/HS. 368 pages. ISBN-13: 978-038573667
Issue: Teenage Criminal Behavior

Dessen, Sarah. **Lock and Key.** Viking Juvenile, 2008. MS/HS. 432 pages. ISBN-10: 067001088X.
Issue: Abandonment

George, Madeline. **Looks**. Viking Juvenile. MS. 240 pages. ISBN-13: 978-0670061679
Issues: Eating disorders and bullying

Giles, Gail. **Right Behind You**. Little, Brown Young Readers, 2007. MS/HS. 308 pages. ISBN-10: 0316166367
Issue: Guilt and rehabilitation

Halpin, Brendan. **How Ya Like Me Now**. Farrar, Straus and Giroux (BYR), 2007. MS/HS. 208 pages.
ISBN-10: 0374334951
Issue: Mentally ill parent

Hijuelos, Oscar. **Dark Dude**. Atheneum, 2008. HS. 448 pages ISBN-13: 978-1416948049
Issue: Teenage runaway and heroin addiction

Hillmer, Timothy. **Ravenhill.** University of New Mexico Press, 2007. HS. 239 pages. ISBN-10: 0826339859
Issue: School violence

Hopkins, Ellen. **Identical**. Margaret K. McElderry, 2008. HS. 576 pages. ISBN-10: 1416950052
Issue: Incest

Hopkins, Ellen. **Impulse**. Margaret K. McElderry , 2007. HS. 672 pages. ISBN-10: 1416903569
Issue: Suicide

Hopkins, Ellen. **Fallout**. Margaret K. McElderry, 2010. HS. 672 pages. ISBN-13: 978-1416950097
Issue: Parental drug addiction

Hopkins, Ellen. **Tricks**. Margaret K. McElderry; 1 edition, 2009. HS. 640 page. ISBN-13: 978-1416950073
Issue: Teen Prostitution

Hyde, Catherine Ryan. **The Year of My Miraculous Reappearance**. Knopf Books for Young Readers , 2007. MS/HS. 240 pages. ISBN-10: 0375832572
Issues: Social isolation and abandonment

Joyce, Graham. **TWOC (Taken Without Owner's Consent).** Viking Juvenile, 2007. HS. 224 pages. ISBN-10: 0670060909
Issues: Guilt and mental illness

Kuehnert, Stephanie. **I Wanna Be Your Joey Ramone**. MTV, 2008. HS. 352 pages. ISBN-10: 1416562699
Issue: Abandonment and substance abuse

Lamarche, Phil. **American Youth.** Random House, 2007. HS. 240 pages. ISBN-10: 1400066050
Issue: Guilt and substance abuse

Madigan, L.K. **Flash Burnout**. Houghton Mifflin Books for Children, 2009. MS/HS. 336 pages.
ISBN-13: 978-0547194899
Issue: Parent with Meth Addiction

Marchetta, Melina. **Jellico Road**. HarperTeen, 2008. MS/HS. 432 pages.
ISBN-13: 978-0061431838
Issues: Parental abuse and abandonment

McMann, Lisa. **Wake**. Simon Pulse, 2008. MS/HS. 224 pages. ISBN-13: 978-1416974475
Issues: Parental abuse and alcoholism

Peters, Julie Anne. **By the Time You Read This, I'll Be Dead**. Hyperion Book CH, 2010. HS. 224 pages.
ISBN-13: 978-1423116189
Issue: Bullying

Rapp, Adam. **Punkzilla**. Candlewick, 2009. HS. 256 pages. ISBN-13: 978-0763630317
Issues: Teenage runaway and drug abuse

Reinhardt, Dana. **Harmless**. Wendy Lamb Books, 2007. MS/HS. 240 pages. ISBN-10: 0385746997
Issue: Guilt when a lie spirals out of control

Reinhardt, Dana. **How to Build a House: a novel**. Wendy Lamb Books, 2008. MS/HS. 240 pages. ISBN-13: 978-0375844539
Issues: Divorce and dealing with a natural catastrophy

Rhodes-Courter, Ashley. **Three Little Words**. Atheneum, 2008. MS/HS 320 pages. ISBN-10: 1416948066
Issue: Abuse in the foster care system

Rosoff, Meg. **What I Was**. Viking Adult, 2008. MS/HS. 224 pages. ISBN-10: 0670018449
Issues: Social isolation and abandonment

Sachs, Marilyn. **The Fat Girl**. Flux, 2007. MS. 226 pages. ISBN-10: 0738710008
Issue: Obesity

Saenez, Benjamin Alire. **Last Night I Sang to the Monster**. Cinco Puntos Press; 1 edition, 2009. HS. 304 pages.
ISBN-13: 978-1933693583
Issue: Alcoholism

Schrefer, Eliot. **The School for Dangerous Girls**. Scholastic Press, 2009. MS/HS. 256 pages.
ISBN-13: 978-0545035286
Issue: Institutional abuse

Scott, Elizabeth. **Living Dead Girl**. Simon Pulse, 2008. HS. 176 pages. ISBN-13: 978-1416960591
Issues: Abduction and sexual abuse

Scott, Elizabeth. **Stealing Heaven**. HarperTeen , 2008. MS. 320 pages. ISBN-10: 0061122807
Issues: Mother's criminal activities and irresponsibility

Strasser, Todd. **Boot Camp**. Simon & Schuster Children's Publishing, 2007. HS 256 pages. ISBN-10: 141690848X
Issue: Parental and institutional abuse

Tharp, Tim. **The Spectacular Now**. Knopf Books for Young Readers, 2008. HS. 304 pages.
ISBN-13: 978-0375851797
Issue: Teen alcoholism

Vaught, Susan. **Big Fat Manifesto**. Bloomsbury USA Children's Books, 2007. MS/HS. 320 pages. ISBN-10:
1599902060
Issue: Obesity

Waters, Daniel. **Generation Dead.** Hyperion Book CH, 2008. MS/HS. 400 pages. ISBN-13: 978-1423109211
Issue: Prejudice

Woodson, Jacqueline. **After Tupac & D Foster**. Putnam Young Adult, 2008. MS. 160 pages.
ISBN-13: 978-0399246548
Issue: Abandonment

Wiess, Laura. **Such a Pretty Girl.** Pocket Books, 2007. HS 224 pages. ISBN-10: 1847390382
Issue: Incest and pedophilia

Wiess, Laura. **Leftovers.** MTV, 2008. HS. 256 pages .ISBN-13: 978-1416546627
Issues: Parental neglect and a sexual predator

Zalben, Jane Breskin. **Leap**. Knopf Books for Young Readers, 2007. MS. 272 pages.
ISBN-10: 0375838716
Issues: Paralysis and Abandonment
Zarr, Sara. **Sweethearts**. Little, Brown Young Readers, 2008. MS/HS. 224 pages.
ISBN-10: 0316014559
Issue: Parental abuse and pedophilia

Zarr, Sara. **Story of a Girl**. Little, Brown Young Readers, 2007. HS. 208 pages.
ISBN-10: 0316014532
Issues: Promiscuity and social isolation

Essential Question
Where and how do young people find strength in the face of overwhelming adversity?
Guiding Questions for Literature Circles
1) What are the issues the main character in your book is facing?

2) How do these problems affect his/her every day life?

3) Which characters in the story add to or create the problems? How?

4) Which characters in the story provide support? Describe the support and how the main character reacts.

5) What are the main character's psychological methods of coping? (Denial, Silence, Lying, etc.)

6) What positive outside activities does the main character turn to for strength?

   (Sports, Music, Religion, Academics etc.) How do the activities help?

7) What negative activities, if any, does the main character get involved in for relief?

(Drugs, Alcohol, Cutting or hurting herself in other ways, Promiscuity, etc.)

8) Do the problems get resolved? If so, how does the main character work toward the resolution?

9) What do you think the main character's future will be like?

10) In your opinion, is the ending hopeful or depressing? Why?

11) Would you recommend this book to other students? Why or why not?

BOOK BUNDLE: TEENS DEALING WITH DEATH

Coping with the death of a friend or loved one is not easy for people of any age. For children and young adults the experience may impact who they become as adults. Reading about how the main characters deal with death in their lives may inform the readers about coping mechanisms and support systems that enable the young person to move on from the devastating experience. The following list includes books that focus on loss and the grieving experience.

Asher, Jay. **13 Reasons Why.** Razorbill, 2007. HS. 304 pages. ISBN-10: 1595141715
Issue: Death of a classmate (suicide)

Baratz-Logsted, Lauren. **Secrets of My Suburban Life**. Simon Pulse, 2008. MS. 240 pages. ISBN-13: 978-1416925255
Issue: Death of mother

Charlton-Trujillo, E.E. **Feels Like Home.** Delacorte Books for Young Readers, 2007. MS/HS. 224 pages. ISBN-10: 0385733321
Issue: Accidental death of a friend and death of a parent

Cohn, Rachel. **You Know Where to Find Me**. Simon & Schuster Children's Publishing, 2008. MS/HS. 208 pages. ISBN-10: 0689878591
Issues: Suicide of a cousin

Crutcher, Chris. **Deadline.** HarperTeen, 2007. HS. 320 pages. ISBN-10: 0060850892
Issue: Terminal illness

De la Pena, Matt. **We Were Here**. Delacorte Books for Young Readers, 2009. MS/HS. 368 pages. ISBN-13: 978-038573667

Issue: Death of a Sibling

Dogar, Sharon. **Waves.** Chicken House Ltd, 2007. MS/HS. 352 pages.
ISBN-10: 1905294247.
Issue: Death of a sibling

Downham, Jenny. **Before I Die.** Definitions, 2007. HS. 336 pages. ISBN-10: 1862304874
Issue: Terminal illness

Ephron, Delia. **Frannie in Pieces.** HarperTeen , 2007. MS/HS. 384 pages.
ISBN-10: 0060747161
Issue: Death of a parent

Foxlee, Karen. **The Anatomy of Wings**. Knopf Books for Young Readers, 2009. HS. 368 pages. ISBN-13: 978-0375856433

Issue: Death of a sibling

Fukui, Isamu. **Truancy.** Tor Teen, 2008. MS/HS. 432 pages. ISBN-10: 0765317672
Issue: Death of a sibling

Forman, Gayle. **If I Stay**. Dutton Juvenile, 2009. 208 pages. ISBN-13: 978-0525421030
Issues: Death of parents and sibling in a car accident

Giles, Gail. **Right Behind You**. Little, Brown Young Readers, 2007. MS/HS 308 pages.ISBN-10: 0316166367
Issue: Manslaughter involving death of a neighborhood child

Harazin, S. A. **Blood Brothers**. Delacorte Books for Young Readers, 2007. MS/HS. 240 pages. ISBN-10: 0385733649.
Issue: Death of a friend

Herlong, M.H. **The Great Wide Sea**. Viking Juvenile, 2008. MS. 288 pages.
ISBN-13: 978-0670063307
Issue: Death of a parent

Hillmer, Timothy. **Ravenhill**. University of New Mexico Press, 2007. HS. 239 pages.
ISBN-10: 0826339859
Issue: School shooting

Hopkins, Ellen. **Identical**. Margaret K. McElderry, 2008. HS. 576 pages. ISBN-10: 1416950052
Issue: Death of a sibling

Joyce, Graham. **TWOC (Taken Without Owner's Consent).** Viking Juvenile, 2007. HS. 224 pages.
ISBN-10: 0670060909
Issue: Death of a sibling

Kadohata, Cynthia. **Outside Beauty.** Atheneum, 2008. MS. 272 pages.ISBN-13: 978-0689865756
Issues: Disfigurement and abandonment

Koertge, Ron. **Strays.** Candlewick, 2007. MS/HS. 176 pages. ISBN-10: 0763627054
Issue: Death of both parents and ensuing problems in foster care

Lamarche, Phil. **American Youth.** Random House, 2007. HS. 240 pages. ISBN-10: 1400066050
Issue: Accidental shooting and death of a sibling

MacLachlan, Patricia. **Edward's Eyes.** Atheneum, 2007. MS. 128 pages. ISBN-10: 1416927433
Issue: Accidental death of a sibling

Marsh, Katherine. **The Night Tourist.** Hyperion, 2007. MS/HS. 240 pages. ISBN-10: 142310689X
Issue: Death of a parent and unresolved issues of a young person's spirit in the afterlife

Mass, Wendy. **Heaven Looks a Lot Like a Mall.** Little, Brown Young Readers, 2007. MS/HS. 256
pages. ISBN-10: 0316058513
Issue: Teen in a coma reviews her life from heaven

Nelson, Jandy. **The Sky Is Everywhere**. Dial, 2010. MS/HS. 288 pages. ISBN-13: 978-0803734951
Issue: Death of a Sibling

Ockler, Sarah. **Twenty Boy Summer**. Little, Brown Books for Young Readers; Reprint edition, 2010. HS.
320 pages. ISBN-13: 978-0316051583
Issue: Death of a Friend

Oliver, Lauren. **Before I Fall**. HarperCollins; 1 edition, 2010. MS/HS.480 pages.
ISBN-13: 978-0061726804
Issue: Dead teenage girl reflects on life

Peet, Mal. **Tamar**. Candlewick 2007. MS/HS. 432 pages. ISBN-10: 0763634883
Issue: Death of a friend during war and ensuing guilt

Powers, J.L. **The Confessional.** Knopf Books for Young Readers, 2007. HS. 304 pages. ISBN-10:
0375838724
Issue: Racial conflict and death of a classmate

Prose, Francine. **Bullyville.** HarperTeen , 2007. MS/HS. 272 pages. ISBN-10: 0060574976
Issue: Death of a parent in the 9/11 tragedy

Schroeder, Lisa**. I Heart You, You Haunt Me**. Simon Pulse, 2008. MS/HS. 240 pages. ISBN-10:
1416955208
Issue: Accidental death of a boyfriend

Schroeder, Lisa. **Chasing Brooklyn**. Simon Pulse, 2010. MS/HS. 432 pages ISBN-13: 978-1416991687
Issue: Death of a boyfriend

Schroeder, Lisa. **Far from You**. Simon Pulse, 2010. MS/HS. 384 pages. ISBN-13: 978-1416975076

Issue: Mother's death

Spinelli, Jerry. **Eggs**. Little, Brown Young Readers, 2007. MS. 224 pages.
ISBN-10: 0316166464
Issue: Death of a parent

Staples, Suzanne Fisher. **The House of Djinn**. Farrar, Straus and Giroux, 2008. MS. 224 pages. ISBN-10: 0374399360
Issue: Death of a grandfather

Staub, Wendy Corsi. **Lily Dale: Awakening.** Walker Books for Young Readers, 2007. MS. 240 pages.
ISBN-10: 0802796540
Issue: Death of mother

Supplee, Suzanne. **When Irish Guys Are Smiling**. Puffin, 2008. MS. 224 pages. ISBN-10: 0142410160.
Issue: Death of mother

Young, E.L. **Storm: The Infinity Code**. Dial, 2008. MS. 336 pages.
ISBN-10: 0803732651.
Issue: Death of a parent

Wolf, Allan. **Zane's Trace**. Candlewick, 2007. MS/HS. 208 pages. ISBN-10: 0763628581
Issue: Deaths of a parent and grandparent

Yeomans, Ellen. **Rubber Houses**. Little, Brown Young Readers, 2007. MS.160 pages. ISBN-10:
031610647X
Issue: Death of a sibling from cancer

Essential Question: How do young people deal with the death?
Guiding questions for literature circle.

1) Whose death is the main character dealing with and what is his/her relationship to this person?

2) What problems arise for the main character?

3) How does the main character attempt to deal with these problems?

4) Which characters in the story provide support? Describe the support and how the main character reacts

to it.

5) What ultimately helps alleviate the pain most successfully?

6) How is the main character similar or different from you? How would you have tried to handle your

sadness?

7) What do you think the main character's future will be like?

8) In your opinion, is the ending hopeful or depressing? Why?

9) Would you recommend this book to others? Why or why not?

BOOK BUNDLE: YOUNG ATHLETES

       Stories about sports are not always just a play by play of the big game, although that is, of course, usually involved. Frequently, the main character has a problem that may or may not be sports related, and he or she works through it by focusing on his or her athletic prowess and passion for the game. Reading these stories will inform readers not only about the sport involved, but more importantly about dealing with problems with integrity and determination. The following is a list of new titles which includes the sport involved and the problem the main character faces.

Beam, Matt. **Getting to First Base with Danalda Chase**. Dutton Juvenile, 2007. MS. 192 pages. ISBN-10: 0525475788
Issues: Girlfriend problems and trying to make the baseball team

Bradbury, Jennifer. **Shift**. Atheneum, 2008. MS. 256 pages. ISBN-13: 978-1416947325

Issues: Parental abuse and cross country bike riding

Choyce, Lesley. **Wave Warrior**. Orca Book Publishers, 2007. MS/HS. 105 pages. ISBN-10: 1551436477
Issues: Learning to surf and dealing with terminal illness

de la Pena, Matt. **Mexican WhiteBoy**. Delacorte Books for Young Readers, 2008. MS. 256 pages. ISBN-13: 978-0385733106

Issues: Baseball and racial tension

Dessen, Sarah. **Along for the Ride**. Viking Juvenile, 2009. MS. 384 pages. ISBN-13: 978-0670011940

Issues: Skateboarding, bike riding, and dealing with grief

Feinstein, John. **Change-Up: Mystery at the World Series**. Knopf Books for Young Readers, 2009. MS. 320 pages. ISBN-13: 978-0375856365

Issue: Baseball and cover-up of criminial behavior

Guttman, Dan. **Getting Air**. Simon & Schuster Children's Publishing, 2007. MS. 240 pages. ISBN-10: 0689876807
Issues: Skateboarding and surviving a plane crash

Headley, Justina Chen. **Girl Overboard**. Little, Brown Young Readers, 2008. MS/HS. 352 pages. ISBN-13: 978-0316011303
Issues: Snow boarding and dealing with injury

Hornby, Nick. **Slam.** Putnam Juvenile, 2007. HS. 304 pages. ISBN-10: 0399250484
Issues: Skate boarding and teen pregnancy

Kluger, Steve. **My Most Excellent Year: A Novel of Love, Mary Poppins, & Fenway Park**. Puffin; Reprint edition, 2009. MS/HS. 416 pages. ISBN-13: 978-0142413432
Issues: Baseball and dealing with grief

Korman, Gordon. **Pop**. Balzer + Bray, 2009. MS. 272 pages. ISBN-13: 978-0061742286

Issues: Football and Alzheimers

Lupica, Mike. **The Big Field.** Philomel, 2008. MS. 288 pages. ISBN-10: 0399246258
Issues: Baseball and Dad's lack of support

Lupica, Mike. **Million Dollar Throw**. Philomel, 2009. MS. 244 pages. ISBN-13: 978-0399246265

Issues: Football and financial problems

Lupica, Mike. **Summer Ball.** Philomel, 2007. MS. 256 pages. ISBN-10: 0399244875
Issues: Basketball and problems with the coach

Lupica,, Mike. **Two-Minute-Drill: Mike Lupica's Comeback Kids.** Philomel, 2007. MS. 176 pages. ISBN-10: 0399247157
Issues: Football and problems with learning disabilities

Mackey, Weezie Kerr. **Throwing Like a Girl**. Marshall Cavendish Children's Books, 2007. MS. 271 pages. ISBN-10: 07614534
Issues: Baseball and moving to a new high school senior year

Myers, Walter Dean. **Game**. Harper Teen, 2008. MS. 224 pages ISBN-10: 0060582944
Issues: Basketball and getting a college scholarship

Murdock, Catherine. **The Off Season**. Houghton Mifflin, 2007. MS/HS. 288 pages. ISBN-10: 0618686959
Issues: Female on the football team and sibling with a devastating injury

Newton, Robert. **Runner**. Knopf Books for Young Readers, 2007. MS. 224 pages. ISBN-10: 0375837442
Issues: Running and death of a parent and injury of a friend

Parker, Robert B. **The Boxer and the Spy**. Philomel, 2008. MS/HS. 224 pages. ISBN-13: 978-0399247750
Issues: Boxing and solving the mystery of a friend's death

Parker, Robert B. **Edenville Owls**. Puffin, 2008. MS. 208 pages. ISBN-13: 978-0142411612
Issues: Basketball and solving a mystery

Schroeder, Lisa. **Chasing Brooklyn**. Simon Pulse; 1 edition, 2010. MS/HS. 432 pages ISBN-13: 978-1416991687

Issues: Triathlon and death of a loved one

Smith, Charles R. **Chameleon**. Candlewick; 1 edition, 2008. MS/HS. 384 pages. ISBN-13: 978-0763630850

Issues: Basketball and gang violence

Trueman, Terry. **7 Days at the Hot Corner**. HarperTeen, 2007. MS/HS. 160 pages. ISBN-10: 0060574941
Issues: Baseball and dealing with the best friend revealing that he is gay.

Weaver, Will. **Saturday Night Dirt**. Puffin, 2008. MS. 272 pages. ISBN-10: 014240392X
Issues: Stock car racing and a variety of self esteem problems

Weaver, Will. **Super Stock Rookie**. Farrar, Straus and Giroux (BYR); 1 edition, 2009. MS. 208 pages. ISBN-13: 978-0374350611

Issues: Stock car racing and cheating

Weaver, Will. **Checkered Flag Cheater**. Farrar, Straus and Giroux (BYR); 1 edition, 2010. MS/HS. 208 pages. ISBN-13: 978-0374350628

Issues: Stock car racing and cheathing

Wiles, Deborah. **The Aurora County All-Stars**. Harcourt Children's Books, 2007. MS. 256 pages. ISBN-10: 0152060685
Issues: Baseball and conflicting loyalties

Zadoff, Allen. **Food, Girls and Other Things I Can't Have.** Egmont USA, 2009. MS/HS. 320 pages. ISBN-13: 978-1606840047
Issues: Football and problems with obesity

Essential Question: How do sports impact the characters' lives?

Guiding Questions for Literature Circle

1) What sport is the main character(s) playing?

2) What is his/her relationship with his/her coach?

3) How do the main character's parents feel about his/her participation in sports?

4) What challenges in his/her life is the main character(s) facing?

5) Do sports help or increase the problems? How?

6) Are the main characters' friends also athletes? How does this impact their relationship?

7) How are you similar to the main character(s)? Different?

8) Does the climax of the book involve a sporting event? Explain

9) Is the ending uplifting or depressing?

10) Would you recommend this book to others?

BOOK BUNDLE: SEXUAL IDENTITY

Sexual identity issues have always been a problem for teens, but today society is more tolerant and students are more comfortable discussing them. Many schools have curriculums that include counseling students about being open to diversity in people's sexual preferences. Reflective of this tolerance is the growing body of young adult literature that focuses on this issue or includes it in a subplot. The following list of titles includes a short synopsis and the sexual identity issue explored in the book.

Bantle, Lee. **David Inside Out**. Henry Holt and Co. (BYR); 1 edition, 2009. MS/HS. 192 pages. ISBN-13: 978-0805081220

Although high school junior David Dahlgren has a girlfriend, he finds himself more attracted to a   cross country teammate Sean. When they begin a secret sexual relationship, David struggles with guilt and the desire to come out to his family and friends. Sean, however, is in denial and their hot and cold   relationship has David filled with emotional turmoil which he longs to resolve.

Burd, Nick. **The Vast Fields of Ordinary**. Dial, 2009. HS. 320 pages. ISBN-13: 978-0803733404

During an eventful summer before college, Dade Hamilton watches his parents marriage implode, his relationship with sort of boyfriend Pablo fizzle, and the media's obsessive coverage of an autistic girl's disappearance unfold. He toils away at a boring job at Food World and feels lost and invisible, until he meets Alex Kincaid, an openly gay drug dealer, with whom he falls in love.

Brothers, Meagan. **Debbie Harry Sings in French**. Henry Holt and Co. (BYR); 1st edition, 2008. MS/HS.   240 pages. ISBN-13: 978-0805080803

After Johnny's father dies and his mother withdraws from life, he sinks into a bout of alcoholism that results in his going to rehab, where he discovers solace in the music of Blondie, a punk rock band whose lead singer is Debbie Harry. He loves her voice, her fierce look and the power behind her music. When his mother sends him to live with his uncle in South Carolina, he falls in love with Maria, a fellow outcast, who encourages him to find his "inner Debbie Harry" by competing in a drag contest in Atlanta.

Frazer, Megan. **Secrets of Truth and Beauty**. Hyperion Book CH, 2009. MS/HS. 352 pages. ISBN-13: 978-1423117117

Dara, a former Little Miss Maine, is now more than pleasingly plump. When she is assigned a multimedia autobiographical project at school, she decides to focus on society's obsession with thinness. After her parents and teacher overreact to what they think is her mental instability, Dara leaves Maine to visit her estranged older sister who works on a goat farm which harbors homeless lesbian teens. There Dara finds acceptance and friendship which give her a self-confidence she has long been lacking.

Hartinger, Brent. **Split Screen: Attack of the Soul-Sucking Brain Zombies/Bride of the Soul Sucking Brain Zombies**. HarperTeen, 2007.

HS. 304 pages. ISBN-10: 0060824085

In this companion to *Geography Club* two books in one tell the stories of best friends Min and Russel who sign up to be extras on the set of a zombie film. In *Attack of the Soul-Sucking Brain Zombies,* Russel must choose between his long-distance boyfriend and a close-to-home ex who wants to get back together. In *Bride of the Soul-Sucking Brain Zombies,* Min struggles to accept her cheerleader girlfriend's decision to stay in the closet.

Hopkins, Ellen. **Impulse**. Margaret K. McElderry , 2007. HS. 672 pages. ISBN-10: 1416903569

After failed suicide attempts, three teens bond in a psychiatric hospital. In alternating chapter- in-verse the stories of Vanessa, Tony, and Conner are told, revealing dysfunctional family relationships. Tony deals with bisexual issues.

Hopkins, Ellen. **Tricks**. Margaret K. McElderry; 1 edition, 2009. HS. 640 page. ISBN-13: 978-1416950073

Five teens driven to prostitution through five different journeys all end up in Las Vegas where they struggle to find a way out of the hopelessness that has come to define their lives.

Juby, Susan. **Another Kind of Cowboy**. HarperTeen, 2007. MS/HS. 352 pages. ISBN-13: 978-0060765170

Alex, who is struggling with his sexuality, has longed to switch from competing in Western riding to dressage. Through fortuitous circumstances he ends up a competition worthy dressage horse and enrolls in lessons at a local stable. There he meets Chloe, a spoiled rich girl with an attitude and a hard-to-handle horse, and the two forge an unlikely friendship. When Chloe gets involved in too much partying and Alex "comes out," they depend on their friendship to help them navigate their problems.

Kluger, Steve. **My Most Excellent Year: A Novel of Love, Mary Poppins, & Fenway Park**. Puffin; Reprint edition, 2009. MS/HS. 416 pages. ISBN-13: 978-0142413432

In alternating voices three Boston teens describe their most excellent year for a class assignment. T.C. is a die-hard Red Sox fan who is "the cool kid everyone wants to be." He has a crush on Alejandra, who is the daughter of an ambassador, who has political aspirations for his daughter, even though she wants to be a performer. Augie is T.C.'s best friend, who is obsessed with Broadway musicals and a boy named Alex.

Lecesne, James. **Absolute Brightness.** HarperTeen, 2008. HS. 480 pages. ISBN-13: 978-0061256271

When Leonard Pelkey, a flamboyant 14-year-old, arrives in Neptune, NJ to live with his cousin Phoebe's family, she is aghast and is sure he will be an outcast. Then she is surprised to find that many people, especially the clients at her mother's beauty salon. embrace his ideas for makeovers of their bodies and minds. When he is brutally murdered, Phoebe is overwhelmed and vows to get to the bottom of his senseless death.

Levithan, David. **Love is the Higher Law**. Knopf Books for Young Readers, 2009. HS. 176 pages. ISBN-13: 978-0375834684

Three Manhattan teens deal with the emotional aftermath of the 9/11 attacks. Claire, who was at school, Peter, who was waiting outside Tower Records to buy the latest Dylan album, and Jasper, who was asleep when the planes hit the twin towers, are at first casual acquaintances, but they are drawn together through sharing their impressions of the tragedy. A romance between Peter and Jasper is fostered by Claire as the three struggle with their feelings about each other and the world around them.

Levithan, David and John Green. **Will Grayson, Will Grayson**. Dutton Juvenile, 2010. HS. 304 pages. ISBN-13: 978-0525421580

In alternating chapters two characters named Will Grayson tell the story of Tiny Cooper, "The world's largest person who is really, really gay." Heterosexual Will Grayson is Tiny's best friend and homosexual will grayson, who writes in lower case letters because he's clinically depressed, becomes Tiny's boyfriend. Together they tell a story of friendship, infatuation and changing to become the person you really want to be.

Lo, Malinda. **Ash**. Little, Brown Books for Young Readers; 1 edition, 2009. MS/HS. 272 pages. ISBN-13: 978-0316040099

In this retelling of *Cinderella*, Ash, the Cinderella character, is again a beleaguered servant under her stepmother's control. However, her fairy godfather is actually an alluring fairy with whom she makes a soul sacrificing pact so that she can attend the royal ball. Although the prince meets and is attracted to Ash, she is more interested in Kaisa, the king's huntress who has enthralled Ash when they meet in the woods and Kaisa teaches Ash to hunt. Will Ash have to sacrifice all to escape her oppressive existence and find true love?

Murdock, Catherine. **The Off Season**. Houghton Mifflin, 2007. MS/HS. 288 pages. ISBN-10: 0618686959

In this sequel to *Dairy Queen* D.J. Schwenk is playing linebacker on the high school football team, hanging out with the quarterback of the rival football team, and helping out on her family's struggling dairy farm. Her best friend, who is a lesbian, reveals her sexual preference and leaves home to be with her girlfriend.

Na, An. **The Fold**. Putnam Juvenile, 2008. MS. 192 pages. ISBN-13: 978-0399242762

Joyce Park longs to be as beautiful as her older sister so that she can capture the attention of John Ford Kang, a popular, gorgeous classmate. When Joyce's wealthy aunt offers her cosmetic surgery to add a fold to her eyelids, she is at first appalled, then tempted. Little does she know her sister is struggling with her desire to come out to her family and confess she is in love with her best girlfriend.

Ryan, Sara. **The Rules for Hearts.** Viking Juvenile, 2007. HS. 272 pages. ISBN-10: 0670059064

In this sequel to *Empress of the World* Battle Hall Davies joins her brother in   Portland, Oregon for the summer before her first year of college. Her attraction to one of the girls she is living with creates complications.

St. James, James. **Freak Show**. Dutton Juvenile, 2007. HS. 224 pages. ISBN-10: 0525477993

Billy Bloom, teenage drag queen, arrives at conservative Eisenhower Academy in his full regalia and is soon beaten to a bloody pulp. When the quarterback on the football team comes to his defense, Billy is smitten. This familiar outcast runs for homecoming queen story has an unusual twist, because this time a "queen" wants to be Queen.

Trueman, Terry. **7 Days at the Hot Corner**. HarperTeen, 2007. MS/HS. 160 pages. ISBN-10: 0060574941

A baseball fanatic who plays third base for his high school's team, Scott Latimer is thrown for a loop when his best friend, Travis, reveals that he's gay. This happens during the citywide baseball tournament, so now, in addition to worrying about playing well in the seven-day tournament, Scott anxiously awaits the results of an HIV test that he gets in secret. He fears he may have contracted AIDS after a batting cage incident, in which he wound up with Travis's blood on his hands.

Weinheimer, Beckie. **Converting Kate**. Viking Juvenile, 2007. MS/HS. 288 pages. ISBN-10: 0670061522

Having moved to Maine with her mother, to live and work at her Great-Aunt Katherine's B & B, 16-year-old Kate has, in her own mind, already left the Church of the Holy Divine. Kate's disgust with her mother's rigid religious beliefs begins when her mother refuses to have a funeral for her ex-husband, Kate's dad, who is a non-believer, and escalates as she realizes how uncharitable her mother is to anyone not of her faith. Kate's search for something to believe in requires courage, strength, and the support of the homosexual minister of a nearby church.

Wittlinger, Ellen. **Parrotfish.** Simon & Schuster Children's Publishing, 2007. HS. 304 pages. ISBN-10: 1416916229

Angela, a transgendered high-school junior, *knows* that she's a boy trapped in a girl's body, so cuts her hair short, buys boys' clothing, and announces that her name is now Grady. Beginning a new life as a boy, of course, is fraught with problems. Grady encounters reactions ranging from outright hostility to loving support during his turbulent year of transition.

Woodson, Jacqueline. **After Tupac & D Foster**. Putnam Young Adult, 2008. MS. 160 pages. ISBN-13: 978-0399246548

Three African American girls weather the years from ages 11 to 13 while listening to Tupac Shakur's music and worrying about his legal troubles and shootings. A subplot about one girl's older brother, a gay man serving prison time after being framed for a hate crime, compliments the girls' story.

Essential Question: How do sexual identity or gender issues impact a teen's life?

Guiding Questions for Literature Circles

1) Which character(s) in the novel is struggling with issues of sexual or gender identity? Explain

2) How are these issues impacting his/her life?

3) Which characters in the story add to the problems? How?

4) Which characters are supportive and how do they show their support?

5) Does the main character seek out GLBT support groups, and if so, how do they help?

6) Do characters in the novel change their opinion about sexual identity or gender issues? If so, what was their original opinion and how does it change?

7) How has your opinion or knowledge about these issues changed from reading this novel?

8) Would you recommend this book to others?

BOOK BUNDLE: DYSTOPIAN SOCIETIES

Literature about dystopian societies can be defined as novels that present alternative realities or worlds set in the present or the future where the living conditions are for some reason appalling. Dystopian novels generally include themes involving morality, violence, lack of free will, lack of freedom, conformity, and/or government control. Teen readers find these novels appealing because they involve adolescent characters who have views with which the reader can sympathize. Many adolescents can relate to the themes of dystopian literature. Issues of control, conformity, corruption and lack of freedom may be encountered as an adolescent grows toward adulthood. These dystopian novels may help adolescents deal with their own struggles in life and give them hope that they too make the world a better place like the characters do in the novels. Having students read these novels and come up with their own definitions of dystopia can be a great catalyst for discussion.

NEW DYSTOPIAN NOVELS

Adlington, L.J. **Cherry Heaven**. HarperTeen , 2008. MS. 464 pages. ISBN-10: 006143180X

Bachorz, Pam. **Candor**. EgmontUSA, 2009. MS/HS. 256 pages. ISBN-13: 978-1606840122

Bacigalupi, Paolo. **Ship Breaker**. Little, Brown Books for Young Readers; 1 edition, 2010. MS/HS. 336 pages. ISBN-13: 978-0316056212

Bodeen. S. A. **Compound**. Feiwel & Friends, 2008. MS. 256 pages. ISBN-10: 0312370156

Brooks, Kevin. **Being.** The Chicken House, 2007. MS/HS. 336 pages. ISBN-10: 0439899737

Collins, Suzanne. **The Hunger Games**. Scholastic Press, 2008. MS/HS. 384 pages. ISBN-13: 978-0439023481

   Catching Fire. Scholastic Press, 2009. MS. 400 pages. ISBN-13: 978-0439023498

   Mockingjay. Scholastic Press, 2010. MS/HS. 400 pages. ISBN-13: 978-0439023511

Condie, Ally. **Matched**. Dutton Juvenile, 2010. MS. 369 pages.ISBN-13: 978-0525423645

Dasher, James. **The Maze Runner**. Delacorte Books for Young Readers; First Edition edition, 2009. MS. 384 pages. ISBN-13: 978-0385737944

De Vita, James. **The Silenced.** Eos, 2007. MS/HS. 512 pages. ISBN-10: 0060784628

Doctorow, Cory. **Little Brother**. Tor Teen, 2008. MS/HS. 384 pages. ISBN-13: 978-0765319852

Fisher, Catherine. **Incarceron**. Dial, 2010. MS.448 pages. ISBN-13: 978-0803733961

Fukui, Isamu. **Truancy**. Tor Teen, 2008. MS/HS. 432 pages. ISBN-10: 0765317672

Goodman, Allegra. **The Other Side of the Island**. Scribe Publications, 2008. MS. 272 pages. ISBN-13: 978-1921372292

Malley, Gemma. **The Declaration**. Bloomsbury USA Children's Books, 2007. MS. 320 pages. ISBN-10: 1599901196

Ness, Patrick. **The Knife of Never Letting Go**. Candlewick, 2009. MS/HS. 496 pages. ISBN-13: 978-0763645762

Patneaude, David. **Epitaph Road**. EgmontUSA, 2010. MS/HS. 272 pages. ISBN-13: 978-1606840559

Pfeffer, Susan Beth. **The Dead and the Gone**. Harcourt Children's Books; 1 edition, 2008. MS. 336 pages. ISBN-13: 978-0152063115

Shusterman, Neal. **Unwind**. Simon & Schuster Children's Publishing, 2007. MS/HS. 352 pages. ISBN-10: 1416912045

Sleator, William. **Test**. Amulet, 2008. MS/HS. 240 pages. ISBN-10: 0810993562

Strasser, Todd. **Boot Camp**. Simon & Schuster Children's Publishing, 2007. HS. 256 pages. ISBN-10: 141690848X

Westerfeld, Scott. **Extras.** Simon Pulse, 2007. MS/HS. 432 pages. ISBN-10: 1416951172

Essential question: What personal qualities and issues drive a character(s) to rebel against what is happening in a dystopian society?

Guiding Questions for Literature Circles

1) Describe the setting of the dystopian society in your novel.

2) Who are the protagonists of the story? Antagonists?

3) What issues threaten the health and/or happiness of the main characters? (Ex. morality, violence, lack of free will, lack of freedom, conformity, government control)

4) What is the catalyst that motivates the main characters to rebel against what is happening?

5) Have you ever experienced anything that would help you understand the frustration the main characters are feeling? If so, what?

6) How does the main character(s) help to make the dystopian society a better place?

7) What is the theme of the book and how does the author convey it?

8) What do you think the future will be like for the main characters?

9) How do you feel about the ending? Is it hopeful or depressing?

10) Would you recommend this book to others? Why or why not?

Stories with a Dash of Science

Although scientific elements have long been available in science fiction stories, generally the author is speculating about what may be possible in the future. Many new young adult titles reviewed in this book include a smattering of science that might be fun for readers to delve into more deeply. Science journalist, E.L. Young, has even gone so far as to include an author's note detailing genuine research and inventions upon which she has based her ideas. Perhaps she will lead the way in encouraging other science journalists to write books for young adults that dish up scientific ideas in a delightfully palatable story. The following entries include a short synopsis of each title and then a suggestion for the area of scientific study that could be paired with the book.

Avi, **The Seer of Shadows**. HarperCollins, 2008. MS. 208 pages. ISBN-10: 0060000155
Scientific Study: Photographic processes and how they have evolved from the 19th century.

Brande, Robin. **Evolution, Me and Other Freaks of Nature**. Knopf Books for Young Readers, 2007. MS/HS. 272 pages. ISBN-10: 0375843493
Scientific Study: Evolution of the human species

Ferguson, Alane. **The Circle of Blood**. Viking Juvenile, 2008. MS/HS. 256 pages. ISBN-10: 0670060569 (Forensic Mystery Series)
 Scientific study: Autopsy process

Ferris, Aimee. **Girl Overboard**. Puffin, 2007. MS/HS. 224 pages. ISBN-10: 0142407992
Scientific study: Marine biology

French, S. Terrell. **Operation Redwood**. Amulet Books, 2009. MS. 368 pages.
 ISBN-13: 978-0810983540

Scientific study: Old growth forests

Hawking, Lucy and Stephen. **George's Secret Key to the Universe.** Simon & Schuster Children's Publishing, 2007. MS. 304 pages. ISBN-10: 1416954627 (Series)
Scientific study: Astronomy or Physics (Authors have included sidebar "mini-lessons" which would help students limit their topic by choosing one of them to investigate.)

Henry, April. **Torched**. Putnam Juvenile, 2009. MS/Hs. 224 pages. ISBN-13: 978-0399246456
Scientific Study: Ecology

Hiaasen, Carl. **Scat**. Knopf Books for Young Readers, 2009. 384 pages. ISBN-13: 978-0375834868
Scientific study: Endangered species and environmental issues

Hobbs, Will. **Go Big or Go Home**. HarperCollins, 2008. MS. 192 pages. ISBN-13: 978-0060741433
 Scientific study: Meteorites and extraterrestrial bacteria

Kelly, Jacqueline. **The Evolution of Calpurnia Tate**. Henry Holt and Co. (BYR); 1 edition, 2009. MS. 352 pages. ISBN-13: 978-0805088410
Scientific Study: Botany and evolution
Kerr, P. B. **One Small Step**. Margaret K. McElderry, 2008. MS. 320 pages. ISBN-13: 978-1416942139
 Scientific study: Rocketry and astronaut training.

McDonald, Abby. **Boys, Bears and a Serious Pair of Hiking Boots**. Candlewick; 1 edition, 2010. MS/HS. 304 pages. ISBN-13: 978-0763643829
Scientific Study: Environmental Activism

Patterson, James. **Maximum Ride: The Final Warning**. Little, Brown and Company, 2008. MS. 272 pages. ISBN-10: 0316002860
Scientific study: Global warming

Patterson, James. **Max**. Little, Brown and Company, 2009. MS. 320 pages. ISBN-13: 978-0316002899
Scientific study: Ocean Pollution

Spinelli, Jerry. **Smiles to Go.** Joanna Cotler, 2008. MS. 256 pages. ISBN-10: 0060281332
Scientific study: Proton decay, astronomy, the String Theory

Testa, Dom. **The Comet's Curse**. Tor Teen, 2009. MS. 240 pages. ISBN-13: 978-0765321077
Scientific study: Astronomy and space travel (The author has included a reader's guide which includes writing and research suggestions, as well as discussion questions.)

Vaught, Susan. **Big Fat Manifesto**. Bloomsbury USA Children's Books, 2007. MS/HS. 320 pages, ISBN-10: 1599902060
Scientific study: Bariatric surgery

Young, E.L. **Storm: The Infinity Code**. Dial, 2008. MS. 336 pages. ISBN-10: 0803732651.
Scientific study: Black Holes or the scientific aspect of the development of military weapons (See author's note for a variety of suggestions.)

ESSENTIAL QUESTION: How has the author incorporated scientific elements that enhance the story and make it a compelling read?

1) Briefly summarize the plot of the story.

2) What scientific elements do you think the author researched to add to the story?

3) List each scientific element and where it was incorporated into the plot.

4) How do the scientific elements enhance the story?

5) Are any of the characters scientific experts on the topics involved? If so, who?

6) Do the scientific elements help make the story more believable? If so, how?

7) Is the author trying to make a political statement about the scientific ideas? Explain

8) What is the theme of the story? Are the scientific ideas related?

9) Are there futuristic ideas that are substantiated by the scientific elements?

10) Do further research on one or more of the elements. What did you find that might add to the story?

In creating your own book bundles and questions for literature circles, you might be interested in **Richard Peck's Ten Questions to Ask about a Novel**.[16]

1) What would this story be like if the main character were of the opposite sex?

2) Why is the story set where it is?

3) If you were to film this story, what characters would you eliminate if you couldn't use them all?

4) Would you film this story in black and white or color? Why?

5) How is the main character different from you?

6) Would this story make a good TV series? Why or why not?

7) What's one thing in the story that's happened to you?

8) Reread the first paragraph of Chapter 1. What's in it to make you read on?

9) If you had to design a new cover for the book, what would it look like?

10) What does the title tell you about the book? Does it tell the truth?

---

[14] Norton, Michael, "Richard Peck's 10 Questions to Ask about a Novel." http://www.michellejnorton.com/?p=67, October 20, 2009.

SHARING NEW YOUNG ADULT LITERATURE WITH COLLEAGUES

Each semester the Boulder Valley School District has offered a course which gives language arts teachers and librarians credit for reading and reviewing new young adult literature. If the participants want credit, they must complete the following requirements.

1) Each participant much read 10 young adult books that have been published within the last five years.

2) A one page review (see the example on the following page) must be written for each book. The review must include:
- Title, author, publisher, copyright date and number of pages
- A half page summary of the book
- A writing prompt
- Discussion questions
- Cross-curricular connections
- Genre identification
- Cautions regarding inappropriate material for younger audiences
- Rating (out of five stars) as to the quality of the writing and audience appeal
- Reviewer's contact information

3) Participants attend class once a month to share reviews. Copies of each review are emailed to all the class members who may print them out if they wish..

4) Teachers meet informally with colleagues in their building to share information about the new books they've read.

5) If three participants read and positively review a title, it is automatically put on the district approved titles list.

6) The reviews are compiled and put on the district website so that all teachers in the district may access them.

For teachers and librarians who are reading these books anyway, it is a fun way to get credit for their work. The discussions frequently include brainstorming ideas as to how to use the books in the classroom, and the cautions are extremely helpful in forewarning teachers and librarians about books that are a bit risky to use in the classroom, but are great reads.

Forever in Blue by Ann Brasheres. Delacorte Press, 2007. MS/HS. 384 pages.

The fourth and final installment in the traveling pants series includes many mature issues because the girls are now in college. Lena enrolls in a summer painting program at school where she meets Leo, a gifted artist. Because they can't afford to hire the model for the extra painting sessions they want to do, they pose nude for each other. This, of course, evolves into a sexual relationship. Just when she thinks she is finally over Kostos, he appears at her door wanting to marry her. He has divorced his wife, who conned him into marrying her by falsely implying she was pregnant. Carmen heads off to a summer theatrical program, assuming she will be a member of the stage crew. However, she auditions for a part and lands it. Unfortunately, her sophisticated roommate, who seems to have cast a spell over Carmen, is jealous and sabotages her. When Bridget's boyfriend Eric goes back to Mexico to coach soccer for the summer, Bridget joins a dig for an ancient city on the coast of Turkey. There is a mutual attraction between her and an archaeology professor. Unfortunately, he is married. Finally, Tibby gives into Brian's pleas to become intimate, only to have the condom break. After a pregnancy scare, she breaks up with Brian, thinking she is no longer in love with him. When he starts dating Lena's sister Effie, Tibby realizes how wrong she really is. Brian has never stopped loving Tibby, and when she gets up the courage to tell him how she feels, he stops seeing Effie. Effie is furious. When Lena sides with Tibby, Effie steals the traveling pants and heads off to Greece. After Effie loses the pants, all four girls go to Greece to find them. Although they don't find the pants, they do enjoy being together.

Writing Prompt: How do the traveling pants impact each of the girl's lives in this book? Do you think they are magic? Why or why not?

Discussion Questions:
1) Why does Lena send Kostos away when he comes to America?
2) Why did Bridget go to Turkey and what problems does she encounter?
3) Why does Tibby break up with Brian? Why does she change her mind?
4) Why does Julia sabotage Carmen's acting efforts? Why does Carmen care about what Julia thinks?

Topics: Friendship, jealousy, sexual intimacy

Genre: Realistic Fiction

CAUTION: SEXUAL CONTENT

Rating: **** This book is a great read and a fitting ending to the popular series. Appropriate for mature middle and high school readers.

Contact Person: Sharon Nehls, Southern Hills Middle School, snehls@comcast.net

Works Cited

Blasingame, James. *Books That Don't Bore "Em*. New York: Scholastic Teaching Resources, 2007. Print.

Bucuvalas, Abigail. "Teaching Social Awareness ? An Interview with Larsen Professor Robert Selman." Web. 8 July 2009.

Coleman, Betsey and Charles. *Integrating Technology in a *Best Practices* Language Arts Classroom*, Colorado Teen Literature Conference, April 5, 2008.

"David Clement-Davies." *Wikipedia, the free encyclopedia*. Web. 21 Oct. 2009.

<http://en.wikipedia.org/wiki/David_Clement-Davies>.

Guiley, Rosemany. *The Encyclopedia of Angels*. New York: Checkmark Books., 2004. Print

Gurian, Michael. *Boys and Girls Learn Differently! A Guide for Teachers and Parents*. New York: Jossey-Bass, 2002. Print.

Krensky, Steven. *The Monster Chronicles*. Minneapolis: Lerner Publications Company, 2007. Print.

"LiteratureCircles.com : What are literature circles?" *Welcome to Literature Circles*. Web. 6 Aug. 2007.

<http://www.literaturecircles.com/article1.htm>.

Lye, John. "Narrative Point of View: Some Considerations." Web. 8 June 2008.

<http://www.brocku.ca/english/courses>.

Norton, Michael. "Richard Peck's 10 Questions to Ask about a Novel." Web. 21 Oct. 2009.

<http://www.michellejnorton.com/?p=67>.

Polette, Nancy, and Marjorie Hamlin. *Exploring Books with Gifted Children*. Littleton: Libraries Unlimited, 1980. Print.

Steele, Kim. "Voice Definition." *Kim's Korner for Teacher Talk*. Web. 21 Oct. 2009.

<http://www.kimskorner4teachertalk.com/writing/sixtrait/voice/definition.html>.

Sullivan, Michael. *Connecting Boys with Books: What Libraries Can Do*. New York: ALA Editions, 2003. Print.

Sullivan, Michael. "Why Johnny Won't Read." *School Library Journal* 1 Aug. 2004. *School Library Journal*. 1 Aug. 2004. Web. 10 July 2008. <http://www.schoollibraryjournal.com/article/CA439816.html>.

Wirtz, Jason. "Creating Possibilities: Embedding Research into Creative Writing." *English Journal* Mar. 2006: 23-27. Print.

Young, Becky. "Have You Read Any Good Poems Lately? Novels in Verse" Web. 21 Oct. 2009.

<http://www.courses.unt.edu/efiga/HistoryAndEthnography/TrendsProjects/young/home_pagebecky_young.htm>.

www.ingramcontent.com/pod-product-compliance
Lightning Source LLC
LaVergne TN
LVHW081316060426
835509LV00015B/1533